DECORATIVE CUT FLOWERS

DECORATIVE CUT FLOWERS

AN ILLUSTRATED GUIDE TO THE IDENTIFICATION AND CARE OF OVER 500 VARIETIES AND CULTIVARS

COEN GELEIN AND NEES JOORE

CASSELL

Contents

Decorative Cut Flowers first published in the UK 1988 by Cassell, an imprint of Cassell plc, Artillery House, Artillery Row, London SW1P 1RT

Original title: *Snijbloemen uit alle windstreken.* First published in the Netherlands by Trendboek BV, Zonnebaan 12D, 3606 CA Maarssenbroek.

Photography: Nees Joore, † VBA
Translation: Carol Stennes
Glossary: Suzette E. Stumpel-Rienks
Final editing: Jac. G. Constant, PAMPUS ASSOCIATES.
Design: Ron Putto, PAMPUS ASSOCIATES.
Coordination: Jan E. van Gelderen, PAMPUS ASSOCIATES.
Word processing: Yvonne Taverne, BOEKBEELD
Typesetting: Caspari BV, Heerhugowaard
Lithography: Gerlings BV, Amsterdam
Printing: Koninklijke Smeets Offset, BV Weert

English translation checked for technical accuracy and approved by Peter Barnes, Botanist at the Royal Horticultural Society Garden at Wisley, England.

© 1988 Coöperatieve Vereniging Pampus Associates u.a., Amsterdam
© 1988 Trendboek BV
This edition © Cassell

British Library Cataloguing in Publication Data
Gelein, Coen
Decorative cut flowers: an illustrated guide to the identification and care of over 500 varieties and cultivars.
1. Cut flowers. Production – Manuals
I. Title II. Joore, Nees III. Snijbloemen uit alle Windstreken.
English
635.9'66

ISBN 0 304 32233 4

Foreword

Although we all know what is meant by the term cut flowers (or at least we think we do), it is extremely difficult to give a precise definition of *cut flowers*. It is a concept unknown to botany, and the phrase itself can be misleading since this book will mention varieties which are not *cut* but sometimes broken or pinched off the plant, and others that are not *flowers*, but leaves, branches or fruits. Nor would it help to call them *vase flowers*, for among cut flowers we include plants or parts of plants that seldom or never end up in a vase, but are used in corsages, floral arrangements, funeral wreaths, and so on.

Commercial use provides the best guide. In the international flower trade, cut flowers are parts of plants which have ornamental value when they are cut off or removed from the plant, which will keep for a time (perhaps with the addition of special substances or by using special methods) and which, in addition, can stand up to transport over certain distances. However because the international cut flower trade is extremely lucrative each year large sums are invested in increasing the assortment. In the first place, this is brought about by a constant search for new cultivars and variations in colour and form by means of crossing and other methods of refinement. But scientific research also plays a crucial role in improving the keeping properties of sorts that wither rapidly, increasing the ornamental value of plants that are inadequate in this respect, and strengthening others which are too vulnerable to transport and which would otherwise be of little importance as commercial cut flowers.

The result of all this activity is that the cut flower assortment becomes larger each year and that more and more sorts fall under the definition given above. In short, the cut flower is a product very much in motion. For the first time, this book gives a fascinating survey of this dynamic product. Although it contains but a selection of the many hundreds of plants from all parts of the world which play a role in the international cut flower trade, it includes the sorts and cultivars that are leaving their mark on the industry's supply at the threshold of the 1990s.

That it was possible to make such a selection is due to the author's very close involvement in what, without any exaggeration, may be called the nerve centre of the international cut flower trade: the Associated Aalsmeer Flower Auctions (VBA). This cooperative organization not only dominates the internationally prominent Dutch flower cultivation, but it is also the world trade centre for the international flower trade. The cooperation of the VBA made it possible to photograph many of the sorts and cultivars described by the author in top condition.

It was a deep shock to the author, the VBA and the compilers of this book that the man who did this photography, Nees Joore, passed away so suddenly shortly after the completion of his work. The flowers on his grave have since faded; the flowers that he photographed are part of the value of this book.

Acanthaceae

The acanthus family (*Acanthaceae*) is quite large. It has some 250 genera, with a total of more than 2000 species. Originally they were tropical shrubs or herbaceous plants which were chiefly found in Indonesia, India and tropical Central and South America. Several of them are also grown as pot plants outside the tropics because of their ornamental value. Well-known examples are *Aphelandra*, *Beloperone*, *Fittonia* and *Thunbergia*.

The flowers are hermaphrodite and stand alone or are grouped in cultivarmes or compound umbels. The large bracts enclose the flowers and form part of their decorative value. The flowers themselves are irregular in form, or labiate and tetramerous or pentamerous. Two or three stamens are borne on the fused petals. The superior ovary has two cells.

Acanthus mollis
Bear's breeches
NAME: *Acanthus* is derived from the old Greek *akanthos*, meaning 'thorn' or 'prickle' and denotes the prickly toothed leaves. *Mollis* = soft and refers to the hair on the leaves.
DESCRIPTION: The large oval leaves can grow up to 40 cm long and 20 cm wide. They are deeply lobed and cut, covered beneath with soft hair and a dark, glossy green above. The firm straight stem is about 80 cm long and bears a long, spike-shaped inflorescence of 40-50 cm in length. The decorative value is formed by the greenish-purple bracts. The purple and cream flowers form in their axils.
ORIGIN: Mediterranean area, as far east as Yugoslavia.

CULTIVATION: Temperate zones, outdoors.
AVAILABILITY: Limited, in July and August.
CARE: The flower spikes must be entirely fully-grown to keep the stem top from drooping. Remove quite a number of leaves to lessen the moisture loss. Use cut-flower food for herbaceous plants.
KEEPING PROPERTIES: 8-10 days.
USES: Primarily in mixed bouquets.
SCENT: None.

Acanthus mollis

Polianthes tuberosa

8

Agavaceae

Amaranthaceae

The agave family (*Agavaceae*), composed of only 20 genera, contains over 2000 sorts of monocotyledonous plants which mostly grow in fairly dry spots in the tropics and subtropics. This family, which is closely related to the lily family (*Liliaceae*), comprises well-known house plants such as *Cordyline*, *Dracaena* (dragon-tree) and *Yucca*. Many *Agavaceae* are succulents and have narrow, pulpy leaves, sometimes with spiny margins, as the various sorts of the *Agave* genus, sometimes with smooth edges, as *Dracaena* and *Cordyline*. Generally speaking, the plants of this family have adapted themselves to life in a dry environment. The leaves have a small surface area, thickened cell walls, a thick epidermis, a large root system and a heightened cell pressure, thus making possible a better moisture uptake.

The flowers are hermaphrodite and sometimes dioecious; they generally are arranged in plumes. The perianth consists of two whorls of petals rolled up into tubes. Six stamens stand at their base. The ovary may be either superior or inferior. The fruits are berries or capsules; the seed is surrounded by much extra food.

Some members of the genus *Agave* are economically significant for the fine white fibre which is made from the leaves. It is especially suitable for processing into rope. These species are planted on a large scale, in Southeast Asia and other places. In Mexico two alcoholic drinks are derived from other agave sorts: the national drink *pulque*, which is scarcely consumed outside Mexico, and the much better known *tequila*.

The amaranth family (*Amaranthaceae*) - 65 genera, nearly 1000 species - is chiefly native to the tropics, subtropics and temperate zones of Africa and America. They are shrubs and herbaceous plants with smooth-margined leaves which are spread around or opposite on the stem.

The hermaphroditic, regularly formed flowers stand alone along a spike-shaped inflorescence and have 4-5, sometimes fused, perianth segments which are usually dry, membranous and without colour. The 1-5 stamens are often fused into a tube at the base and bear petal-like appendages. Remarkably coloured bracts enclose the flowers. The oblique flowers are generally infertile and bear prickles or hairs. The superior ovary has a single compartment; the fruit is a berry or a nut.

The family is divided into two subfamilies: the *Amaranthiodeae*, which include the genera *Amaranthus* and *Celosia*, have stamens with four pouches and an ovary with one to many egg cells. The *Gomphrenioideae*, which include the decorative plants *Gomphrena*, *Iresine* and *Alternanthera* (pigweed), have stamens with two pouches and an ovary with only a single egg cell.

Several members of the amaranth family are cultivated, primarily in the tropics, as vegetables or for their edible seeds. An example of the former is the Surinamese amaranth (*Amaranthus dubius*).

Polianthes tuberosa
Tuberose

NAME: *Polianthes* is a contraction of two Latin words and means 'plant with whitish flowers'. *Tuberosa* = tuberous.

DESCRIPTION: The flower stem can reach 1 m in length and is covered with white, very fragrant rose-shaped flowers which have a diameter of approx. 4 cm. The tuberose used to be much cultivated for the perfume industry in southern France.

ORIGIN: Not precisely known; probably Mexico.

CULTIVATION: Limited, in southern France, Israel and southern Africa.

AVAILABILITY: In winter and early spring from Israel and southern Africa; in summer and autumn from southern France.

CARE: Cut off a bit of the stem; add cut-flower food for bulb flowers or herbaceous plants to the water.

KEEPING PROPERTIES: They are strong flowers, and will keep for 10-14 days, depending on how long they have been transported.

USES: In bridal work and corsages; sometimes in flower arrangements and mixed bouquets.

SCENT: Very fragrant.

Amaranthus caudatus

Amaranthus cruentus

Amaranthus cruentus,
syn. *A. paniculatus,*
syn. *A. chlorostachys*
Princess feather

NAME: See *A. caudatus. Paniculatus* means 'plume-shaped'.

DESCRIPTION: A sturdy, straight stem of 60-80 cm, which is reddish in the red cultivars. The leaves are light green; the upright inflorescence is a branched flower cluster, and the central branch is the longest. The tiny flowers are very close together. They are red (such as 'Pygmy Torch' and 'Roter Dom') or green (e.g. 'Pigmy Viridius') depending on the cultivar.

ORIGIN: First cultivated in North America in the 18th century, from unknown ancestors.

CULTIVATION: All flower-growing areas of the world.

AVAILABILITY: From July to the end of September.

CARE: Cut off a bit of the stem; use cut-flower food for herbaceous plants.

KEEPING PROPERTIES: If the flowers are in full bloom, 10-16 days. The leaves wither earlier and may then be removed.

USES: In floral arrangements, in decorative work and in bouquets of dried flowers.

SCENT: None.

Amaranthus caudatus
Love-lies-bleeding (red)
Tassel flower (green)

NAME: The Latin name is composed of two Greek words: the negative *a* and *marainesthai*, meaning 'to waste away': so it is a plant with flowers that never fade. *Caudatus* means 'tail-shaped'.

DESCRIPTION: An annual plant with a straight, sturdy stalk of approx. 80 cm and light green leaves. The inflorescence consists of 'tails' of 20-40 cm, which were red in the original plant. The cultivar group 'Albiflorus' (or 'Viridius') has a pale green inflorescence.

ORIGIN: Tropical South America.

CULTIVATION: All flower-growing areas of the world, especially the red form.

AVAILABILITY: From July to October, with a peak in August-September.

CARE: Remove lower leaves, cut into the stem. Use cut-flower food for herbaceous plants.

KEEPING PROPERTIES: If the bloom is sufficiently developed: 8-12 days. Immature flowers will droop.

USES: In mixed bouquets and decorative floral work.

SCENT: None.

Celosia argentea 'Plumosa'

Celosia argentea 'Cristata'

Gomphrena globosa

Celosia argentea 'Plumosa'
Chinese wool flower, Plume celosia

NAME: The genus name is derived either from the Greek *kélon*, a piece of dry wood, or from *kélis* = blood stain. The former could refer to the dry membraneous perianth, or flower envelope, of the plant; the latter to the red spot exhibited by a type occurring on Java. *Argentea* means 'silver-coloured' (the sheen on the stalk), *plumosa* = 'plume-shaped' (the inflorescence).
DESCRIPTION: The thick, fleshy stalks have somewhat oval leaves and are about 1 m long. At the end they bear a large plume flower branched like a feather with a clear main plume. The colours are scarlet, red, purple or yellow.
ORIGIN: Tropical Africa, but now wild in the entire tropical belt.
CULTIVATION: In flower-growing areas with a temperate climate, as a hothouse flower; grown outdoors in Kenya and other countries.
AVAILABILITY: From May until September, chiefly hothouse flowers.
CARE: The flowers spot very easily. Remove the lower leaves, cut into the stem, use cut-flower food for herbaceous plants.
KEEPING PROPERTIES: 8–10 days.
USES: In floral arrangements and large floral work. The flowers can also be dried.
SCENT: None.
ORIGIN: The cool mountainous areas of Chile.

Celosia argentea 'Cristata'
Chinese wool flower, Cock's comb

NAME: See *C. argentea 'Plumosa'*. *Cristata* means shaped like a cock's comb or crest and refers to the shape of the inflorescence.
DESCRIPTION: See *C. argentea 'Plumosa'*. The stem is somewhat longer (up to 1 m); the tiny flowers are generally red and form a broad, comb-shaped inflorescence. The improvement of this plant chiefly took place in Japan.
ORIGIN: Tropical Africa; now wild in the entire tropical belt.
CULTIVATION: In Europe and Japan, in the hothouse; in Africa (e.g. Kenya) outdoors.
AVAILABILITY: From May until September.
CARE: See *C. argentea 'Plumosa'*.
KEEPING PROPERTIES: 12–16 days; the leaves generally turn yellow after a week.
USES: In floral arrangements and large floral work.
SCENT: None.

Gomphrena globosa
Globe amaranth

NAME: *Gomphrena* is a corruption of *Gromphaena*, the old Latin name for a plant with red and green leaves which was used as a medicine for coughing up blood. *Globosa* = globe-shaped, the shape of the inflorescence.
DESCRIPTION: A branching herbaceous plant covered with soft hairs, of which the leaves half encircle the stem. The globular inflorescence is at the top of the stem; the small flowers are surrounded by two coloured bracts. There are white, pink, orange, red, purple and salmon varieties.
ORIGIN: The tropics and subtropics of America.
CULTIVATION: All flower-growing areas of the world.
AVAILABILITY: From July to the end of September. The flowers are sometimes sold dried.

CARE: Remove lower leaves, cut a bit off the stem, use cut-flower food for herbaceous plants. When buying them, make sure that the inflorescence is fully-grown.
KEEPING PROPERTIES: 7–12 days. They keep less well in autumn and during periods with little sunlight.
USES: In mixed bouquets and floral work. Also as dried flowers.
SCENT: None

Amaryllidaceae

The amaryllis family (*Amaryllidaceae*) is a close relative of the lilies (*Liliaceæ*) and the irises (*Iridaceae*). Botanists are divided on the question of which plant genera belong to this family. As to the cut flowers, there is difference of opinion only with respect to the genus *Agapanthus*, which some would place in the amaryllis family because of the umbel, and despite the superior ovary. We have not done so; in our view, this sort belongs in the lily family.

Most *Amaryllidaceae* are bulbous plants; some, however, have a rootstock, such as *Alstroemeria* and *Clivia*. Many members of the amaryllis family are native to tropical and subtropical areas; others, such as the snowdrop and the daffodil, originated in Europe.

The inflorescence is basically an umbel on a leafless stem, but sometimes the 'umbel' consists of a single flower, as in the trumpet daffodil. The flowers have two whorls of floral bracts, sometimes with a corolla, as the trumpet (or cup) in the daffodil. The stamens also stand in whorls of three; the inferior ovary has three compartments. The fruit is sometimes a capsule which bursts open, in other cases a berry. Internationally speaking, the daffodil is the most important ornamental flower of this family.

△ Alstroemeria aurantiaca   ▽ Alstroemeria hybrid

Alstroemeria aurantiaca
Peruvian lily

NAME: The genus of *Alstroemeria* is named after the Swedish jurist Clas Alstroemer (1736-1794). He was a pupil of Linnaeus. In addition to doing a great deal of work for agriculture and stock raising, he went as a researcher to South America and from there he sent Linnaeus seeds of *A. pelegrina*. *Aurantium* is the Latin name for orange; in this case it refers to the colour of the flower.

DESCRIPTION: The flowers of this perennial plant with tuberous roots are 4-5 cm long and grow in umbels on a stem which is thickly covered with lanceolate leaves. The inner sepals are pointed; they are striped red with reddish-brown spots. The outer ones are blunt; they have orange spots and are somewhat green at the tip. The most frequently cultivated cultivar is the deep orange 'Orange King'. The clear yellow 'Aurea' is much rarer.

ORIGIN: The cool mountainous areas of Chile.

CULTIVATION: All flower-growing areas with a temperate climate and not too severe winters.

AVAILABILITY: End of June - end of August.

CARE: Cut away the white parts of the stem, remove lower leaves. Use cut-flower food for herbaceous plants. Change the water frequently, since the flower rapidly pollutes it.

KEEPING PROPERTIES: 10-12 days.

USES: Singly or in mixed bouquets; also in decorative arrangements.

SCENT: None.

Alstroemeria hybrids
Peruvian lily
NAME: See *A. aurantiaca*.
DESCRIPTION: Large flower umbels on long stems (1.20-1.50 m). The colour assortment is large and ranges from pink, salmon, orange, red and lilac to white tints and some others. All flowers are markedly striped, usually in yellow, on the inner whorl of sepals. See also *A. aurantiaca*.
ORIGIN: The plant's ancestors come from the cool mountainous areas of Brazil, Chile and Peru; initially most hybrids were developed in England, but later in the Netherlands as well.
CULTIVATION: All important flower-growing areas.
AVAILABILITY: Throughout the year, with a peak between June and August. From October to May there is a limited supply to Western Europe from Kenya.
CARE: See *A. aurantiaca*. The pedicels are obliquely attached to the stem and are therefore easily damaged. For this reason, the flowers are sold in bunches of ten in a plastic wrap.
KEEPING PROPERTIES: 14-16 days.
USES: Sold in bunches; used in bridal bouquets, corsages, funeral work and floral arrangements.
SCENT: None.

Hybrids
The assortment of *Alstroemeria* hybrids is increasing every year. At present it is primarily blue tints which are being sought. Most hybrids come from five ancestors: *A. pelegrina*, with large lilac flowers, already cultivated by the Incas in Peru; *A. ligtu* from Chile, which brought the pink colour into the assortment and *A. brasiliensis* (the wine red); *A. psittacina*, native to northern Brazil (*psittacina* means 'parrot coloured'), bearing dark red flowers with yellow and red stripes and green-tipped petals. Lastly, *A. aurantiaca* brought the orange and yellow colours into the present assortment. Presently the most important hybrids are:
'Rosario' A pink cultivar of the 'butterfly' type, so called after the flower shape. The buds are not susceptible to dehydration. This cultivar blooms later than most others. 'Rosario' is the most frequently cultivated *Alstroemeria* hybrid.
'Jacqueline' is also much grown. It is another hybrid of the 'butterfly' type. The main blossom time is in May and June; the winter bloom is of little significance.
'Lilac Glory' has a very striking pink colour and blossoms largely between March and September. After that the supply decreases.

'King Cardinal' is a red cultivar which retains its colour during sunny summers. The main blossom time starts in March and continues into the autumn. The winter bloom is minimal.
'Yellow King' is a brightly coloured yellow cultivar which yields 85% of this cultivar blossoms in April-July.

Amaryllis belladonna
Cape belladonna, Belladonna lily
NAME: Roman writers such as Ovid and Virgil used the name of *Amaryllis* for a beautiful shepherdess. It is the Latin translation of the Greek *Amarullus*, derived from a word which means 'sparkling'. *Belladonna* is Italian for 'beautiful lady'. In addition to the beauty of the flower, this name also refers to eye drops prepared from deadly nightshade (*Atropa belladonna*) which unnaturally enlarge the pupil of the eye. This was formerly considered a mark of beauty in a woman.
DESCRIPTION: A bulbous plant with a plump bulb and long narrow leaves which are about as long as the flower stem. At the end of this stem grows a cultivarme of 8-10 bell-shaped flowers. In the bud they are upright, in bloom they hang. The colour assortment varies from light pink to carmine red and white.
ORIGIN: South Africa. First cultivated in the Netherlands about 1620.
CULTIVATION: Commonly grown in southern Africa; limited cultivation in all other flower-growing areas.
AVAILABILITY: Limited, in August and September; in spring sometimes from southern Africa.
CARE: The flower is sold when the first buds have opened slightly. Cut a bit off the stem; use cut-flower food for bulb plants.
KEEPING PROPERTIES: The first flowers wilt after 6-7 days, the last ones after approx. 3 weeks.
USES: Especially in floral arrangements; the white cultivar also in church decorations.
SCENT: The flower has a very pleasant, soft scent.

△ Amaryllis belladonna   ▽ Crinum x powellii

Crinum x powellii
(no popular name)
NAME: *Crinum* is the Latin form of the Greek *krino*, which means 'lily' and refers to the flower shape. *Powellii* is for the American florist Charles W. Powell (1854-1927).
DESCRIPTION: The plant is a cross between *C. bulbispermum* and *C. moorei*, both of which come from southern Africa. The cross-breeding took place in England in 1858. It is a bulbous plant with long flower stems (up to 80 cm). The flowers stand in groups of 6-10 and face downwards and outwards. They are pink or white; the stamens are just as long as the tubular flowers and have red anthers.

ORIGIN: See above.
CULTIVATION: Limited, in all flower-growing areas of the world
AVAILABILITY: In late summer and in spring.
CARE: For them to keep well, the first buds must be quite open. Cut off a bit of the stem; use cut-flower food for bulb plants.
KEEPING PROPERTIES: The first flowers wilt after approx. 10 days, the last after 3 weeks.
USES: Sometimes in bouquets, more often in large floral work and in flower arrangements.
SCENT: Hardly any.

Urceolina amazonica,
syn. *Eucharis grandiflora*
Amazon lily

NAME: *Urceolina* is derived from *urcellus* (= jar) and refers to the shape of the flower. *Amazonica* means 'of the Amazone'.

DESCRIPTION: A bulbous plant with 2-4 leaves which are approx. 30 cm long and 12 cm wide. The long stem of about 50 cm bears 5-8 flowers close together. They are 10 cm in diameter and of a strikingly vivid white. The 1-2 cm long corolla, which opens to the side, has somewhat greenish markings. The former genus name *Eucharis* (= charming) refers to the particular beauty of the flower.

ORIGIN: Tropical Colombia; the plant was first cultivated in Belgium in 1853.

CULTIVATION: All flower-growing areas with hothouse cultivation; in India outdoors.

AVAILABILITY: Throughout the year, with peaks in February-May and in October-November.

CARE: Cut off a bit of the stem; use cut-flower food for bulb plants in water. The flower cannot withstand cold (minimum temperature 15° C).

KEEPING PROPERTIES: 7-10 days; longest if only one flower is open when they are bought.

USES: Especially in floral work such as bridal bouquets and corsages, although the thick, hollow stem is difficult to work with. In a vase, generally as a single flower.

SCENT: Soft and very pleasant.

Urceolina amazonica, syn. Eucharis grandiflora

Galanthus nivalis
(Common) Snowdrop

NAME: The popular name refers to the early bloom (February), sometimes when there is still snow on the ground, and to the bell-shaped flower. *Galanthus* means something like 'milk flower', *nivalis* = snow white; both words of course refer to the flower's colour.

DESCRIPTION: A single nodding flower grows on the approx. 12 cm long stem of this bulb plant. The outer petals are about 2 cm long and stand out somewhat; the inner ones are somewhat shorter and stand upright. The tops of the latter are somewhat notched; at the indent there is a green spot. The two linear leaves are blue-green.

ORIGIN: Europe, the Caucasus and Asia Minor. Cultivated since medieval times.

CULTIVATION: Southern France; in the Netherlands, on the West Frisian island of Texel.

AVAILABILITY: Early spring.

CARE: Slit the stem; use cut-flower food for bulb plants.

KEEPING PROPERTIES: In a warm room only a few days; at lower temperatures 2-3 weeks.

USES: In vases; also in bridal bouquets and corsages.

SCENT: None.

Haemanthus katharinae
'Roi d'Albert', syn. 'König Albert'
Blood flower

NAME: *Haemanthus* is composed of *haema* (= blood) and *anthos* (= flower). *Katharinae* refers to Empress Catherine.

DESCRIPTION: On an umbel-shaped inflorescence of 20 cm in diameter stand a large number of star-shaped orange-red small flowers with long, protruding stamens which increase the ornamental value. The thick, fleshy stem is approx. 40 cm long. The 3-5 leaves, broad and oval, appear while the plant is blooming and have a short apparent stem.

ORIGIN: The tropical parts of South Africa (around 90 sorts, most of which were first cultivated in the last century).

Galanthus nivalis

CULTIVATION: Limited, in all flower-growing areas with hothouse cultivation.

AVAILABILITY: Limited, throughout the year.

CARE: The flowers on the umbel should be at least half open. Cut into the stem; use cut-flower food.

KEEPING PROPERTIES: Approx. 10 days. The flowers will turn blue at temperatures below 15° C.

USES: Because of its price, the flower is found almost only in exclusive floral work.

SCENT: None.

△ Hippeastrum hybride 'Red Lion' ▽ Haemanthus katherinae 'Roi d'Albert'

Hippeastrum hybride 'Appelbloesem'

Hippeastrum hybrids
Amaryllis

NAME: *Hippeastrum* literally means 'horseman star' (*astron* = star); the name refers to the star-shaped flowers of the original sorts.

DESCRIPTION: The bulb produces one or two hollow flower stems of 50-70 cm. On each stem grow 3-4 flowers which are red, pink, salmon, white or two-toned, depending on the cultivar. The 50 cm long dark green leaves appear after the flowers when they bloom early and at the same·time as the flowers when they bloom late.

ORIGIN: Southern and Central America and the Caribbean; depending on the sort, in dry forests and savannahs and in the damp rain forests of the tropics and subtropics.

CULTIVATION: All flower-growing areas of the world, but especially in the Netherlands and southern Africa.

AVAILABILITY: Throughout the year, with a peak in February and March.

CARE: The flowers may not be cooled. Cut into the stem and use cut-flower food for bulb plants.

KEEPING PROPERTIES: 14 days, provided the flowers are not yet opened when purchased. The temperature may not go below 15° C.

USES: Mostly in large floral work; to a very limited degree in a vase.

SCENT: None.

Cultivars

The improvement of *Hippeastrum* took place primarily in England and the Netherlands. It is presently in the Netherlands that the largest number of new cultivars are developed. The most important parents are *H. vittatum*, *H. reginae* and *H. leopoldii*. The first crossbreeds had striped flowers with narrow petals. In 1865 De Graaf crossed the existing hybrids in Leiden with *H. psittacinum* and thus obtained the cultivar '**Empress of India**'. Today's cultivars with a variety of colours and large, well-shaped flowers come from this ancestor. The most important among them are:

'**Red Lion**', the most frequently cultivated variety, with lovely round and wide, red petals. The flowers stand wide open at right angles to the stem, which makes for easy viewing.

'**Appelbloesem**', the most frequently cultivated pink cultivar. Keeping properties, flower shape and the colour of the bud are strikingly good, which gives this cultivar a large commercial value.

'**Ludwig Dazzler**', the best known white cut flower cultivar. The flower bud is vividly coloured; the heart of the flower shows little green. The white cultivars are very seldom used as cut flowers. The *Hippeastrum* assortment is very large and is still growing every year. A few promising new cultivars are 'Oscar' (red), 'Hercules' (cerise) and 'Christmas Gift' (white, very lovely). New cultivars are offered in a limited supply, because it takes a very long time before they can be produced on a large scale.

Leucojum aestivum

'Mount Hood'

'Carlton'

Leucojum aestivum
Snowflake

NAME: The Greek *leukoion* means 'plant with lovely white flowers'; it is a name which has been given to several plant sorts. *Aestivum =* summer and refers to the time it blooms, although the popular name calls up a different picture.
DESCRIPTION: The nodding white flowers have yellowy-green spots at the tips and grow in umbels of 3-8. They look rather like large snowdrops. The stem, 30-40 cm long, is slightly longer than the 4-7 linear leaves.
ORIGIN: Central and Eastern Europe, Southwest Asia and the Caucasians; now grows wild in the northeast of the United States. The plant was first cultivated in the Netherlands in 1594.
CULTIVATION: All flower-growing areas in temperate zones.
AVAILABILITY: May-June.
CARE: One-third of the flower umbel must be open. Cut into the stem; use cut-flower food for herbaceous plants.
KEEPING PROPERTIES: 7-10 days.
USES: In a vase and in floral work.
SCENT: None.

Narcissus pseudonarcissus
Daffodil

NAME: Narcissus is the Latin form of the Greek Narkissos, the name of a youth who was transformed into a flower by the gods (see page 18). The name is also thought to be related to the Greek word narkos = to stun, intoxicate. It would then refer to the strong scent of some wild narcissus species.
DESCRIPTION: A large number of cultivars have been developed since the Romans first brought the original wild sorts into cultivation. They are all bulbous plants with round stems and bluish-green, strap-shaped leaves up to 2 cm wide. The cultivated daffodils can be distinguished into eight important groups on the basis of their flower shapes: the trumpet narcissus or daffodil, the large corolla narcissus, the short corolla narcissus, the double-flowered narcissus, the jonquil, the polyanthus, the split corolla narcissus and the poet's narcissus. See further under 'Cultivars'.
ORIGIN: South-western Europe.
CULTIVATION: Primarily in southern England and the Channel Islands (outdoors) and in the Netherlands (forced, under glass).
AVAILABILITY: From October till the end of April, with a peak between January and March.
CARE: The narcissus stem gives off slime, which has an unfavourable effect on its keeping properties. A special preservative has been developed to counter this. Another possibility: put the flowers into water and change it after 24 hours. Cut into the stems; use plenty of water.

KEEPING PROPERTIES: 6-12 days, but shorter in October and November and at high room temperatures.
USES: In a vase, also in mixed bouquets. Further in floral work, especially the small-flowered polyanthus.
SCENT: Varies with different sorts.

Cultivars

'Golden Harvest' (trumpet narcissus or daffodil) was the top cultivar in this group for years. Corona (the 'trumpet') and petals are both deep yellow. The cultivar has a lengthy blossoming period and can also be made to bloom late (August/September).
'Ice Follies' (trumpet narcissus or daffodil) is a very recent cultivar which is gaining popularity. Corona and petals are both completely white.
'Carlton' is an entirely yellow large corolla narcissus of excellent quality. Large corolla narcissi distinguish themselves from daffodils in that the length of the corona (also called the cup) is no more than one-third of the length of the petals. If the cup is larger, then the plant is a trumpet narcissus.
'Flower Record' (large corolla) produces a great many flowers. The petals of this cultivar are creamy white, the corona is tinged bright orange towards the edge.
'Verger' is a short corolla narcissus, that is, the length of the corolla is clearly less than one-third of the length of the petals. The cultivar bears one flower per stem. The petals are white, the corona orange-red. The cultivar is less frequently cultivated than the various yellow cultivars.
'Cheerfulness' is a multi-flowered 'polyanthus' type with creamy white, fragrant flowers. Each stem bears several flowers, in contrast to

the double-flowered cultivar **'Texas'** (yellow with red), for instance, which bears only one flower per stem.
Narcissus jonquilla, a wild species from the western part of the Mediterranean, is a small-flowered jonquil with a very pleasant scent. It is primarily available in April.
'Geranium' is a cultivar belonging to the polyanthuses, another member of which is the well-known cultivar **'Paper White'**, which is brought to blossom in gravel and water indoors at the end of the year. They are simple-flowered and strongly aromatic polyanthuses. 'Geranium' has bright white petals and an orange-red corona.
'Laurens Koster' is another polyanthus with a very lovely, pale yellow colour and a strong, pleasant scent. It keeps very well.
Narcissus poeticus **'Actaea'** is the most frequently cultivated cultivars of the poet's narcissus. The cultivar has one flower per stem. The petals are white, the small corolla yellow to deep orange. The flowers are strongly scented.
Split-corona narcissi bear one flower per stem. The flowers are frilled and the corona flat and deeply cut. Split-corona narcissi come in numerous shades of yellow; sometimes they are two-coloured. These cultivars are gaining popularity primarily in modern flower arrangement.

△ 'Tahiti' ▽ 'Actaea'

△ 'Cheerfulness' ▽ 'Flower Record'

△ 'Geranium' ▽ Narcissus, split-corona

Narcissus jonquilla

Revenge for unrequited love

The daffodil or narcissus, by far the most important commercial flower of the amaryllis family, is said to owe its name to the Greek legend of Narcissus.

Narcissus was the son of the river god, Kephissus, and the nymph Leiriope. He grew to be a ravishingly handsome young man with whom a great many girls fell in love. But quite in vain, for Narcissus had other things on his mind and took scarce notice of the female beauty which fluttered around him. One of his admirers, the nymph Echo, found his indifference particularly annoying. She asked the goddess of revenge, Nemesis (according to others: Aphrodite, the goddess of love), to punish the recalcitrant Narcissus.

The goddess went about this in her own way. Once, after a strenuous hunt, when Narcissus was quenching his thirst in a stream, he fell in love with his own reflection. In fact, he was so mesmerized by what he saw that he could not move from the spot. When he finally came in danger of dying of malnutrition, the gods felt sorry for him. They changed Narcissus into a white flower with an orange-yellow heart.

Many poets have sung the praises of the flower and the legend. Linnaeus immortalized both in his way by calling a bulbous plant from the Balkans after the Greek demi-god: Narcissus poeticus, the poet's narcissus.

Nerine bowdenii and **N. sarniensis**
Spider lily (*N. bowdenii*)
Guernsey lily (*N. sarniensis*)

NAME: The Latin name comes from the Greek sea-god Nereus. *Bowdenii* is the Latinized name of a botanist, *sarniensis* a derivative of Sarnia, the Latin name for the British island of Guernsey. *N. sarniensis*, almost certainly a descendent of bulbs from a stranded ship which came from South Africa, was cultivated on this island.

DESCRIPTION: A bulb plant with a bare stem around 50 cm long topped by a multifloral umbel. The umbel of *N. bowdenii* bears ten to twelve bright red flowers of 6-8 cm; *N. sarniensis* has an umbel consisting of eight to twelve shiny, bright orange flowers of 7-8 cm in length. Other less generally available nerine sorts are *N. undulata* syn. *N. crispa* which has a shorter stem and an umbel with eight to twelve pale pink flowers, and *N. flexuosa* 'Albo', with an umbel of ten to twelve white flowers.

ORIGIN: South Africa.

PRODUCTION: Chiefly the Netherlands; the island of Guernsey for *N. sarniensis*. AVAILABILITY: Although originally an autumn flowerer, thanks to temperature treatment of the bulbs, *N. bowdenii* is commonly available in all seasons, with a peak from August to the end of December.

Nerine flexuosa 'Alba'

CARE: When purchased, the flowers should have fully grown buds which are just about to open. Fill the vase with water at 10-12° C; use cut-flower food. Do not put the flowers in a cold place; low temperatures will cause them to tinge blue.

KEEPING PROPERTIES: Twelve to eighteen days, depending on the temperature.

USE: Especially in floral work; also in bridal work and corsages, and in a vase.

SCENT: None.

Cultivars

The most commonly available cultivar of *N. bowdenii* is **'Favorite'**; of *N. sarniensis* it is **'Corusca Major'**. The dozen nerine sorts are crossed with a related sort, *Lycoris africana*, which has golden flowers, in attempts to increase the range of colours.

On a limited scale, crosses are also available of *N. sarniensis* and *N. flexuosa* in red, orange, salmon, pink and cerise tints.

'Corusca Major'

Aquifoliaceae

The holly family (*Aquifoliaceae*) has only two genera, of which the genus holly (*Ilex*) is the most important: the leaves are ornamental while the wood is used in inlay work.

The *Aquifoliaceae* are trees or shrubs with alternate, often leathery leaves. They are closely related to the *Celastraceae*. The regularly formed greenish-white flowers are generally unisexual (and then usually dioecious) and are grouped in short racemes. They have four sepals fused at the base, four petals and four stamens. The superior ovary has three or more cells; the fruit is a coloured berry with a single stone.

'J.C. van Tol'

Ilex aquifolium
Holly

NAME: *Ilex* is the former Latin name for the holly or holm oak. It was given to the holly because the leaves of both sorts bear a superficial resemblance. *Aquifolium* is a contraction of *acus* (= needle) and *folium* (= leaf) and refers to the needle-like prickles of the holly leaf.

DESCRIPTION: Among the approx. 400 *Ilex* species, *I. aquifolium*, with more than 50 cultivars, is by far the most important. This tall shrub can grow up to 8 m high and, depending on the cultivar, has dark green, gold or silver-speckled leaves, various plant shapes and a variety of berry colours. The small, white flowers stand in groups in the axils and develop into small berries in the autumn.

ORIGIN: Western, Central and Southern Europe, North Africa and Western Asia, into China. The holly has been cultivated since ancient times.

CULTIVATION: All countries with a temperate climate.

AVAILABILITY: November and December.

CARE: Much holly is used dried. If you put live branches in a vase, use a cut-flower food designed for shrubs.

KEEPING PROPERTIES: In water 4-5 weeks, dry 7-10 days. Berries and leaves will shrink.

USES: Especially in floral arrangements at Christmas time. This preference stems from the midwinter feasts of the Iron Age Teuton peoples of Germany, for whom holly was a sacred tree.

SCENT: None.

Cultivars

'**J.C. van Tol**' is a cultivar with many large, bright orange-red berries and only slightly dentate leaves. It is primarily cultivated for the berry; the shrub itself is less popular because it is rather widespreading in growth.

'**Bacciflava**' is a cultivar with yellowish berries which has been cultivated since 1688. The berry colour varies from yellow to light orange. The cultivar is chiefly used in modern floral work.

Ilex verticillata
Deciduous holly

NAME: *Verticillata* means 'whorled' and refers to the arrangement of the berries. See further *I. aquifolium*.

DESCRIPTION: In contrast to *I. aquifolium*, this species of holly loses its leaves in the winter. The plant is dioecious; the female plants bear large numbers of bright red berries on leafless branches. For the berry formation, it is necessary for male plants to be in the vicinity. The branches of this holly species are fairly thin, sturdy and light brown.

ORIGIN: Central and north-eastern America. First cultivated in England in 1736.

CULTIVATION: Widespread in temperate climates.

AVAILABILITY: November-December.

CARE: Cut into the branch, use cut-flower food for shrubs. The berries are sensitive to ethylene (from ripening fruit) and will soon drop off under the influence of this gas.

KEEPING PROPERTIES: In water 4-5 weeks, dried 5-7 days.

USES: In floral work and Christmas decorations; sometimes, too, alone in a vase.

SCENT: None.

'Bacciflava'

Araceae

The arum family (*Araceae*) has over 2000 species, divided between more than 100 genera. They are herbaceous and monocotyledonous. Many grow in the tropics, but some are also native to Europe. In temperate regions the family is represented by plants such as the sweet flag (*Acorus calamus*), the somewhat rarer snakeweed (*Calla palustris*) and the cuckoo-pint (*Arum maculatum*).

In addition to their normal roots, many tropical arums also develop prop and aerial roots to absorb water and minerals. Some sorts are cultivated for their edible roots or berries, but the family derives its economic value primarily from a number of ornamental plants.

The inflorescence consists of a spathe, which is large and brightly coloured in some sorts, but in others small and green. The flowers are found on a blunt-ended spadix, but not at the end of it; they have 4-6 stamens.

The flowers of a few Araceae give off a smell of decay; this is how they attract insects to pollinate them: for example, the genus *Arum*, which has unisexual flowers. Other genera, such as *Anthurium*, have hermaphrodite flowers. They mature at different times to prevent self-pollination.

Anthurium andreanum hybrids, syn. *A x cultorum*

Flamingo plant, Tail flower, Wax flower, Oil-cloth flower, Painter's palette

NAME: *Anthurium* (from *anthos* = flower and *aura* = tail) literally means 'tail flower'. *Andreanum* refers to the Paris garden architect E. F. André, editor of 'Revue horticole', after whom this flower was named in 1876.

DESCRIPTION: A plant with a fairly short stem, quite a few aerial roots and shiny, heart-shaped leaves with palmate venation. From the coarsely veined, shiny, heart-shaped and rather leathery red, salmon, white or pink spathe, the top of which is sometimes green, grows a fairly thick, straight but somewhat inclined spadix. On this spadix the female flower parts mature first. Only when they have finished do the stamens develop. This makes self-pollination impossible.

ORIGIN: The rain forests of Colombia. Cultivation and improvement first took place in Belgium and France.

CULTIVATION: *In vitro* culture, primarily in the Netherlands. Also on the Hawaiian islands and, to a more limted extent, in all flower-growing areas of the world.

AVAILABILITY: Throughout the year, although limited in the period from January to March.

CARE: The flowers must be mature upon purchase: the spadix has a granular appearance and the neck of the stem is sturdy. Less mature flowers will droop; when they are overripe, the spadix is less attractive but they can be kept longer. The flowers are sold with the stem in a small vial of water. After purchase remove the vial, cut a bit off the stem and put the flower in fresh water. No cut-flower food is needed. Optimum temperature is 18°C. At higher temperatures they will not keep so long and the flowers will turn blue. The use of florist's plastic foam lessens their keeping properties.

KEEPING PROPERTIES: 10-18 days. See also under 'Care'.

USES: Especially in floral work. Alone, in bouquets, sometimes with leafy material.

SCENT: None.

Cultivars

'**Avoclaudia**' is one of the finest red cultivars with a bright red flower that is less likely to discolour. A new red cultivar is 'Tropical'; it is rapidly gaining in popularity.

'**Avoanneke**' is the most frequently cultivated pink cultivar. The flower colour fades in bright sunlight in spring.

'**Oranje Favoriet**' ('Orange Favourite') is one of the most popular orange cultivars; the other is '**Avonette**'. The colour is bright orange, with a striking sheen.

'**Cuba**' is a clear white cultivar, with a green point on the spadix. It is outstanding for its colour and productivity. Another white cultivar, with a mother-of-pearl sheen on the spathe, is '**Hoenette**': very distinctive with good keeping qualities.

'Avoclaudia'

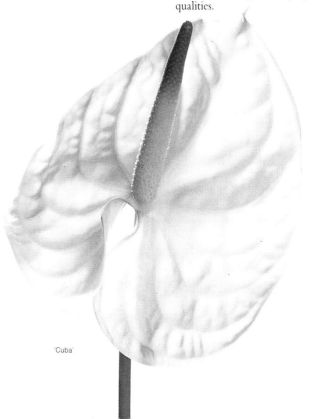

'Cuba'

Anthurium scherzerianum

Anthurium scherzerianum
Flamingo flower

NAME: *Scherzerianum* is in honour of the Viennese globe traveller and political economist K. von Scherzer (1821-1903). See also *A. andreanum*.

DESCRIPTION: An almost stemless herbaceous plant with dark green leaves 20 cm long, which are somewhat rounded at the foot and have a somewhat lighter middle nerve. The flower stem is the same length as the leaves. The orange, somewhat curved spadix is surrounded by an oval to oblong spathe which is usually red but may also be red and white speckled, salmon or greenish-white.

ORIGIN: Tropical rain forests of South America. First cultivated in Germany in 1862.

CULTIVATION: All flower-growing areas of the world, especially as a pot-plant.

AVAILABILITY: Throughout the year, with a peak in March/April.

CARE: Cut off a bit of the stem; put in water with cut-flower food. The spadix must have a granular appearance when they are purchased. The flowers cannot withstand cold; minimum temperature 16°C.

KEEPING PROPERTIES: 10-14 days.

USES: Floral work with leafy material.

SCENT: None.

Arum Italicum
Cuckoo-pint

NAME: *Arum* is the Latin form of the old Greek *aron*; *italicum* means 'from Italy'.

DESCRIPTION: A perennial bulb plant with lanceolate leaves on long stems. The unisexual flowers are grouped on a tuberous spadix surrounded by a greenish spathe.

At the end of the spadix is a violet, club-shaped bulge. Under this bulge is a band of thread-like appendages. On this band are located the male flowers, a zone with infertile projections, and the female flowers, in that order. The female flowers, consisting of a sessile stigma and an ovary, ripen earlier than the male flowers. The flowers are cross-pollinated by tiny flies; the smell of decay from the tip of the spadix attracts them and the infertile projections hold them in place. They are not released until the projections dry out, after the pollination of the female flowers. Then the male flowers mature. The cuckoo-pint blooms in April; its lovely orange berries ripen on the spadix from June till September.

ORIGIN: Native to Central and Southern Europe. Now spread as far as Scotland to the north and the northern Ukraine to the east.

CULTIVATION: Limited, in flower-growing areas with a temperate climate.

AVAILABILITY: From June until October; peak in July-September.

CARE: Cut a bit off the stems; change the water regularly. Cut-flower food helps to keep the water clean.

KEEPING PROPERTIES: 10-20 days.

USES: The stem, up to 60 cm long, and the spadix covered with berries are primarily used in floral arrangements.

SCENT: None.

Spathiphyllum 'Mauna Loa'
Peace lily, Spathe flower

NAME: *Spathiphyllum* is composed of the Latin words *spatha* (= sheath) and *phyllum* (= leaf). 'Mauna Loa' is a cultivar name after a volcano on Hawaii.

DESCRIPTION: The flowers are 10-20 cm long and grow on a stem of 40-50 cm. The spadix is creamy white, the upright spathe is bright white. The plant itself is a herbaceous perennial with glossy dark green leaves, 25-40 cm long and about 18 cm wide; the flower stem is longer than the leaves.

ORIGIN: Tropical South and Central America, including Mexico and Colombia (36 species). 'Mauna Loa' comes from America and is the result of a cross between *S. floribunda* and a hybrid from the Hawaiian Islands, 'McCoy'.

CULTIVATION: United States; also flower-growing areas elsewhere in the world. In the Netherlands, production via *in vitro* tissue culture is increasing.

AVAILABILITY: Throughout the year, with a peak in May.

CARE: Cut into stem, use cut-flower food. Temperature not lower than 15°C.

KEEPING PROPERTIES: 2-3 weeks.

USES: Modern flower work; in a vase in combination with leafy material.

SCENT: None.

Arum italicum

Spathiphyllum 'Mauna Loa'

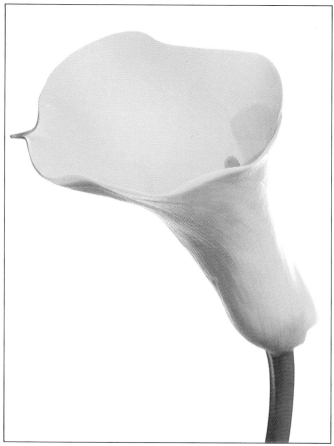

Zantedeschia elliotiana

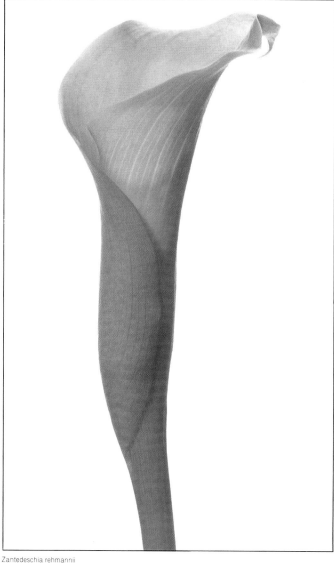

Zantedeschia rehmannii

Zantedeschia aethiopica
Calla, Arum lily

NAME: The genus of *Zantedeschia* is named after the Italian doctor and botanist G. Zantedeschi (1773-1846). *Aethiopica*, derived from the Greek, literally means 'growing in the land of the Moors'; also, 'sunbaked'. Botanists formerly used the word to indicate an African origin.
DESCRIPTION: The 1 m long flower stem of this perennial bears a funnel-shaped spathe with flattened edges. It is white, and surrounds a yellow spadix which is almost as long as the spathe.
ORIGIN: South Africa; first cultivated in the Netherlands in 1687.
CULTIVATION: Primarily in England, Germany and the Netherlands, but also elsewhere in the world.
AVAILABILITY: Throughout the year, with a peak in the period from February to May.
CARE: Cut off a bit of the thick, fleshy stem; use cut-flower food.
KEEPING PROPERTIES: 10-14 days at a temperature of 8-15°C; less at higher temperatures.
USES: In funeral work and church decorations; in England, also in bridal work. Sometimes in a vase.
SCENT: Slightly fragrant.

Zantedeschia rehmannii
Pink calla

NAME: As well as the Italian Zantedeschi (see *Z. aethiopica*), the plant is also named after the Swiss physician and author on the use of flowers, Joseph Zavier Rehman (1753-1831).
DESCRIPTION: The 8 cm long, narrow funnel-shaped spathe of this sort varies from light pink to pinkish-red, as does the spadix. The plant grows to around 40 cm high. It has narrower leaves than the other *Zantedeschia* species.
ORIGIN: The South African province of Natal.
CULTIVATION: Primarily in southern Africa; to a very limited extent elsewhere.
AVAILABILITY: May-June for plants of European origin. Supply from southern Africa in November and December.
CARE: Cut a bit off the stem; use cut-flower food.
KEEPING PROPERTIES: 10-14 days.
USES: Especially in floral work. Sometimes as a single flower in a vase, in combination with leafy material.
SCENT: Slight.

Zantedeschia elliotiana
Yellow calla

NAME: In addition to being named after the Italian Zantedeschi (see *Z. aethiopica*), this sort is also named after the English captain, Elliot, in whose park at Farnborough, Hampshire, the plant first bloomed in Europe in 1896.
DESCRIPTION: A funnel-shaped, golden yellow spathe of approx. 10 cm long, surrounding a shorter yellow spadix. The flower stem of this perennial tuberous plant is about 60 cm long; its oval, heart-shaped leaves are speckled white.
ORIGIN: The highlands of southern Africa.
CULTIVATION: Primarily southern Africa; to a lesser extent England and the Netherlands. On a very limited scale elsewhere.
AVAILABILITY: June-July for flowers of European origin. In November-December from southern Africa.
CARE: Cut a bit off the stem; use cut-flower food.
KEEPING PROPERTIES: 12-16 days.
USES: Especially in floral work; occasionally in a vase.
SCENT: Slight.

Asclepiadaceae

The 250 genera of the milkweed family (*Asclepiadaceae*) contain 2000 species. They are primarily herbaceous climbers, plants, shrubs and trees from the tropics. Most of them are native to South America; some succulent types grow in southern Africa. Many sorts contain a milky juice. Well-known decorative plants from this family belong to the genera of *Hoya*, *Ceropegia*, *Stapelia* (carrion flower), *Asclepias* (milkweed plant), and *Stephanotis* (Madagascar jasmine). Only the last two are used as cut flowers.

The leaves of the *Asclepiadaceae* are generally opposite and mostly have entire edges. The inflorescence is usually a compound umbel, but can be a simple umbel. The hermaphrodite flowers are regularly formed. The five sepals are fused, just as the five petals, which are twisted or touch one another. The corolla and stamens bear appendages. The filaments are short or absent; the anthers are fused with the ovary, forming a tiny pillar. The ovary is semi-inferior and consists of two nearly detached carpels with a style and a five-lobed stigma.

The anthers have two pouches in which the pollen is compressed into a lump; when pollination takes place, it is transported as a whole. Each lump of pollen has its own transport arm. In the subfamily *Cyanchoideae* the lumps are linked, two by two, by a gland.

Stephanotis floribunda

Asclepias tuberosa
Milkweed, Swallow wort, Butterfly weed
NAME: The genus is named after Asklepios, the ancient god of the art of healing. *Tuberosa* = tuberous.

DESCRIPTION: A stem of 50-60 cm supports an umbel with numerous flowers of which the petals are orange-yellow and the corona bright orange. The plant has long, lanceolate leaves.

ORIGIN: North America; first cultivated in England in 1669.

CULTIVATION: All flower-growing areas with a temperate climate.

AVAILABILITY: From June until September.

CARE: Most of the flowers in the umbel should be open when they are purchased. After purchase, remove the lower leaves, cut a bit off the stem and add cut-flower food to the water.

KEEPING PROPERTIES: 7-12 days.

USES: Single, also in mixed bouquets.

SCENT: Slightly aromatic.

Stephanotis floribunda
Madagascar jasmine
NAME: *Floribunda* = richly flowering; *stephanotis* is derived from the Greek words *stephanos*, for 'wreath', and *ous*, for 'ear'. The name refers to the five tips of the petals of the corona, which form a wreath.

DESCRIPTION: The Madagascar jasmine is an evergreen climbing shrub with shiny, dark green leaves. The white flowers, 5 cm in diameter, have a spreading perianth. They grow in umbels in the leaf axils.

ORIGIN: Madagascar; first cultivated in England in 1839.

CULTIVATION: Frequently as a potted plant, in Denmark and other countries. As a cut flower, in all flower-growing areas on a limited scale.

AVAILABILITY: Throughout the year, with a peak in June and July.

CARE: As cut flowers, they are supplied in a plastic bag and must be used immediately.

KEEPING PROPERTIES: Very short

USES: Primarily because of the very short stem, almost exclusively in bridal work, corsages, and so on.

SCENT: Very fragrant.

Asclepias tuberosa

Aspidiaceae

Berberidaceae

The aspidium or shield fern family (*Aspidiaceae*) contains several genera of ferns, including *Arachniodes, Cyrtomium, Didymochlaena, Dryopteris* and *Polystichum*. Some are native to the tropics and subtropics of Asia; others, such as *Didymochlaena,* occur in the entire tropical belt. All shield ferns have scaly stems. The spores are spread over the underside of the leaves.

Arachniodes adiantiformis,
syn. *Ruhmora adiantiformis*
Leather fern
NAME: *Arachniodes* means 'with spiderweb-like hair' and is derived from the Greek word for spiderweb: *arachnion. Adiantiformis* literally means: resembling the *Adiantum,* or the fern sort which we know as maidenhair.
DESCRIPTION: 30 to 50 cm long bipinnate fronds with oblong leaf segments which have roughly dentate margins. They have a leathery structure, grow closely on a hairy, creeping rootstock, and are shiny green. The groups of brown spores are dotted over the underside of the leaf.
ORIGIN: Southern Africa, South America, New Zealand.

CULTIVATION: Especially in the United States (California); to a limited extent, in the Netherlands (hothouse cultivation).
AVAILABILITY: Throughout the year.
CARE: Cut off the dried part of the stem. Use cut-flower food.
KEEPING PROPERTIES: 3-4 weeks.
USES: In bouquets and in flower arrangements.
SCENT: None.

The barberry family (*Berberidaceae*) has from five to six hundred species classified into 13-16 genera. Some of these species are clearly related, such as *Berberis* and *Mahonia*; others have only a few characteristics in common. The most important criterion for classifying species into this family is that they bear more resemblance to one another than to species from other families.

The *Berberidaceae* are native to the temperate zones of Europe, Asia and America and to the mountains of South America. The leaves, compound or simple, are fairly far apart and generally lack stipules. In the genus *Berberis*, the leaves on the long shoots have evolved into spines; the true leaves are on the short shoots.

The flowers of the barberry family stand in plumes or racemes and are hermaphrodite. The perianth consists of 4-6 segments. The six stamens stand opposite the inner petal segments; the stigma may be without a style. The ovary is superior and has one compartment; the fruit is often fleshy, as in *Berberis* and *Mahonia*. The seed has an upright embryo. Many plants of this family are grown as decorative shrubs.

Mahonia aquifolium
Hollygrape, Barberry, Oregon grape
NAME: The plant is named after the American herb specialist of Irish origin Bernard M. Mahon (1775-1816). *Aquifolium* is the old scientific name for the holly and refers to the sharp leaf margins.
DESCRIPTION: The ornamental value of the plant lies in its pinnate leaves which are dark green, but turn a beautiful bronze in the winter. The young shoots bear 5-11 narrow

oval leaves, each about 6 cm long. They are prickly and serrate. In April-May the Oregon grape bears small yellow flowers in cultivarmes which later grow into beautiful bluish-black berries.
ORIGIN: North America.
CULTIVATION: All temperate climate zones.
AVAILABILITY: From September to March, with a peak in November/December.
CARE: Cut off a bit of the branch and put it in water. Cut-flower food is not necessary.
KEEPING PROPERTIES: In water 3-4 weeks; dry, up to 7 days.
USES: In floral work, especially around Christmas.
SCENT: None.

Arachniodes adiantiformis

Boraginaceae

The nearly 2000 species of the borage family (*Boraginaceae*) - annual and perennial herbs, shrubs, trees and climbing plants - are largely native to the Mediterranean, but also occur in practically all temperate and subtropical areas of the world. Well-known representatives in our areas are the comfrey (*Symphytum officinale*) and the viper's bugloss (*Echium vulgare*). Another well-known member is borage (*Borago officinalis*). The stems of the plants are covered with rough hairs; the leaves, which generally stand apart, are also hairy. They are simple and without stipules. On the inner side of the upper epidermis, the leaves show deposits of calcium carbonate, or cystolits. The regularly formed flowers are mostly hermaphrodite. They form simple or composite inflorescences, which are curled up in their young condition. The five sepals are usually partly joined as are the five corolla lobes. The flowers are bell-shaped, sometimes with scales in the throat. The five stamens, generally of unequal length, are borne on the petals and often have appendages on the filaments. The fruit is a four-chambered schizocarp (sometimes containing a stone). Many members of the borage family are cultivated for the ornamental value of the flowers; others, such as viper's bugloss and borage, for bee-keeping.

△ Heliotropium arborescens   ▽ Myosotis hybrid

Heliotropium arborescens
Heliotrope, Cherry pie

NAME: The name of the plant is derived from the Greek words *helios* (= sun) and *tropos* (= turn): a plant that turns towards the sun. *Arborescens* means 'tree-like; forming a definite stem'.
DESCRIPTION: A semishrub with short, hairy leaves and deep purple flowers which grow in bunches. Heliotrope is usually cultivated as an annual plant; it is then soft and herbaceous.
ORIGIN: Peru. The plant was first cultivated in England in 1740.
CULTIVATION: On a limited scale, in all flower-growing areas of the world.
AVAILABILITY: From April until September.
CARE: Remove lower leaves, cut a little off the stem; use cut-flower food for herbaceous flowers.
KEEPING PROPERTIES: 5-8 days.
USES: In floral work and summer bouquets.
SCENT: Strong and very pleasant.

Myosotis hybride
Forget-me-not

NAME: *Myosotis* means 'mouse-ear' and refers to the form of the leaves.
DESCRIPTION: Perennial herbaceous plants, 30-40 cm high, and with hairy leaves and stems. The lanceolate leaves are stalkless and are about 4 cm long and dark green. The lovely deep blue flowers are approx. 0.5 cm in diameter. They grow far apart in long spikes. Commonly cultivated hybrid cultivars are 'Isolde Krotz' and 'Ruth Fischer'; there is some cultivation of pink and white cultivars. Also cultivated for use as cut flowers are the marsh forget-me-not (*M. palustris*) and the wood forget-me-not (*M. sylvatica*).
ORIGIN: Europe, Northern Asia.
CULTIVATION: Flower-growing areas in temperate climates, especially Germany and Switzerland.
AVAILABILITY: From late April until August.
CARE: Half of the flowers should be open when purchased. Remove lower leaves, cut a bit off the stem, use cut-flower food for herbaceous plants. KEEPING PROPERTIES: 10-12 days; the flowers will discolour somewhat.
USES: In a vase, in bouquets (especially Biedermeier style) and in corsages.
SCENT: None.

Bromeliaceae

The bromeliad family (*Bromeliaceae*) has a total of 60 genera and more than 2000 species. In addition, numerous cultivars and hybrids have been developed over the years. The genera *Aechmea*, *Ananas*, *Billbergia*, *Cryptanthus*, *Guzmania*, *Neoregelia*, *Nidularium*, *Tillandsia* and *Vriesea* are the most important ones in flower growing.

The bromeliad family is native to tropical and subtropical South America. Many genera grow as epiphytes on other plants, but without being parasitic. Others, such as *Aechmea*, grow terrestrially (= on the ground) and have a much better developed root system. All of them are herbaceous plants with short stems and a rosette of leaves.

The fasciate leaf bases, which are sometimes coloured at the tip (*Neoregelia*) or have prickles (*Aechmea*), often form a basin in which the plants catch water. These sorts have a different sort of root on the base of the leaf with which they absorb water from the basin. True epiphytes bear special hair structures, called trichomes, at the leaf base for the uptake of water.

The inflorescence is monocarpic, which means that, after flowering, the plant can only continue to grow from the side buds. The flowers grow in spikes, racemes or plumes. They are hermaphrodite and regular in form, and often form in the axil of the coloured bracts (*Tillandsia*) or in the basin (*Neoregelia*). Calyx and corolla are ternate and the flower has six stamens.

In the wild, the flowers are pollinated by birds and insects. The stigma is ripe once the pollen has been released. The ovary with three cells may be either inferior or superior. The fruit is a berry or a capsule. The seed sometimes contains pinnate appendages, for example in *Vriesea*.

Aechmea fasciata
Achmea

NAME: *Aechmea* means 'lance point' and refers to the thorny, pointed tip of the outer calyx leaf. *Fasciata* = banded or striped, referring to the markings on the leaf.

DESCRIPTION: The plant consists of a funnel-shaped leaf rosette of leaves with blunt tops and prickly points. The leaf margin is sharply prickled and the leaf has silver-coloured, somewhat woolly cross stripes. The inflorescence is in the shape of a pyramid and entirely pink, with fairly long, prickly dentate pink bracts and pink spathe petals. The corolla initially tends to purple and turns blue as it matures.

ORIGIN: Eastern Brazil.

CULTIVATION: The plant was first cultivated in England in 1826 and is now cultivated in all flower-growing areas of the world.

AVAILABILITY: Throughout the year (thanks to the use of bloom regulators); the plant normally blossoms in summer.

CARE: Cut a bit off the stem; use cut-flower food. Dried, the flower can be kept for 1-2 days.

KEEPING PROPERTIES: In water, 6-8 weeks.

USES: Especially in modern flower arrangement.

SCENT: None.

Guzmania 'Amaranth'
Guzmania

NAME: The plant is named after the 19th-century Spanish pharmacist and naturalist A. Guzman. 'Amaranth' is the cultivar name and refers to the colour of the flower.

DESCRIPTION: The fairly thin leaves form a leaf rosette; they are green, with reddish lines at the base of the leaves. The spathe leaves are purple-red, as are the involucres; the corolla is white.

ORIGIN: The *Guzmania* species are native to the north of South America and to Costa Rica. They were much cultivated during the period from 1776-1870, primarily in England. The present hybrid cultivars, including 'Amaranth', were developed in the Netherlands.

CULTIVATION: In all flower-growing areas of the world (hothouse cultivation).

AVAILABILITY: Throughout the year, thanks to the use of growth regulators which can influence the blossoming time.

CARE: Cut a bit off the stem; add cut-flower food to the water. Later, if necessary, cut into the stem again and change the water.

KEEPING PROPERTIES: Approx. 2 months.

USES: In modern flower arrangement; also very pretty in a vase.

SCENT: None.

Aechmea fasciata

Cultivars

Guzmania '**Grand Prix**' This hybrid cultivar was developed in the Netherlands, as was 'Amaranth', and one of the most important ancestors of both was *G. lingulata*. Involucres and spathe leaves are bright red, the corolla leaves are white. The flower stem is 50-60 cm long and is slightly reddish. Care and keeping properties same as for 'Amaranth'.

Guzmania wittmackii A species with a more wide-open inflorescence, with narrow red spathe leaves and involucres, white corolla leaves tending to lilac and a green stem around 60 cm long. In addition to the red sort, there is also a purplish-red form. The flowers will keep exceptionally well: about 4 months, even at high temperatures.

△ Guzmania 'Amaranth' △ ▷ Guzmania wittmackii ▽ Tillandsia leiboldiana

Neoregelia carolinae
Blushing bromeliad

NAME: The plant is named after the German botanist and writer E.A. von Regel from Gotha, director of the Botanical Garden in Zürich and of the Imperial Botanical Garden in St. Petersburg (now Leningrad). *Carolinae* refers to Princess Carolina Louise (1723-1783), the wife of grand duke Karl Friedrich of Baden. She corresponded a great deal with Linnaeus and formed the plan (which she never carried out) to publish a book of all the 10,000 plants he described.

DESCRIPTION: A flat plant with a broad, funnel-shaped rosette. The leaves, 30 cm long and 5 cm wide, stand out horizontally and are shiny green. The innermost leaves turn shiny red, the other leaves redden only at the base. The corolla leaves are purple and stand in the basin. The most frequently cultivated cultivar is 'Meyendorffia' (bright red). Other sorts often seen are the speckled cultivars 'Tricolor' (white centre stripe, green leaf margins) and 'Flandia' (white leaf margins).

ORIGIN: Eastern Brazil.

CULTIVATION: The plant was first cultivated in Switzerland in 1857 and is now grown in hothouses all over the world.

AVAILABILITY: Throughout the year.

CARE: Shake the earth from the roots; wrap the damp roots in plastic foil or sphagnum.

KEEPING PROPERTIES: Several months.

USES: The entire plant is used in floral arrangements.

SCENT: None.

Tillandsia leiboldiana
Tillandsia

NAME: The plant is named after the Finnish writer and botanist E. Till-Landz (1640-1693) and von Leibold, about whom nothing is known.

DESCRIPTION: The stemless plant has green, smooth-margined leaves of 30 cm long and a flower stem of 40-50 cm. The spathe petals are 8-10 cm long and around 3 cm wide; the lower ones have green tips. The corolla petals are a beautiful blue and form a lovely contrast with the red spathe petals.

ORIGIN: The area from Southern Mexico to Costa Rica.

CULTIVATION: The plant was first cultivated in 1886, but only became popular around 1975. It is now grown in all hothouse cultivating areas of the world.

AVAILABILITY: Throughout the year, by regulating the blossoming time.

CARE: Cut off a bit of the stem, use cut-flower food.

KEEPING PROPERTIES: Around two months.

USES: In modern floral work.

SCENT: None.

Campanulaceae

The bellflower family (*Campanulaceae*) consists primarily of annuals and biennials, perennials and a few semishrubs. All are dicotyledonous. The 35 or so genera, with over 600 species, primarily grow in the temperate areas of the northern hemisphere. A few genera are native to South America.

The leaves of the plants are simple and are borne alternately, opposite one another or in whorls. The bell-shaped flowers are grouped in cultivarmes, spikes or capitula and have both calyx and corolla. The base of the calyx is fused with the ovary, which is generally inferior and consists of 2-5 united carpels. The flowers have five corolla lobes and stamens and a single style; the number of stigmata is the same as the number of carpels.

The flowers are pollinated by insects, which are attracted by the nectar. It is produced at the foot of the style and is generally hidden by the broad bases of the stamens. To avoid self-pollination, the five stamens ripen in the bud, while the stigmata are still immature. When the flower opens, the stamens wilt. After a while the stigma lobes mature and cross-pollination can take place. The fruit is a capsule in most genera, rarely a berry.

The Campanulaceae contain a milky juice. Instead of starch, they have certain sugar compounds which are also found in dahlia tubers.

Campenula glomerata 'Superba'

Campanula glomerata
Canterbury bells

NAME: *Campanula* (= bell) refers to the shape of the flower; *glomerata* (= ball of yarn) refers to the arrangement of the flowers in the inflorescence.

DESCRIPTION: Perennial plant with long, coarse-haired leaves with irregularly serrate margins and a somewhat heart-shaped stem at the base. The top leaves, which are oval, surround the sturdy stem of 40-50 cm. The deep violet-blue flowers stand in dense capitula at the end of the stem; they are shaped like broad funnels, are slightly hairy and 2-3 cm long. The flower corolla is cut to one-third of its length into oval, pointed tips. The calyx is lanceolate, with pointed tips. The cultivar 'Superbe' has sturdy stems and a lovely inflorescence.

ORIGIN: Europe, Western Asia, Siberia.

CULTIVATION: The plant was first cultivated in Germany in 1561 and is now grown outdoors in the temperate zones of Western Europe and other areas.

AVAILABILITY: End of May - July.

CARE: The flowers should be half open when purchased. Remove lower leaves, cut a bit off the stem, use cut-flower food for herbaceous plants.

KEEPING PROPERTIES: 10-14 days.

USES: In a vase; also in bouquets.

SCENT: None.

Campanula medium
Canterbury bells

NAME: *Campanula* = bell; *medium* is in this case derived from the Italian *erba media*, the popular name for the plant. This probably has to do with the fact that Canterbury bells have appendages between the thin calyx petals.

DESCRIPTION: A biennial plant which spends the winter as a rosette of root leaves. The root leaves are long, oval to oblong in shape, and half encircle the stem; they are hairy and dentate or serrate. The leaf base flares into a winged stem. The leaves on the stem are much smaller. The flowers are broad and bell-shaped, have short stems, and hang gracefully in large, pyramidal cultivarmes. The flowers of the ancestral species are violet-blue, 7-8 cm long and 5 cm across. There are also white, pink and light blue cultivars. In the cultivar called 'Calycanthema' (= calyx flower) the calyx lobes are enlarged and fused and are of the same colour as the corolla. They are also called 'Cup and saucer Canterbury bells'.

ORIGIN: Southern Europe, southern Germany and southern England.

CULTIVATION: The plant was first cultivated in France in 1500 and is now grown in all temperate flower-growing areas. It needs winter cold for the bud formation.

AVAILABILITY: From the end of May until July.

CARE: Remove the lower leaves, cut a bit off the stem, put the branches in water with cut-flower food for herbaceous plants.

KEEPING PROPERTIES: 8-14 days, if the flowers are still closed upon purchase.

USES: In a vase; in mixed bouquets.

SCENT: None.

Campanula persicifolia
Bellflower

NAME: *Campanula* = bell; *persicifolia* means 'having leaves as the peach'.

DESCRIPTION: The plant has smooth, unbranched stems and long, narrow, smooth, slightly serrate leaves ending in a point. The leaf base extends a long way down the stem. The flowers stand wide open and are around 3 cm long; they are lightly cut, have a diameter of 5 cm and are grouped in loose racemes. The calyx lobes are finely lanceolate, with smooth margins and hairless points. 'Alba' is the white form of what was originally a lilac-blue flower. It was discovered in England in 1771.

ORIGIN: Central and southern Europe, the Balkans. The plant was first cultivated in Belgium in 1554.

CULTIVATION: Outdoors, in all flower-growing areas.

AVAILABILITY: Normally starting in early August; when forced in hot-house cultivation they can come on the market as early as May.

CARE: Upon purchase, the buds should be fully grown but not yet open. Remove lower leaves, cut off a bit of the stem, use cut-flower food for herbaceous plants.

KEEPING PROPERTIES: See *Campanula medium*.

USES: See *Campanula medium*.

SCENT: None.

Cultivars

C. persicifolia 'Caerulea' is a bright blue variant from the wild sort.

Platycodon grandiflorus
Chinese bellflower, Balloon flower

NAME: The genus name is a contraction of the Greek words *platus* (= wide, flat) and *kodon* (= bell). *Grandiflorus* means 'bearing large flowers'.

DESCRIPTION: A perennial plant approx. 50 cm high with oval to lanceolate blue-green leaves whose margins are irregularly dentate. The flowers are wide-mouthed bells which, in their unopened state, have the form of a balloon. They are approx. 7 cm across. The wild sort is lilac blue; there is also the white form, 'Albus', and a pink one.

ORIGIN: North and East Asia.

CULTIVATION: The lilac-blue form was first cultivated in Austria in 1773, the white form in Germany in 1896. Today the flower is grown in all temperate zones. It is especially popular in Japan.

AVAILABILITY: June to August.

CARE: When purchased, the buds must be just ready to open. Remove lower leaves, cut off a piece of the stem, use cut-flower food for herbaceous plants.

KEEPING PROPERTIES: 7-12 days.

USES: In a vase and in floral arrangement.

SCENT: None.

Campanula medium

Campanula persicifolia 'Alba'

Campanula pyramidalis

Trachelium caeruleum

Campanula pyramidalis
Chimney bellflower

NAME: *Campanula* = bell; *pyramidalis* means 'pyramidal in shape' and refers to the form of the inflorescence.

DESCRIPTION: A 1-1½ m high perennial plant with tuberous roots and shiny green leaves with secretory serrate margins. The upper leaves have no stem, the lower ones do. The flowers, which were originally blue (there is now also a white form, 'Alba'), stand upright and have a wide-mouthed bell shape. The lower flowers are stemmed; at a later stage of the bloom, the calyx tips fold back.

ORIGIN: Mediterranean.

CULTIVATION: The plant was first cultivated in England in 1830 and is now grown in all flower-growing areas with a temperate climate.

AVAILABILITY: From June until August.

CARE: Remove lower leaves, cut a bit off the stem, use cut-flower food for herbaceous plants.

KEEPING PROPERTIES: 12-15 days.

USES: In a vase; in mixed bouquets.

SCENT: None.

Trachelium caeruleum
Blue throatwort

NAME: The genus name is derived from the Greek *tracheia* = throat: the plant was formerly used to treat neck and throat aches. *Caeruleum* means 'dark blue'.

DESCRIPTION: A perennial plant but, because it cannot withstand frost, generally cultivated as an annual. The bright green leaves are nettle-like and oval, with a pointed tip. The flower stem, often more than 80 cm long, bears an umbel with a large number of small, light purple, bell-shaped flowers.

ORIGIN: The western part of the Mediterranean region, chiefly Portugal.

CULTIVATION: West European flower-growing areas, especially the Netherlands.

AVAILABILITY: From July until November (outdoors and hothouse).

CARE: When purchased, a few flowers should be open; the others should be closed but no longer green. Immature flowers cannot be kept long. To stop them wilting, they must always be transported in water. Always use cut-flower food.

KEEPING PROPERTIES: 8-12 days, provided they are well-treated.

USES: In a vase; in mixed bouquets.

SCENT: None.

Caprifoliaceae

Most of the honeysuckle family (*Caprifoliaceae*) are small trees or shrubs often climbing, although a small number of herbaceous plants are also found among the 20 genera with 450 species. They are native all over the world, with the exception of certain parts of Africa, but are best represented in North America and East Asia.

The leaves of the honeysuckle family are simple and opposite. Some sorts (for instance, the guelder rose and the snowball tree) have nectaries, or honey glands on the leaf stalks.

The flowers are hermaphrodite. Their inflorescence is a raceme or cyme. The flowers have four or five calyx lobes which are fused with the ovary to form a calyx tube. The corolla usually has five lobes in two segments. The five stamens (sometimes one is missing) stand on the corolla tube. The single style bears an enlarged stigma. The fruit is generally a berry.

Viburnum opulus

Symphoricarpos albus
Snowberry

NAME: *Symphoricarpos* is a contraction of the Greek words *sumphuein*, which means 'to fuse', and *karpos* = 'fruit'. The name refers to the fusing of the follicles. *Albus* means white, the colour of the berries.

DESCRIPTION: A broad bush with many runners and bare twigs. The leaves, 4-7 cm long, have very short stalks; they are bluntly oval and often lobed. The pink flowers are grouped in dense bunches. The plant derives its ornamental value from the 10-12 mm white berries which acquire this colour in late summer and can be used until November. An often-seen cultivar is 'White Hedge', with ascending branches and large, snow-white berries.

ORIGIN: Eastern Canada and the northern United States.

CULTIVATION: In flower-growing areas with moderate to severe winters.

AVAILABILITY: From August until November, with a peak in September/October.

CARE: Cut a bit off the branch and put it in clean water. Change the water regularly; cut a bit off the stem each time.

KEEPING PROPERTIES: After two weeks the berries will begin to turn brownish. This happens earlier to branches harvested late in the season.

USES: In flower arrangements, in floral work and for decorations.

SCENT: None.

Viburnum opulus 'Sterile'
Snowball tree

NAME: *Viburnum* is an old Latin plant name derived from *vière* (= to bend or plait). It might refer to the bending twigs of the plant. *Opulus* is the former Latin name of a maple to which the snowball bears a superficial resemblance. *Sterile* means infertile; the snowball tree is the infertile form of *V. opulus*, a berried shrub which is generally known as the guelder rose.

DESCRIPTION: Long, straight, woody branches with fresh green 3-lobed leaves and a globular inflorescence, initially greenish. The many flowers in the globe change colour in ripening to clear white, which is why it is called the snowball tree.

ORIGIN: The guelder rose is native to Europe, some of the non-European Mediterranean and to north Asia. The infertile form came about in the Netherlands spontaneously in 1594.

CULTIVATION: Chiefly in the Netherlands, especially in the vicinity of Aalsmeer.

AVAILABILITY: From December until May, with a peak between January and March.

CARE: The inflorescence must be entirely fully-grown but still a bit green when purchased. Cut off a bit of the stem and put it in lukewarm water (15-20° c) with cut-flower food for shrubs.

KEEPING PROPERTIES: 12-14 days; in a cool spot a little longer.

USES: In a vase, in mixed bouquets and in large decorations in churches, at exhibitions, etc.

SCENT: None.

Symphoricarpos albus

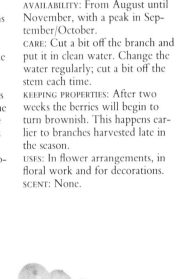

Caryophyllaceae

The pink family (*Caryophyllaceae*) is richly represented in the entire Mediterranean area, but members of it grow in nearly all temperate areas of the world. The various campion sorts (*Melandrium* or *Silene* species) are well-known. Some genera, such as *Cerastium* and *Stellaria* (chickweed), are even cosmopolitan.

All pink types (80 genera: over 2000 species and many thousands of cultivated cultivars) are annual or perennial herbaceous and dicotyledonous plants. Some, such as *Dianthus arboreus*, grow into sub-shrubs. The simple, opposite leaves have smooth margins. In some sorts, such as the carnation, they are even fused to encircle the stem at the nodes.

The flowers are mostly at the ends of the stems. They are radially symmetrical and generally hermaphrodite. In the carnation, the base of the calyx has a few bracts. The flowers have 4 or 5 petals, but they are often so deeply cut or serrated that it looks like many more. The number of stamens is usually 8-10 - twice the number of petals. The ovary consists of 2-5 carpels, with an equal number of separate styles. The fruit is a capsule.

Dianthus barbatus
Sweet William

NAME: The name *Dianthus* is derived from the Greek words *dios*, 'god', and *anthos*, 'flower': so it means 'divine flower'. The name was initially chosen for the scented flowers of *Dianthus caryophyllus*, the gillyflower or clove pink. *Barbatus* means 'bearded' or 'wearing long hair' and here refers to the long involucral bracts.

DESCRIPTION: The plants, which reach a height of around 50 cm, are grown from seeds (as biennials) or cuttings. They have shiny leaves, generally green, which are broad lanceolate in form, with short stems and five nerves. The inflorescence is a dense umbel, with long involucral bracts. The flowers themselves are 2-3 cm across; the involucral bracts consist of oval scales. The most frequent colours are red and pink, both in many shades, as well as salmon and white. In addition, there are cultivars with a band of a different colour. Cultivars with very dark flowers have darker leaves as well.

ORIGIN: The mountain meadows of Central and Southern Europe. The plant has been cultivated since 1500.

CULTIVATION: All cut flower-growing areas with a temperate climate.

AVAILABILITY: From December until August, with a peak (95%) in May and June.

CARE: The florist should have the flowers in water with a special compound to stop the leaves yellowing. Remove lower leaves, cut off a bit of the stem and add cut-flower food for herbaceous plants to the water.

KEEPING PROPERTIES: 7-10 days.

USES: In a vase, also in mixed bouquets.

SCENT: None.

Dianthus barbatus

Cultivars

Mixed: Some 90% of the supply consists of mixed Sweet Williams cultivated from seed. The mixture is composed of cultivars such as 'Scarlet beauty' (bright red), 'Newport Pink' (salmon pink), 'Crimson' (copper red), 'Pink Beauty' (bright pink), 'Diadem' (red with a white centre) and 'Nigricans' (dark leaf, reddish-black flowers). Such a mixture is termed 'formula mixture'.

Red ('Cerise'): A selection which is propagated by taking cuttings. If the cuttings are cooled, the planting and blossoming times can be spread out, which makes supply of this selection possible as early as November.

White: This Sweet William selection is also obtained by means of cuttings. The colour of the leaf is light yellow-green.

Dianthus caryophyllus 'Teicher'
Gillyflower, Clove pink

NAME: *Dianthus* means 'divine flower'; the name was chosen for its pleasant scent. *Caryophyllus* means 'clove-like' and, in addition to referring to the family name, it also points to the scent, which is like that of cloves.
DESCRIPTION: The plant, growing 50-60 cm high, is not hardy and is generally grown as a biennial. The lanceolate leaves have five nerves and are a frosty blue. The flowers stand in squat, rounded, more or less filled cymes; in this cultivar, they have mixed colours. The petals are somewhat dentate; the four involucral bracts are short, blunt and contiguous.
ORIGIN: Mediterranean.
CULTIVATION: The plant was cultivated by the Greeks and came to Western Europe in 1270. It is grown in all areas with outdoor cut-flower cultivation.
AVAILABILITY: June-July.
CARE: When buying them, make sure that the flowers are in specially treated water (to stop them wilting through ethylene formation). After purchase, place them in water with cut-flower food for carnations.
KEEPING PROPERTIES: 10-14 days, provided they have been treated.
USES: In a vase, also in mixed bouquets, and in flower arrangement.
SCENT: Spicy and fragrant.

'Teicher'

Dianthus plumarius
Border pink, Garden pink

NAME: *Dianthus* = divine flower; *plumarius* is derived from the Latin *pluma*, which means 'feather'. The name relates to the finely cut petals of the flower.
DESCRIPTION: The plant forms loose clumps with ascending stems and grows to about 25 cm. The linear leaves are frosted bluish-green; the white or pink flowers grow in groups of 2 or 3 and are strongly scented. The petals are obovate, deeply cut with fine hairs at the base. The calyx has four scales which are much shorter than the calyx itself.
ORIGIN: The mountain meadows of Central Europe.
CULTIVATION: The garden pink was first cultivated in Belgium in 1565 and is now grown in many flower-growing areas. The most frequently cultivated cultivar is 'Diamant', with white flowers.
AVAILABILITY: June and July.
CARE: At the florist's, garden pinks should be in specially treated water to stop them wilting due to ethylene formation. At home, add cut-flower food to the water.

KEEPING PROPERTIES: 8-12 days, provided they have been treated.
USES: In a vase, in Biedermeier bouquets and in flower arrangement (in bridal work, for instance).
SCENT: Highly aromatic; slightly pungent.

Dianthus caryophyllus hybrids
Carnation

NAME: *Dianthus* = divine flower; *caryophyllus* = clove-like.
DESCRIPTION: Non-hardy perennial plants which are propagated from cuttings and can reach a height of 1.50 - 1.80 m. The lanceolate leaves are frosted blue. There is, finally, one main flower per branch; the weaker flowering branches which the plant develops in addition are removed before the growth period. The flowers are well-filled; depending on the cultivar, the petals are serrate to finely dentate. The colour also differs according to the cultivar.
ORIGIN: Mediterranean, at least the ancestors. The first crosses came about at the end of the last century in America; for this reason, the flower is sometimes called 'American carnation'.
CULTIVATION: All important cut flower-growing areas, such as Italy, France, the Netherlands, the United States, Israel and in recent years also in Spain and Kenya.
AVAILABILITY: Throughout the year; in summer from Western Europe, in the other months chiefly from Israel and Kenya.
CARE: At the florist, the flowers must stand in specially treated water to stop them wilting through the formation of ethylene. After purchase put them in water with cut-flower food for carnations. Keep fruit away from the flowers, for it also produces ethylene.
KEEPING PROPERTIES: 6-16 days, depending on the temperature. At high temperatures the life span is short.
USES: In a vase, in mixed bouquets and in flower arrangement or for decorations.
SCENT: Some cultivars are aromatic, others are not.

Cultivars

There are numerous cultivars of carnations, the colours of which range from white to deep purple; some are even two-coloured. The flower shape shows variations as well. Among the most important cultivars are:
'Scania', the most frequently cultivated red carnation. The cultivar is striking for its brilliant red colour which is retained in the winter months. It is slightly scented.
'Pallas' has large yellow flowers with a few tiny pink stripes. It is quite strongly scented and keeps very well.
'Charmeur' is a cross between the spray carnation 'Exquisite' and the large-flowered carnation 'William Sim'. It has a sturdy stem and not very large flowers, but they keep excellently. The lilac pink mutant 'Rose Charmeur' and the very pale

'Charmeur'

Spraycarnation 'Orange Ministar'

lilac 'Primeur' were developed from 'Charmeur'.

'**Nora**' is the most frequently cultivated pink carnation. It has lovely fluted petals with very finely dentate margins. One advantage of the cultivar is its excellent stem quality, even in winter.

'**White Sim**' is the most frequently cultivated white carnation cultivar. It is fairly old, but its excellent quality keeps it popular.

Dianthus caryophyllus hybrids
Spray carnation

NAME: See Carnation.

DESCRIPTION: In contrast to the carnation, which bears only one flower per stem, the spray carnation has a compound inflorescence, giving it a less static appearance. There are a great many varieties, of which around sixty are generally cultivated. The colour assortment is large and contains several two-coloured sorts: white with red edges, yellow with orange or red, etc. The flowers keep a long time, but in winter they sometimes have fragile stems, a result of lack of light during the growth period.

ORIGIN: Spray carnations were developed in the United States by crossing *D. caryophyllus* with the French long-flowering carnations and with large-flowered American carnations.

CULTIVATION: See Carnation.
AVAILABILITY: See Carnation.
CARE: See Carnation.
KEEPING PROPERTIES: See Carnation.
USES: See Carnation.
SCENT: None.

Cultivars

'**Silvery Pink**', which grows quickly and has pretty and full flowers, is one of the most frequently cultivated pink cultivars. In the winter months the raceme formation is not as good.

'**Barbara**' has cherry-pink flowers and is one of the most frequently cultivated spray carnation cultivars, for one reason because of its high production.

'**Yellow Ministar**' is a yellow-flowering mutant from the cultivar 'Ministar' and is characterized by a high production and a very good quality.

'**Ministar**' has the same characteristics as the previous cultivar; the flowers are orange with red stripes.

'**Red Ministar**' is also a mutant from 'Ministar' with the same characteristics but brilliant red.

'**Albivette**' is the best quality white spray carnation in the present assortment. The cultivar was raised by the Garden Plant Breeding Institute in Wageningen.

'**Eolo**' is the lilac-pink small-flowered spray carnation, a so-called micro-carnation. During the summer months, the cultivar has a very high production.

'White Sim'

'Bristol Fairy'

'Karina'

Dianthus caryophylhus hybrids
Chinesine or **Diantini carnation**

NAME: see Carnation

DESCRIPTION: A group of spray carnations with small, practically simple flowers, with a lovely coloured band in the centre. This marking came about by crossing *D. caryophyllus* with *D. chinensis*.

OTHER DATA: See Carnation

Gypsophila paniculata
Chalk plant

NAME: *Gypsophila* is derived from the Greek *gypsos* (= chalk, gypsum) and the Greek word *philein*: to love. In other words: a plant that likes chalky soil. *Paniculata* means: 'with a paniculate (much branched) inflorescence'.

DESCRIPTION: A much branched perennial plant, which can grow up to 1 m high. The grey-green lanceolate leaves are around 7 cm long; the numerous small flowers, white or pink, are grouped in dense, wide panicles.

ORIGIN: The Mediterranean and Eastern Europe, as far as Siberia.

CULTIVATION: The plant was first cultivated in the United Kingdom in 1759 and is now grown in all flower-growing areas of the world, but primarily in the Netherlands and Israel. Cultivation has greatly increased since propagation from cuttings and tissue culture have become possible.

AVAILABILITY: Throughout the year, with peaks in March/April and November/December.

CARE: Upon purchase, most of the flowers in the panicle should be open; the florist should have the flowers in specially treated water. At home, put them in water with cut-flower food for carnations.

KEEPING PROPERTIES: 2-3 weeks, provided they are treated.

USES: Especially in mixed bouquets.

SCENT: None.

Cultivars

'**Bristol Fairy**' is the most frequently cultivated chalk plant variety, largely because it can be grown both outdoors and in the hothouse. The white flowers are fairly large. Numerous named selections have been developed from this cultivar, including 'Perfecta' and 'Romano'. They are quite difficult to distinguish.

'**Flamingo**' is the most important pink cultivar. Others are 'Pink Veil' and 'Rose Valley'.

Gypsophila elegans
Chalk plant

NAME: *Gypsophila* = chalk-loving; *elegans* means 'elegant'.
DESCRIPTION: An annual plant with broad stems in fork-shaped branchings. It grows to about 50 cm high and has long linear leaves. The numerous flowers are white, pink or red. They are roughly 1-2 cm in diameter and are grouped together in wide, loose compound panicles. The petals are somewhat hairy on the outside.
ORIGIN: Asia Minor, the Caucasus. The plant was first cultivated in the United Kingdom in 1820.
CULTIVATION: All areas with seed flower cultivation.
AVAILABILITY: June-July.
CARE: Cut a bit off the stem (usually with roots); use cut-flower food for carnations. Most flowers should be open when purchased.
KEEPING PROPERTIES: 14-18 days, provided the water is kept clean.
USES: Especially in mixed bouquets.
SCENT: None.

Cultivars

'**Roem van Rijnsburg**' is a cultivar with much larger flowers than the original sort; the flower diameter is around 2 cm. It is the most frequently cultivated chalk plant cultivar. The flowers are white. A white cultivar on its way up is 'Snow Fountain', which grows slightly more erect.
'**Karmozijn**' is a cultivar with dark, deep red flowers. Like the dark red cultivar 'Carminea', it is available much less frequently than the white cultivars.

'Roem van Rijnsburg'

Lychnis viscaria
Campion

NAME: The old Greek plant name *Lychnis* is derived from *lychnos*, which means 'lamp'. It refers to the flower's bright colour. *Viscaria* (= sticky) refers to the sticky exudation on the stem, beneath each node.
DESCRIPTION: A sticky perennial plant of around 50 cm high and with slightly red flushed, almost unbranched stems. The oblong leaves are about 10 cm long and end in a pointed tip. The carmine red flowers, around 15 mm across, are grouped in compound umbels and form small plumes. The club-shaped calyx (6-15 mm) has 10 strong nerves; the petals have nearly smooth, sometimes slightly frilled margins.

ORIGIN: From Central Europe to Japan. The original sort was first cultivated in England in 1596; the most frequently cultivated cultivar, the double-flowered 'Plena', was discovered there in 1596.
CULTIVATION: Cut flower-growing areas with a temperate climate.
AVAILABILITY: From May until July.
CARE: Cut off a bit of the stem; use cut-flower food for carnations.
KEEPING PROPERTIES: 6-10 days, depending on the temperature.
USES: In a vase and in mixed summer bouquets.
SCENT: Slightly scented.

Lychnis chalcedonica
Jerusalem cross

NAME: *Lychnis*: see Campion. *Chalcedonica* refers to the place the plant was first found: Chalcedon (now Kadikoy) on the eastern side of the Bosporus, opposite Constantinople (now Istanbul).
DESCRIPTION: A perennial plant growing up to 1 m high, with light green, elongated oval, rough-haired leaves with a rounded, heart-shaped leaf base. The 2-3 cm flowers are grouped in dense umbel-shaped bunches. The corolla petals are divided.
ORIGIN: From Central Russia to Asia Minor. The plant was first cultivated in Germany in 1561.
CULTIVATION: Cut flower-growing areas with a temperate climate and outdoor cultivation.
AVAILABILITY: June-July.
CARE: The florist should have the flowers in specially treated water. At home, put them in water with cut-flower food for carnations.
KEEPING PROPERTIES: 6-9 days, depending on the temperature.
USES: Especially in mixed summer bouquets.
SCENT: None.

Saponaria vaccaria 'Wit'

△ Lychnis chalcedonica ▽ Saponaria vaccaria 'Rosabella'

Saponaria vaccaria,
syn. *Vaccaria hispanica*
Soapwort

NAME: *Saponaria* is derived from
the Latin *sapo* (= soap) and refers
to the cleansing effect of the plant's
sap. *Vaccaria* comes from *vacca* (=
cow); the plants are said to be very
good feed for cattle.

DESCRIPTION: Annual plant with
bluish-green stems of 50-60 cm
long, with fork-shaped branchings
at the top. The broad leaves are
lanceolate and somewhat fused at
the bottom of the stem. The white
or pink flowers stand on long
stems in loose compound umbels.
The calyx is initially tubular but
later grows into a balloon with
five wings. The corolla is just as
long as the calyx.

ORIGIN: Central Europe, Mediterranean area and the Caucasus. The
plant was first cultivated in England in 1596.

CULTIVATION: Primarily in the
Netherlands (outdoors).

AVAILABILITY: July-August; by forcing, sometimes as early as May.

CARE: Remove leaves from the
stem, cut a bit off the stem, use
cut-flower food for carnations.

KEEPING PROPERTIES: 7-12 days.

USES: In a vase; extensively in mixed bouquets.

SCENT: Slight.

Cultivars

'**Rosabella**', a cultivar with lovely
deep pink flowers. It is a mutant of
the original sort, which bears
white, pink-veined flowers.

'**Wit**' is a clear white selection
from the previous sort. This colour
is grown less often than the pink
form.

Celastraceae

The *Celastraceae* family, composed of some 50 genera, contains more than 800 sorts of dicotyledonous trees and bushes, but especially climbing or twining plants and 'tree stranglers'. They occur in the tropics, the subtropics and in temperate zones. One representative of the *Celastraceae* is the spindle tree (*Euonymus europaeus*).

The leaves of these plants are opposite or alternate. Sometimes they are leathery and in some sorts they have stipules. The small, greenish flowers are unisexual or hermaphrodite and often stand in compound umbels. The sepals and petals are grouped under or on a fleshy disc. The three to five sepals are discrete or fused at the base; in some varieties they are absent. The number of stamens is equal to the number of sepals; they are implanted on the disc, alternated by the petals. The supe-rior ovary, with 3-5 fused carpels, has two or three cells. Each cell has two or even many more ovules which lie along the axis in the ovary. The short style has 2-4 stigmata. The fruit is a berry, a stone fruit or a capsule. The seeds are enclosed in a brightly coloured seed coat.

Some varieties are economically significant, although to a limited degree. For instance, the leaves of *Catha edulis* are used in preparing Arabian tea and mead; some *Euonymus* sorts yield wood and a rubber-like latex; and *E. europaeus* is used in the manufacture of soap. Some sorts are grown as ornamental shrubs. In the cut-flower world two sorts play a role, not for their flowers, but for the beautifully coloured berry fruits and the autumnal colours of the leaves.

Celastrus orbiculatus
Celastrus
NAME: *Celastrus* is the Latin form of the old Greek plant name *kelastros*. *Orbiculatus* means 'circle-shaped' and refers to the arrangement of the berries.
DESCRIPTION: A woody creeper with pointed leaves, the shape of which is variable; the leaf margins are secretory and dentate. The small greenish flowers stand in axillary racemes. The fruits are deep yellow and remain on the plant even after it loses its leaves. Later they spring open. The aril, the red growth surrounding the seed, forms a lovely contrast with the yellow of the berry. Pretty selections are 'Diane' and 'Herma-phroditus'.
ORIGIN: China and Japan. The plant was first cultivated in Russia in 1860.
CULTIVATION: Limited, in areas with a temperate climate.
AVAILABILITY: October-November; if the branches are cooled, sometimes even in December.
CARE: Cut a bit off the stem; use cut-flower food for shrubs in the water.
KEEPING PROPERTIES: In water, 3-4 weeks.
USES: In floral work; to a limited extent, in a vase.
SCENT: None.

Euonymus europaeus
Spindle tree
NAME: *Euonymus* is the Latin form of the old Greek plant name *Euonumos*, or 'plant having an auspicious name'. The name was meant ironically: it is poisonous, especially the berries. The Romans made an extract from it to combat head lice. *Europaeus* means: 'coming from Europe'.
DESCRIPTION: A deciduous shrub of which the young twigs are green and slightly angular, with lengthwise stripes, and the older ones bear cork frames. The leaves, approx. 6 cm long, are oval; the top is shiny green, the underside bluish green, the leaf margin is finely dentate. The many tiny flowers develop into four-chambered pinkish-red fruits, which are the same shape and colour as the hats worns by cardinals of the Roman Catholic church.
ORIGIN: Europe and Western Asia. The plant was cultivated in ancient times.
CULTIVATION: The shrub is grown on a limited scale as a ground cover, and also occurs wild, at least in temperate areas. The branches are cut off for decorative purposes.
AVAILABILITY: End of August-October.
CARE: Cut off a bit of the branch; use cut-flower food for shrubs in the water.
KEEPING PROPERTIES: 2-3 weeks (in water).
USES: In flower arrangement.
SCENT: None.

Celastrus orbiculatus   Euonymus europaeus

Compositae

The family of the composite flowers (*Compositae*) is the largest flowering plant family in the world: around 25,000 species, classified into some 1100 genera. Representatives of this dicotyledonous family occur all over the world, with the exception of the South Pole area. The composites are scarce in tropical rain forests, but they are richly represented in the semiarid regions of the tropics and subtropics (Cape Province and the Mediterranean area). Most composites are evergreen shrubs or herbaceous perennials with rootstocks. Other perennial composites have tap roots or tubers, or belong to the annual and biennial herbaceous plants. Some sorts are climbers or succulents.

The leaves are generally alternate, but sometimes they are opposite. They can have a great many forms; in some cases they have been reduced to needles or scales. They are sessile or stalked and the margins are often serrated or lobed. Stipules are absent. Many *Compositae* have ducts for resin or milky sap. The flowers are grouped together in heads, encircled at the base by involucres. In certain genera the involucres stand on the shared receptacle. The calyx is either lacking or takes the shape of scales or fuzz. The flowers are unisexual or hermaphrodite; the outer flowers are sometimes infertile.

The corolla consists of five fused petals in the shape of a tube (the tubular or disc flowers); or it may be clearly bilaterally symmetrical, with a short disc and all the radiating florets joined in a sort of ribbon (the ray flowers).

A flower head may consist exclusively of disc flowers (as in *Cirsium*), exclusively of ray flowers (as in the dandelion), or it may be composed of a heart of disc flowers surrounded by a whorl of ray flowers (for example, in the single-flowered chrysanthemum and the Transvaal daisy). In the latter case the ray flowers are often infertile or female. The disc flowers are then hermaphrodite or male respectively. All flowers in the flower head may also be hermaphrodite.

There are five stamens. They usually have discrete filaments and fused anthers and are implanted in the base of the corolla. The inferior ovary has one compartment and bears a style with two stigma lobes.

As it grows, the style pushes the released pollen out of the pollen tube, so that insects can reach it. The stigmata open only later, after which the flower can be pollinated. The fruit, a nut, generally has a hairy pappus or bristles, so that the seeds can be spread by the wind.

Several genera have great economic value: in agriculture, for instance, the sunflower; in flower growing the chrysanthemum and the Transvaal daisy.

The traditional classification of the *Compositae* into 20 genera is no longer adequate. Modern research has shown that many genera have been placed in the wrong groups and that the entire classification should be reviewed. As a result, a number of names printed on the following pages will probably be changed in the future.

Achillea filipendulina
Yarrow

NAME: *Achillea* is derived from the name of the Greek hero, Achilles, who is said to have used the plant to heal wounds. *Filipendulina* means: 'hanging on threads' and refers to the finely dissected leaves.
DESCRIPTION: A perennial plant approx. 1 m high with sturdy, erect striate stems which have a dense leaf cover near the bottom. The leaves are bright green and finely cut and divided. The inflorescence consists of numerous small bright yellow flower heads, which together form a large, flat inflorescence. Commonly grown cultivars are 'Parker' (very suitable as a dried flower), 'Coronation Gold' (with smaller flower racemes and greyish leaves) and 'Gold Plate'.
ORIGIN: Asia Minor and the Caucasians. The plant was first cultivated in the United Kingdom in 1803.
CULTIVATION: All areas with outdoor flower cultivation, except the tropics and areas with severe winters.
AVAILABILITY: From June until September.
CARE: When purchased, at least three-fourths of the flowers should be open (for drying: all of them). Remove lower leaves, cut off a bit of the stem, use cut flower food. To dry: hang the branches upside down in a cool, dry spot.
KEEPING PROPERTIES: Approx. 3 weeks.
USES: In a vase, especially in mixed bouquets; as a dried flower.
SCENT: The leaves are aromatic.

Achillea filipendulina

39

Achillea ptarmica 'Perry's White'

'Moonshine'

Achillea millefolium
Milfoil, Common yarrow

NAME: See also *Achillea. Millefolium* means 'a thousand leaves'.
DESCRIPTION: A perennial plant about 60 cm high with lanceolate pinnate leaves, finely cut at intervals. The flower heads have a diameter of 5 mm and usually bear five ray flowers which are twice as long as the involucres. The white, pink or carmine red flower heads are grouped in dense clusters. The most frequently cultivated cultivars are 'Red Beauty' (late blossoming, purple red), 'Kelwayi' (dark carmine red) and 'Cerise Queen' (light carmine red).
ORIGIN: Entire northern hemisphere. The plant was first cultivated in Switzerland in 1561.
CULTIVATION: All temperate areas with outdoor flower cultivation.
AVAILABILITY: From June until September.
CARE: Remove lower leaves, cut off a bit of the stem, use cut-flower food.
KEEPING PROPERTIES: 2-3 weeks; the colour fades gradually.
USES: In a vase and in mixed bouquets.
SCENT: None.

Achillea ptarmica
Sneezewort

NAME: See also *Achillea. Ptarmica* is derived from the Greek *ptarnusthai* = to sneeze; the plant's smell was said to induce sneezing.
DESCRIPTION: A perennial plant with upright and lightly hairy stalks of roughly 70 cm long. The linear, pointed leaf is more than ten times as long as it is wide and is not hairy. The flower heads stand in clusters; they have a diameter of about 15 mm and bear 10-13 white ray flowers which are larger than the involucre. The most frequently cultivated cultivars are the double flowered 'Perry's White' and 'The Pearl', which is grown from seed.
ORIGIN: Europe and Western Asia. Now also naturalized in the eastern part of North America.
CULTIVATION: All temperate areas with outdoor cut-flower cultivation.
AVAILABILITY: Summer months.
CARE: Remove lower leaves, cut off a bit of the stem, add cut-flower food to the water.
KEEPING PROPERTIES: Approx. 3 weeks.
USES: In a vase, in mixed bouquets and in flower arrangement.
SCENT: None.

Achillea x taygetea 'Moonshine'
Achillea

NAME: See *Achillea. Taygetea* after the Taygetos mountains in South Greece.
DESCRIPTION: The plant, a cross between *A. millefolium* and *A.* 'Clypeolata', has stems of about 50 cm long which are covered up to the inflorescence with finely cut and divided, silver-grey hairy leaves; they grow smaller towards the top. The sulphur yellow flower heads stand in dense clusters which can become up to 15 cm across.
ORIGIN: Unknown.
CULTIVATION: In moderate and subtropical areas with outdoor cut-flower cultivation.

AVAILABILITY: June; a second time in September.
CARE: Remove lower leaves, cut off a bit of the stem, use cut-flower food. The flowers must be three-quarters open.
KEEPING PROPERTIES: 3-4 weeks.
USES: In a vase, in mixed bouquets and in flower arrangement.
SCENT: None.

Ageratum houstonianum 'Schnittwunder'
Floss-flower

NAME: *Ageratum* is derived from the Greek *ageratos*, which means 'never ageing'; the name refers to the long flowering period. The second name is for the Scottish discoverer of the plant, W. Houston (1695-1733), who collected plants in North America and the West Indies.

DESCRIPTION: A perennial plant (however, usually grown as an annual) of 50-60 cm high, lightly hairy with oval, heart-shaped and somewhat serrate leaves; the upper ones often encircle the stem. The flower heads are 5-10 mm across. The lavender flowers are grouped in clusters.

ORIGIN: From Mexico to Peru. The plant was first cultivated in the United Kingdom in 1768.

CULTIVATION: All flower-growing areas with outdoor cultivation.

AVAILABILITY: From June until the end of September.

CARE: The flower heads must be fully-grown when they are purchased. Remove lower leaves, cut off a bit of the stem, use cut-flower food for herbaceous plants.

KEEPING PROPERTIES: 8-14 days.

USES: In a vase, and in flower arrangements such as in Biedermeier bouquets.

SCENT: Slightly scented.

Anaphalis triplinervis

Ammobium alatum
Everlasting sand flower

NAME: *Ammos* means 'sand', *bios* = life: plant that lives in sandy ground. *Alatum* means 'winged' and refers to the wings along the stems.

DESCRIPTION: Annual plant with broad, bright green winged stems. The oblong-oval leaves narrow into a stalk; the upper ones are small, the lower ones are grouped in rosettes. At the end of the approx. 60 cm long stem there are one or more flower heads with a diameter of 3 cm. The bright white, spreading involucre is larger than the yellow disc, which darkens as the flowering progresses.

ORIGIN: Australia. The plant was first cultivated in the United Kingdom in 1822.

CULTIVATION: Flower-growing areas with outdoor cultivation; a great deal in the Netherlands.

AVAILABILITY: From June until September.

CARE: To dry them, buy them when most of the flowers are open. Hang them upside down in an airy place.

KEEPING PROPERTIES: As dried flower, very longlasting.

USES: Chiefly as dried flower. To a limited extent, in a vase and in mixed bouquets.

SCENT: None.

Anaphalis triplinervis
(no popular name)

NAME: *Anaphalis* is an old Greek plant name; *triplinervis* means 'having three nerves'.

DESCRIPTION: A woolly plant with white hairs and oblong-oval leaves of 7-20 cm long, which encircle the stem and contain 3-5 nerves. The upper side is covered with cobweb-like hair, the underside is woolly. The white flower heads are grouped in clusters. The involucral bracts resemble ray flowers; the disc flowers are close together and extend from the involucres like brushes. The cultivar 'Schwefellicht' is light sulphur yellow.

ORIGIN: Himalayas; the plant has been cultivated since 1824. The related sort *A. margaritacea*, from eastern North America, was first cultivated in England in 1596.

CULTIVATION: European flower-growing areas with outdoor cultivation.

AVAILABILITY: From July until early September.

CARE: In water with cut-flower food for herbaceous plants.

KEEPING PROPERTIES: 10-14 days.

USES: In a vase, and in Biedermeier bouquets; also as dried flower.

SCENT: None.

'Schnittwunder'

Anthemis sancti-johannis

Anthemis sancti-johannis
Roman camomile

NAME: *Anthemis* is the Greek word for camomile and is derived from *anthos* = flower. The addition of *sancti-johannis* in this case refers to the patron saint of the St. Ivan Bilak Cloister in Bulgaria.

DESCRIPTION: A perennial plant of approx. 90 cm high with upright and generally unbranched stems which are somewhat woolly. The lower leaves are finely cut and resemble fingers on a hand. The flower heads, 4-5 cm across, have pale orange ray flowers. The involucral bracts are lanceolate, with a brown, finely cut, fringed edge.

ORIGIN: Bulgaria. The plant was not cultivated until 1925.

CULTIVATION: European cut-flower areas with outdoor cultivation.

AVAILABILITY: From June until August.

CARE: The flowers must be entirely open. Cut a bit off the stem, use cut-flower food for herbaceous plants.

KEEPING PROPERTIES: 10-14 days.

USES: Chiefly in mixed field bouquets.

SCENT: Leaf and flower are aromatic.

Artemisia stelleriana
Wormwood

NAME: The plant is named after Artemisia, a Roman ruler who lived around 325 B.C. According to old herbalists, the plant was good for menstrual complaints. The second name is in honour of the German doctor, G.W. Steller (1709-1745), who led scientific expeditions to the Russian Bering Island and described many animals, including his own discovery, Steller's sea-cow (*Rhytina gigas*).

DESCRIPTION: A vigorously growing perennial plant with many erect, branching stems. The entire plant is covered with silvery-white woolly hair, the leaves are inverted ovals and very finely cut; the unremarkable inflorescence consists of pale yellow-green, thin plumes.

ORIGIN: North-east Asia and western North America. The plant was first cultivated in Russia in 1865.

CULTIVATION: Western European cut-flower areas with outdoor cultivation.

AVAILABILITY: From the end of July until September.

CARE: Remove lower leaves, cut off a bit of the stem, use cut-flower food.

KEEPING PROPERTIES: 3-4 weeks.

USES: In floral work and mixed bouquets, primarily for the silver-grey foliage.

SCENT: Somewhat aromatic.

Aster novae-angliae 'Harrington's Pink'
Michaelmas daisy

NAME: *Aster* is the Latin translation of the Greek *asteros*, which means 'star'; it refers to the shape of the flower heads. *Novae-angliae* is an inflected form of Nova-Anglia (New England), the old name for the English colonies in North America where the plant originally came from.

DESCRIPTION: Approx. 1.50 m high plant with rough hairs, strong stems and 5-12 cm long lanceolate leaves which encircle the stem. The 30-50 ray flowers nod slightly; the involucral bracts are glandular and hairy. The original colour of the flower is lilac; 'Harrington's Pink' is a salmon pink cultivar. There are also red and purple-blue Michaelmas daisies.

ORIGIN: North America. The plant was first cultivated in the Netherlands in 1697.

CULTIVATION: All temperate cut-flower growing areas with outdoor cultivation.

AVAILABILITY: August until October. If the days are artificially shortened, it can be forced to flower as early as the end of June.

CARE: Remove lower leaves if necessary, cut off a bit of the stem, use cut-flower food.

KEEPING PROPERTIES: 2-3 weeks.

USES: In a vase; sometimes in mixed bouquets.

SCENT: None.

Artemisia stelleriana

Aster novi-belgii

△ Aster ericoides   ▽ Aster tongolensis

Aster novi-belgii 'Climax'
Michaelmas daisy

NAME: See also the previous variety. *Novi-belgii* refers to the origin of the sort, the island of Manhattan, which used to be called New Belgium.

DESCRIPTION: A perennial plant, about 1 m high and not very hairy. The stems are densely covered with 7-12 cm long, oblong leaves; they have smooth margins or are somewhat dentate. The flower heads stand in clusters or plumes. The 15-25 ray flowers are grouped around a yellow disc. The original flower colour was violet-lilac. Nowadays there are cultivars registered in all shades of lilac, blue, purple, red and white. *Novi-belgii* is the most frequently cultivated variety of Michaelmas daisy.

ORIGIN: Eastern North America. The plant was first cultivated in France in 1686.

CULTIVATION: All flower-growing areas with a temperate climate.

AVAILABILITY: From August to the end of September. If the days are artificially shortened, it can be forced to flower as early as the end of June.

CARE: Cut off a bit of the stem, remove lower leaves, use cut-flower food.

KEEPING PROPERTIES: Approx. 14 days.

USES: In a vase; sometimes in autumn bouquets.

SCENT: Slight.

Aster ericoides 'Monte Casino'
(no popular name)

NAME: See also Michaelmas daisy. *Ericoides* literally means 'resembling erica', or heather, and refers to the many tiny flowers on the plant, or the small upper leaves.

DESCRIPTION: Perennial plant, 70-90 cm high with smooth, very branching stems. The branchings are nearly horizontal. The leaves are slightly hairy; the lower ones are oblong and dentate, the higher ones are linear and pointed, with smooth margins. The small flower heads are grouped in dense racemes and bear 15-25 white ray flowers. There are also cultivars with pink flowers.

ORIGIN: Canada and the northern United States.

CULTIVATION: Especially the Netherlands and Germany. Its cultivation has greatly increased in popularity since it has become possible to spread out the bloom by artificially shortening its days.

AVAILABILITY: From April until December, with a peak in October.

CARE: Remove lower leaves, cut off a bit of the stem, use cut-flower food.

KEEPING PROPERTIES: 14-18 days.

USES: Primarily ornamental, in mixed bouquets and floral work.

SCENT: None.

Aster tongolensis 'Berggarten'
(no popular name)

NAME: See also Michaelmas daisy. *Tongolensis* means 'coming from Tongolo' (Sichuan, Western China).

DESCRIPTION: A 40-50 cm high perennial plant which is densely hairy and has erect stems each bearing a single flower. The lower leaves are oblong, pointed and generally have smooth edges. The long-stemmed flower heads have a diameter of 5-6 cm and are covered with orange-yellow tubular flowers (the centre) and lilac-blue ray flowers. The involucral bracts are blunt, hairy and have ciliate margins; they are grouped in three rows. *A. tongolensis* is also sometimes called *A. subcaeruleus*.

ORIGIN: Western China. The plant was first cultivated in Germany in 1901.

CULTIVATION: All Western European cut-flower areas with outdoor cultivation, but chiefly in Germany.

AVAILABILITY: May-June.

CARE: Remove lower leaves, cut off a bit of the stem, use cut-flower food.

KEEPING PROPERTIES: 8-14 days.

USES: In a vase and in mixed bouquets.

SCENT: None.

'Wunder von Staefa'

△ Bupthalmum salicifolium   ▽ Calendula officinalis

Aster x frikartii 'Wunder von Staefa'
(no popular name)

NAME: See also *A. novae-angliae*. The plant is also named after the Swiss florist Karl Ludwig Frikart (1879-1964), who made the cross.

DESCRIPTION: A 60-80 cm high perennial plant with erect and very branching stems and large flower heads (7-9 cm). The ray flowers of this cultivar are lilac-blue, the tubular flowers, or centre, are yellow. The leaves have short hairs and smooth edges.

ORIGIN: A cross between *A. amellus* x *A. thompsonii*, made in 1920.

CULTIVATION: Western Europe, especially Germany.

AVAILABILITY: August-September.

CARE: Remove lower leaves, cut off a bit of the stem, use cut-flower food.

KEEPING PROPERTIES: 10-15 days.

USES: Especially in a vase; sometimes in mixed bouquets.

SCENT: None.

Bupthalmum salicifolium
Oxeye

NAME: *Bupthalmum* means 'cow eye' or 'ox eye'. The name is derived from the Greek words *buos* (cow) and *opthalmos* (eye) and refers to the shape of the flower heads. *Salicifolium* means 'willow-leaved' and refers to the leaf shape.

DESCRIPTION: A perennial plant 40-60 cm high and with erect, frequently branched stems. The leaves are broad and lanceolate and slightly hairy. The upper ones are finer and smaller and have short points. The flower heads have a diameter of 5-6 cm and stand on long stems. The ray flowers are golden yellow; the involucral bracts are lanceolate, pointed and grouped in three rows.

ORIGIN: Central Europe, from south-eastern France to central Yugoslavia. The plant was first cultivated in the Netherlands in 1720.

CULTIVATION: Temperate areas with outdoor-flower cultivation.

AVAILABILITY: July and August.

CARE: Remove lower leaves, cut off a bit of the stem, use cut-flower food for herbaceous plants.

KEEPING PROPERTIES: 8-12 days.

USES: In a vase and in mixed summer bouquets.

SCENT: None.

Calendula officinalis
Pot marigold

NAME: *Calendula* is the diminutive form of the Latin *calendae* and is derived from *caldere* = to proclaim. The name refers to the Roman custom of officially and publicly proclaiming the last day of the month. Our word 'calendar' has the same background. For the marigold, it refers to its long blooming period. *Officinale* means 'healing'; herbal lore says the marigold is effective for a variety of ailments.

DESCRIPTION: A 40-50 cm high annual plant covered with soft, secretory hairs. The lanceolate to oblong leaves are spread over the stem and have smooth margins. The single flower heads are 7-10 cm across and may be yellow or exhibit all shades of orange. Generally many-petalled cultivars with a deep orange colour are grown as cut flowers.

ORIGIN: Presumably the Mediterranean, southern Europe and southern England. The flower has been cultivated since ancient times.

CULTIVATION: All flower-growing areas with a temperate climate.

AVAILABILITY: Throughout the year, with a peak in May and June (Western European flowering period).

CARE: The flowers should be entirely open when purchased. Remove lower leaves, cut off a bit of the stem, use cut-flower food for herbaceous plants.

KEEPING PROPERTIES: 6-12 days.

USES: In a vase and in bouquets. The flowers are also used for their pigment and to prepare an alkaline tincture (for insect bites and nettle stings).

SCENT: The plant is strongly scented.

Callistephus chinensis
China aster

NAME: *Callistephus* is derived from the Greek words *kallos* (= beauty) and *stephos*, meaning 'wreath'. The name refers to the lovely wreath of ray flowers of the original simple-flowered sort. *Chinensis* means 'coming from China'.

DESCRIPTION: An annual plant, 50-60 cm high and with very branching stems. The oval-lanceolate leaves are spread over the stem, and their margins are roughly cut. The single flower heads on the ends of the stems differ in shape and colour, depending on the cultivar, but all of them have semi-globular involucres and their outer bracts are leaf-like.

ORIGIN: North and Central Asia. The seeds of the plant came to France in the beginning of the 18th century, where the plant was first cultivated around 1730.

CULTIVATION: All flower-growing areas of the world, but chiefly in Germany and the United States.

AVAILABILITY: From July to October with a peak in August/September.

CARE: Remove lower leaves, cut a bit off the stem, use cut-flower food for herbaceous plants. Change the water regularly; the flowers quickly pollute it.

KEEPING PROPERTIES: 10-16 days.

USES: In a vase, and in bouquets.

SCENT: Faint.

Cultivars

Single This group of cultivars, also called the single Chinese aster, has the flower type of the original sort, although the flower size has been somewhat increased through selection. They are always sold as a mixture, in shades of carmine red, carmine pink, violet-blue and white.

Pompon asters A refinement of the lilliput asters, with medium-sized flowers which make a compact impression. The ray flowers are tubular in shape. The cultivars can be supplied by colour or as a formula mixture. The colour variety is large: all shades of red, pink, samon, blue, cream yellow and white and also scarlet, dark and light blue flowers with white centres.

Giant rays or **Nadeln asters** This group has very fine, narrow ray flowers in a large and well-filled flower head. The colours are white, yellow, salmon pink, dark pink, light and dark blue.

Giant princess aster Very large-flowered asters with broad, flat flower petals and well-filled flowers, with usually somewhat yellow centres. The colour assortment includes bright red, carmine, scarlet and wine red, salmon and dark pink, light and dark blue, yellow and white. The flowers can be cultivated by colour.

Bouquet asters A group of medium-sized flower cultivars with somewhat curved ray flowers and a somewhat globular form. The colours are white, pink, salmon and copper pink, carmine and scarlet, light and dark blue and white.

Duchess asters Originally American cultivars ('Ball') that bloom late and have very large flowers (10-12 cm across). The colour assortment is large: light and dark blue, blue with white, carmine and deep scarlet, dark, light and carmine pink, yellow and white. The broad flower petals curve inward somewhat.

The assortment of summer asters includes a great many other cultivars, such as the new '**Germania**' cultivars, which grow to 100 cm high. Their flowers are large and well-filled and the colour assortment is large; it includes the shades of salmon orange and very pale pink.

A few other groups: Rose asters, Milady asters, Early Beauty asters, Bornthaler asters, Johannistag or Burperana asters (the earliest flowering type), Radio asters (which resemble the Giant rays) and decorative or Madeleine asters. All have the well-known aster colours (see above).

Callistephus chinensis, giant princess

Catananche caerulea
Blue cupidone

NAME: *Catananche* is of Greek origin (katananché) and means 'magic potion to arouse love'. The Thessalian women used the plant to force men to love-making. Modern research has shown that it does not have this property. *Caerulea* means 'dark blue', the colour of the flower.

DESCRIPTION: A perennial plant, 50-70 cm high, with thin, branching erect stems covered with greyish hairs. At the base of the stem is a rosette of grey-green hairy leaves. They are lanceolate and their edges are smooth or finely cut. The flower heads are a subdued blue, while the centre is dark purple. The outside is purple-blue. The involucral bracts are membranous and mother-of-pearl-like; they increase the ornamental value. The thin stem is not very sturdy.

ORIGIN: South-western Europe. The plant was first cultivated in England in 1588.

CULTIVATION: Moderate and subtropical areas with outdoor flower-growing.

AVAILABILITY: From the end of June until August.

CARE: Cut off a bit of the stem, use cut-flower food.

KEEPING PROPERTIES: 8-12 days (in a vase).

USES: In flower arrangement, as a dried flower and (to a limited extent) in a vase.

SCENT: None.

Carthamus tinctorius
Safflower

NAME: *Carthamus* is the mediaeval latinization of the Arabian name of the plant: *kurthum* or *gurdum*. *Tinctorius* means 'yielding dye' and refers to the pigment in the flower.

DESCRIPTION: Annual plant, up to 1 m high; the stems are not hairy and are little branched. The oval leaves are spread over the stem; they encircle it with a heart-shaped base and have prickly dentate edges. The flower heads are approx. 3 cm across and are orange-yellow. The outer involucral bracts are leaf-like.

ORIGIN: Probably the area between Asia Minor and the Indian subcontinent. The plant has been cultivated since ancient times; the Egyptians used it for its dyestuff.

CULTIVATION: Primarily the Netherlands. The plant has gained in popularity in recent years.

AVAILABILITY: From July to the end of September (outdoor cultivation); starting in June (from the hothouse).

△ Carthamus tinctorius   ▽ Catananche caerulea   ▽ Amberboa moschata

CARE: The flower should be well open when purchased. Remove lower branches, cut off a bit of the stem, use cut-flower food.

KEEPING PROPERTIES: 8-14 days.

USES: Chiefly as a dried flower, in bouquets. The dried flowers retain their colour for a long time: in a vase to a limited extent.

SCENT: None.

Amberboa moschata,
syn. *Centaurea moschata*
Sweet sultan, Yellow sultan

NAME: *Amberboa* is derived from a Turkish name for the plant; *moschata* (from the Greek *moschus*) means 'smelling like musk'.

DESCRIPTION: An annual plant with branching stems of 40-60 cm, and finely cut, widely dentate or lobed leaves. The long-stemmed flower heads have a diameter of 4-5 cm and were originally yellow. The flowers have a silky sheen. Nowadays there are also white, pink and red cultivars. The cultivar 'Imperiale' is larger in all respects than the others and is also covered with light grey hairs.

ORIGIN: Eastern Mediterranean area.

CULTIVATION: In flower-growing areas with outdoor cultivation.

AVAILABILITY: From June until August.

CARE: Remove lower leaves, cut off a bit of the stem, use cut-flower food for herbaceous plants.

KEEPING PROPERTIES: 5-8 days.

USES: In field bouquets, floral works and in a vase.

SCENT: Very pleasant.

Centaurea dealbata
Pink cornflower

NAME: *Centaurea* comes from the old Greek plant name *kentauros* = centaur. The centaurs were mythical beings, half man and half horse. *Dealbata* means 'to plaster' and refers to the felt-like white hairs.

DESCRIPTION: A hairy perennial plant with sparsely branched stems. The finely cut leaves have linear divisions with smooth edges. They have long stalks and the underside is covered with silver-white hairs. The single flower heads have a diameter of 4-5 cm and are dark pink (a few cultivars are carmine pink); the involucral bracts have brown, fringed appendages.

ORIGIN: The Caucasus. The plant was first cultivated in the United Kingdom in 1804.

CULTIVATION: All flower-growing areas with a temperate climate.

AVAILABILITY: June-July.

CARE: Remove lower leaves, cut off a bit of the stem, use cut-flower food for herbaceous plants.

KEEPING PROPERTIES: 5-7 days.

USES: In mixed bouquets and in a vase.

SCENT: None.

△ Centaurea macrocephala　▽ Centaurea dealbata

Centaurea montana

Centaurea macrocephala
Yellow cornflower

NAME: See also Pink cornflower. *Macrocephala* means: 'having a large (flower) head'.

DESCRIPTION: A perennial plant of 80-100 cm high, with unbranching stems and rough, elliptical leaves with serrated edges which narrow in the stalk. The single flower heads have a diameter of 8-12 cm. The flower stem is swollen, the flower is golden yellow. The brown fringed involucral bracts are striking.

ORIGIN: The Caucasus, Asia Minor. The plant was first cultivated in Germany in 1800.

CULTIVATION: Temperate areas with outdoor flower cultivation.

AVAILABILITY: From May until October, with a peak in July.

CARE: Cut off a bit of the stem; use cut-flower food. The buds should show good colour when purchased.

KEEPING PROPERTIES: 7-10 days.

USES: In mixed bouquets, in a vase, in flower arrangement and also as dried flower.

SCENT: None.

Centaurea montana
Knapweed

NAME: See also Pink cornflower. *Montana* means 'growing in mountainous areas'.

DESCRIPTION: A perennial plant forming runners with erect stems approx. 60 cm long and oval-oblong leaves with smooth edges which narrow in the stalk. The entire plant is covered with silvery-white hairs. The single flower heads have a diameter of around 6 cm; they have a somewhat purple disc and blue ray flowers. There are also large-flowering cultivars of this sort in blue, pink and white.

ORIGIN: The Alps, Vosges and Jura; Asia Minor. The plant was first cultivated in Germany in 1554.

CULTIVATION: Temperate areas with outdoor flower cultivation.

AVAILABILITY: Especially in May-June.

CARE: Remove lower leaves, cut off a bit of the stem, use cut-flower food for herbaceous plants.

KEEPING PROPERTIES: 5-7 days.

USES: In mixed and field bouquets and in a vase.

SCENT: None.

Centaurea cyanus
Blue cornflower, **Bluebottle**
NAME: See also Pink cornflower. *Cyanus* (from the Greek *kuaneos*) means 'dark blue'.
DESCRIPTION: An annual plant, approx. 50 cm high, whose stem is at first woolly but later becomes hairless; it is not very sturdy. The leaves are generally linear and far apart. The flower heads have a diameter of approx. 4 cm; the flower is long-stemmed and its original colour was blue.
ORIGIN: The central and eastern part of the Mediterranean area; later it also went wild elsewhere as a cornfield weed. The plant was first cultivated around 1480.
CULTIVATION: Outdoor flower cultivation areas in the entire world.
AVAILABILITY: From May to the end of September, with a peak in July.
CARE: Remove lower leaves, cut off a bit of the stem, put them in a clean vase with cut-flower food for herbaceous plants.
KEEPING PROPERTIES: 5-7 days.
USES: In mixed and field bouquets and in a vase.
SCENT: None.

Cultivars
'**Diadeem**' is the most frequently cultivated blue cultivar. Other blue cultivars are '**Victoria**' (early blooming) and '**Blue Boy**' (an older cultivar that manages to remain popular).
'**Pinkie**' distinguishes itself by its well-filled flowers and is the most frequently cultivated pink cornflower cultivar.
'**Red Boy**' is one of the purpled-red cultivars which are much used in cornflower mixtures.
'**Wit**' is a bright white cultivar which is grown only to a limited extent. The flower will turn somewhat brown as it matures.

Chrysanthemum carinatum
NAME: *Chrysanthemum* comes from the Greek words *chrysos* (= gold) and *anthos* (= flower): a plant with golden flowers (many chrysanthemum sorts are yellow). *Carinatum* means 'careening' (from the Latin *carina* = ship's keel) and refers to the shape of the involucre leaves.
DESCRIPTION: Glabrous annual plant, 50-60 cm high with fleshy, doubly cleft leaves which have linear pointed tips. The single flowers, 4-6 cm across, have a dark-coloured disc composed of tubular flowers. Around it are the ray flowers, which were white with a yellow base in the original sort. The most frequently cultivated cultivar, a pale golden yellow, is 'Etoile d'Or'. The cultivation of the plant has led to numerous other colour combinations, but all of them have a coloured ring at the base of the ray flowers. The involucral bracts are slanted. Only the single-flowered cultivars are used as cut flowers.
ORIGIN: North-west Africa; the plant was first cultivated in 1796.
CULTIVATION: Limited, in all areas with outdoor cut flower cultivation.
AVAILABILITY: From June until September.
CARE: Remove lower leaves, cut off a bit of the stem, clean the vase with a bleach solution, use cut-flower food for herbaceous plants.
KEEPING PROPERTIES: About 4 days.
USES: In a vase and in Biedermeier bouquets.
SCENT: None.

Centaurea cyanus

Chrysanthemum carinatum

Chrysanthemum coccineum,
syn. *Pyrethrum roseum*
Painted daisy, Pyrethrum
NAME: See also *C. carinatum. Coccineum* means 'scarlet', the colour of one of the cultivars.
DESCRIPTION: A glabrous perennial plant with unbranched stems. The leaves are finely cut and divided, with linear tips; the upper ones have entire or serrate margins. The single blooms stand on long stems. In the single flowering form the tubular flowers in the centre are yellow and the ray flowers are pink. The cultivated cultivars, both single and double, come in shades of pink, red and creamy white. The most frequently cultivated cultivars are 'Gloriosa' (carmine), 'Pink Ideal' and 'Eileen May Robinson' (bright pink), 'Regent' (red) and 'Mont Blanc' (white).
ORIGIN: The Caucasus, Armenia. The plant was first cultivated in the United Kingdom in 1804.
CULTIVATION: Temperate areas with outdoor cut flower cultivation.
AVAILABILITY: Early May and June.
CARE: When purchased, 2 or 3 wreaths of the tubular flowers should be open. The flowers must not be kept dry too long. Cut off a bit of the stem, use cut-flower food for herbaceous plants.
KEEPING PROPERTIES: 10-14 days.
USES: In a vase; sometimes in mixed bouquets.
SCENT: None.

Chrysanthemum frutescens,
syn. *Argyranthemum frutescens*
White marguerite
NAME: See also *C. carinatum. Frutescens* means 'like a semi-shrub' and refers to the manner of growth.
DESCRIPTION: A very branching somewhat shrubby plant growing up to 1.5 m high with bluish-green leaves deeply cut in feathery shapes with narrow, dentate tips. The numerous flower heads stand on long stems, have a diameter of 8 cm and are shaped like daisies. The most frequently cultivated white cultivar is 'Comtesse de Chambord'. 'Snowflake' is a large-flowered white cultivar. 'Etoile d'Or', a frequently cultivated cultivar, is a pale golden yellow. Its leaves are greener than those of the white cultivars.
ORIGIN: Canary Islands. The plant was first cultivated in England in 1699.
CULTIVATION: As a cut flower, primarily on the French and Italian Riviera. Elsewhere chiefly as a potted plant.
AVAILABILITY: From February until April. As a potted plant, the white marguerite blossoms throughout the summer.
CARE: Remove lower leaves, cut off a bit of the stem, use cut-flower food.
KEEPING PROPERTIES: 2-3 weeks.
USES: In mixed spring bouquets, for instance, with Persian buttercup and anemone. SCENT: None.

The chrysanthemum

The Swedish naturalist Carl Linnaeus (1707-1778) gained fame primarily as the spiritual father of binary nomenclature, plant or animal names consisting of two elements. He gave all living things a Greek or Latin genus name followed by a sort name. This revolutionary system, which was rapidly adopted around the world, put an end to the chaos in plant and animal names which had prevailed until then.

The chrysanthemum, too, was named by Linnaeus. He called the plant Chrysanthemum indicum. Literally: the golden yellow flower which comes from the Indies. And this was a mistake. For, although the chrysanthemum had come to the Netherlands at the end of the 17th century from Batavia (the present Indonesian capital, Jakarta), it was definitely not native to the Dutch East Indies. It had made a detour.

Long before the Christian era, the flower was cultivated in the imperial gardens of China. Where its wild origins lie we do not know; perhaps in China, or in Japan. At any rate, cultivated chrysanthemums had gained great popularity in these countries by 1200; there was a large assortment of garden cultivars by then. The popularity of the plant has remained. Japan has a national festival devoted to the chrysanthemum (the 9th day of the 9th month) on which the flower is honoured as the symbol of longevity. The chrysanthemum is depicted on the imperial weapon and flag, and the Order of the Chrysanthemum is one of the highest Japanese imperial distinctions.

Nowadays the chrysanthemum is among the most important cut flowers in the world; in Japan, the United States and the United Kingdom it is number one. The modern assortment consists almost exclusively of hybrid cultivars, which were obtained by crossings of C. indicum, C. morifolium and a number of different species. New cultivars for the improvement of the assortment come from these three countries, as well as from the Netherlands. Special treatments controlling the length of the day make it possible to bring the flower on the market throughout the year. This year-round cultivation, which originated in the United States, takes place in the hothouse. But traditional cultivation methods remain in use as well, and the flowers bloom at the natural time: in autumn or winter.

Chrysanthemum frutescens

Chrysanthemum varieties

The many chrysanthemums in the modern assortment can be classified in two manners: according to flower size and branch shape (chiefly determined by the method of cultivation) and according to flower shape.

According to the first type of classification, the following groups are distinguished:

Large-flowered chrysanthemums
These have one stem per plant and one flower per stem. They are used in large decorations, in churches, for instance, but their cultivation is diminishing. France and Belgium are still fairly important production areas.

Medium-flowered chrysanthemums
They generally bear several stems per plant but only one flower per stem. They are not cultivated on a large scale, partly because their cultivation is quite labour-intensive: the side buds have to be pinched off.

Bunch chrysanthemums
This type has smaller flowers than the previous ones and bears several flowers per stem. Bunch chrysanthemums presently form 90 per cent of the supply.

The following types of flower shapes can be distinguished:

Single-flowered chrysanthemums
They resemble daisies and have an open centre of tubular flowers.

Pyrethrum and anemone-shaped chrysanthemums
This type has a centre of outgrown tubular flowers, around which are grouped one or more rows of ray flowers.

Multiple-flowered chrysanthemums
The centre of tubular flowers is lacking. The bloom consists exclusively of ray flowers. The way in which they are grouped determines the appearance of the flower: dense or loose globes or ornamentals with flat petals.

Radial or ostrich plume chrysanthemums
The blooms consist exclusively of ray flowers which are rolled outwards lengthwise like long, narrow pipes. The ray flowers are arranged on the receptacle in a spiral shape.

Spider chrysanthemums
The narrow ray flowers of this type are completely curled lengthwise. They are of differing lengths, which gives the flowers an irregular spider shape.

Pompon chrysanthemums
This type has small multiple flowers which are composed entirely of ray flowers. The ray flowers are rolled up lengthwise like funnels; their implantation is regular and fixed.

Finally, a great many cultivars have flower shapes that do not fit in the above categories and so they are classified under the catch-all 'other flower shapes'.

△ 'Gerrie Hoek'

'Harlequin'

'Cassa'

Chrysanthemum indicum-hybrid,
syn. *Dendranthema x grandiflorum,*
syn. *C. x hortorum*
Chrysanthemum, 'Mum'
NAME: See *C. carinatum. Indicum*
means (incorrectly) 'from the Indies'. The plant, originally from
China or Japan, came to the Netherlands by way of Batavia,
through the relations of the Dutch
East Indies Company with Japan.
DESCRIPTION: Very branching
woody shrubs, highly aromatic,
with a leaf shape varying from
coarsely dentate to lobed. The leaf
size is determined by the method
of cultivation: large-flowered
chrysanthemums have much larger
leaves than the same cultivar cultivated as bunch chrysanthemums.
The leaves are greyish-green and
slightly downy. The flower heads
stand in plumes or clusters and can
take many forms.
ORIGIN: China or Japan (uncertain).
CULTIVATION: The entire world,
but chiefly in the United States,
United Kingdom, Japan and the
Netherlands.
AVAILABILITY: Throughout the
year.
CARE: Bunch chrysanthemums are
sometimes sold in plastic foil; the
medium-flowered cultivars are often packed in cellophane bags.
Unwrap them; remove the lower
leaves (so that no leaves touch the
water), cut off a bit of the stem,
use cut-flower food for chrysanthemums.
KEEPING PROPERTIES: Chrysanthemums cultivated outdoors: 7-10
days (the leaves wilt first); year-
round chrysanthemums at least 3
weeks.
USES: For all purposes, but primarily in a vase.
SCENT: Spicy, aromatic.

△ 'Bright Eyes'   ▽ 'Spider'   △ 'Cotton Ball'   ▽ 'Pink Pearl'

Cultivars

'**Pink Pearl**' is a pink-flowering,
single-flowered cultivar which
blooms outdoors as early as August.
'**Gerrie Hoek**', pink in colour, is
one of the many cultivars with
multiple flowers. The assortment
in this group is large; many cultivars are mutants.
'**Bright Eyes**', yellow with a purple centre, is a pompon-shaped
bunch chrysanthemum, a type that
is gaining in popularity; consumers
appreciate the small, compact
flower shape.
'**Long Island Beauty Gold**' is a
golden yellow mutant of the pink
ancestral cultivar. It is a
pyrethrum-flowered cultivar and is
striking for its singular flower
shape.
'**Cremon white**' is an anemone-
flowered medium-size chrysanthemum, a cultivar type remarkable
for the distinctive flower shape.
'**Streamer**' and '**Breitner**' belong
to the group of multiple-flowered
medium-size chrysanthemums and
they are lavender and pink respectively. This cultivar type is among
the most frequently cultivated
chrysanthemums.
'**Prinses Armgard**' (bronze) belongs to the large-flowered multiple chrysanthemums, a type with
an impressive flower shape;
however, the demand for it is
declining.
'**Harlequin**' (light bronze), '**Cassa**'
(white) and '**Regoltime**' (yellow)
are all single-flowered bunch chrysanthemums produced in year-
round cultivation on a large scale.
The colour variation in this group
is very large.
'**White Spider**' is a white spider-
shaped chrysanthemum, a very different group of generally excellent
quality.
'**Cotton Ball**' (white) belongs to
the group of pompom-shaped
chrysanthemums. The year-round
cultivation of this type is gradually
getting started.
'**Dark Flamengo**' is a dark purple, multiple-flowered chrysanthemum. The cultivars of this type
are of excellent quality, but they
are not the most important group
in year-round cultivation.
'**Refour**' is a bright white pyrethrum-flowered cultivar with an
unusual flower shape and an excellent quality.

Chrysanthemum leucanthemum

Chrysanthemum maximum

Chrysanthemum segetum

Chrysanthemum leucanthemum
Ox eye daisy

NAME: See also *C. carinatum*. *Leucanthemum* means 'having white flowers' (from the Greek *leukos* = white, and *anthos* = flower).
DESCRIPTION: Perennial plant, 30-50 cm high, with unbranched stems and thin leaves. The upper leaves encircle the stem and are somewhat dentate, the lower ones are deeply dentate and spatula-shaped. The single flower heads are 4-5 cm across. The tubular flowers (the centres) are yellow, the wreath of ray flowers white.
ORIGIN: Northern hemisphere. The plant was first cultivated in the Netherlands in 1596.
CULTIVATION: Temperate areas with outdoor flower cultivation.
AVAILABILITY: May-July.
CARE: Remove lower leaves, cut off a bit of the stem, use cut-flower food for herbaceous plants.
KEEPING PROPERTIES: 8-10 days.
USES: In a vase, in mixed and field bouquets. Sometimes dyed in the colours yellow, pink, blue green, etc.
SCENT: None.

Chrysanthemum maximum
Shasta daisy

NAME: See also *C. carinatum*. *Maximum* means 'the largest' and refers to the flower size.
DESCRIPTION: A perennial plant with stems 60-80 cm long and long wedge-shaped leaves, the upper ones of which are narrower and finely dentate. The flower heads are somewhat fleshy and have a diameter of 6-8 cm. The ray flowers are white. Multiple-flowered forms are the most frequently cultivated. The flowers are often dyed green, blue, pink and yellow or other colours. Among the present cultivars (also known as *C. maximum*-hybrids) the most frequently cultivated are the double-flowered 'Wirral Supreme', 'Esther Read' and the single-flowered 'Beethoven' (all white).
ORIGIN: Pyrenees.
CULTIVATION: Temperate areas with outdoor cultivation.
AVAILABILITY: Early May - early July.
CARE: When purchased, the middle of the flower should be open; if they are to be dyed, they must be completely open. Remove lower leaves, cut off a bit of the stem, use cut-flower food for herbaceous plants.
KEEPING PROPERTIES: 2-3 weeks.
USES: In a vase, in mixed bouquets, as dyed flowers.
SCENT: None.

Chrysanthemum parthenium

Chrysanthemum parthenium,
syn. *'Matricaria capensis'*
Feverfew
NAME: See also *C. carinatum*. *Parthenium* is derived from the Greek word *parthenois* which means 'virginal' and refers to the white colour of the flower.
DESCRIPTION: A perennial plant, but cultivated as an annual, and smelling strongly of camomile. The slightly branched stems are 60-70 cm long; the leaves are oval, with long, lobed tips. The flower heads stand in dense leafy clusters; their diameter is 2-3 cm. The tubular flowers in the centre are yellow; the ray flowers in the wreath around it were white in the original form, but there are also pale yellow cultivars. Some are single-flowered; 'Snowball' and 'Golden Ball' have double flowers.
ORIGIN: Asia Minor, the Caucasus. The plant has been cultivated since ancient times.
CULTIVATION: Virtually worldwide.
AVAILABILITY: June-August; with artificially lengthened days, until December.
CARE: Remove lower leaves, cut off a bit of the stem, use cut-flower food for herbaceous plants.
KEEPING PROPERTIES: 2-3 weeks.
USES: Especially in mixed bouquets and in floral work.
SCENT: Spicy, like camomile.

Chrysanthemum segetum
Corn marigold
NAME: See also *C. carinatum*. *Segetum* means 'growing in cornfields' and refers to where it grows in its native country.
DESCRIPTION: Annual plant with unbranched to little branched stems, 40-60 cm high. The leaves are lanceolate or spatula-shaped and vary from coarsely dentate to finely cut; the upper ones are somewhat heart-shaped and encircle the stems. The single flower heads have a diameter of approx. 5 cm. The wild form of the flower is yellow; in the cut-flower cultivars the tubular flowers (the centres) are yellow and the ray flowers around it golden yellow.
ORIGIN: Mediterranean.
CULTIVATION: Nearly the entire world.
AVAILABILITY: July-September.
CARE: Remove lower leaves, cut off a bit of the stem, use cut-flower food for herbaceous plants; change the water if necessary.
KEEPING PROPERTIES: 7-12 days.
USES: In a vase and in mixed bouquets.
SCENT: Somewhat spicy.

Cirsium japonicum
Plumed thistle
NAME: *Cirsium* is derived from the old Greek thistle name *kirsion*, which was used as a remedy for varicose veins. Perhaps it is also related to the Latin word *cirrus*, which means 'curl' or 'lock of hair' and might refer to the hair-like flower petals. *Japonicum* means: 'from Japan'.
DESCRIPTION: Annual plant, about 1 m high, the lower leaves of which form a rosette and the upper ones, which are narrower, encircle the stem. The leaves are a bright green. Leaf margins and stems are covered with a great many fine prickles. The flower heads are surrounded by bracts. Two cultivars are commonly cultivated: the dark crimson 'Rose Beauty' and the pale pink 'Pink Beauty'. The lilac-red *C. heterophyllum* is sometimes also cultivated as a cut flower.
ORIGIN: Japan.
CULTIVATION: All cut flower-growing areas of the world.
AVAILABILITY: June-August.
CARE: When purchased, the buds should be open. Cut off a bit of the stem, use cut-flower food for herbaceous plants.
KEEPING PROPERTIES: 2-3 weeks.
USES: In modern flower arrangement; to a limited extent, in a vase and in mixed bouquets.
SCENT: None.

Cirsium japonicum 'Pink Beauty'

53

Coreopsis grandiflora
Tickseed

NAME: *Coreopsis* is derived from *koris* (= bedbug) and *opsis* (= resembling) and refers to the shape of the achenes. *Grandiflora* = large-flowered.

DESCRIPTION: The plant has erect, usually branching, stems of 60-80 cm. The lower leaves are spatula-shaped and have smooth margins; the upper ones have 3-5 leaflets. The flower heads, with a diameter of approx. 7 cm, are fairly long-stemmed. The ray flowers are golden yellow and have 3-4 lobes on the top. The most frequently cultivated cultivar is 'Badengold'.

ORIGIN: Central and south-eastern United States. The plant was first cultivated in the United Kingdom in 1821.

CULTIVATION: In temperate and subtropical areas with outdoor cut-flower cultivation.

AVAILABILITY: July-end of August.

CARE: When purchased, the flower should be at least half open. Remove lower leaves, cut off a bit of the stem, use cut-flower food for herbaceous plants.

KEEPING PROPERTIES: 10-12 days.

USES: In a vase and in mixed bouquets.

SCENT: None.

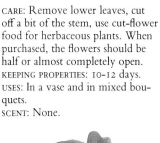

△ Coreopsis grandiflora

△ Coreopsis lanceolata

Coreopsis lanceolata
Tickseed

NAME: See also previous variety. *Lanceolata* means 'lanceolate' and refers to the shape of the leaf-like organs.

DESCRIPTION: This variety differs from *C. grandiflora* in its stems, which are leafy at the base, its single leaves and its long-stemmed flower heads. The flower heads are 4-6 cm across and have 6-10 long, wedge-shaped ray flowers with 3-7 lobes at the top. The stem length is 40-50 cm. Frequently cultivated cultivars are 'Zonnekind' and 'Sunray'.

ORIGIN: Central and eastern United States. The plant was first cultivated in the United Kingdom in 1724.

CULTIVATION: All temperate and subtropical areas with outdoor cut-flower cultivation.

AVAILABILITY: June-July.

CARE: Remove lower leaves, cut off a bit of the stem, use cut-flower food for herbaceous plants. When purchased, the flowers should be half or almost completely open.

KEEPING PROPERTIES: 10-12 days.

USES: In a vase and in mixed bouquets.

SCENT: None.

Cosmos bipinnatus, syn. Cosmea

Cynara scolymus

Dahlia hybrid, decorative 'Glory of Heemstede'

Cosmos bipinnata,
syn. *Cosmea*
Cosmos

NAME: *Cosmos* is the Latin form of the Greek work *kosmos* = ornament. *Bipinnatus* means 'bipinnate' and refers to the opposite leaves.
DESCRIPTION: Annual plant, 1.5 m high; the bipinnate leaves have linear tips. The single flower heads have a diameter of 10-12 cm. The centre, with yellow tubular flowers, is small; around it there are usually eight ray flowers which were originally pink but now may be pink, red or white. A related sort is *C. sulphureus*, with multiple flowers, in various shades of orange.
ORIGIN: *C. bipinnatus* and *C. sulphureus* are native to Mexico. The former was first cultivated in the United Kingdom in 1789, the latter in Spain in 1791.
CULTIVATION: All outdoor flower cultivation areas in the world.
AVAILABILITY: Early July - end of September.
CARE: Remove lower leaves, cut off a bit of the stem, use cut-flower food for herbaceous plants.
KEEPING PROPERTIES: *C. bipinnatus* 6-9 days; *C. sulphureus* 8-12 days.
USES: In a vase, in floral work and in mixed bouquets.
SCENT: The leaves have a slightly spicy aroma.

Cynara scolymus
Globe artichoke

NAME: *Cynara* is the Latin form of the Greek *kunara*, the name for a sort of artichoke. *Scolymus*, from the Greek *skolumos*, was the name for a thistle-like plant with an edible receptacle, which may have been the forerunner of our edible artichoke.
DESCRIPTION: A perennial plant growing up to 2 m high, with grooved stems and very large pinnate and prickly dentate leaves, which are greyish-green on the top while the underside is silvery white. The flower heads have a diameter of 15 cm. They have large receptacles which become pulpy and can be eaten as a vegetable. The triangular involucral bracts have sharp points and are thicker at the base. The inflorescence consists of tubular purple flowers.
ORIGIN: The plant does not grow wild but originated from the cardoon (*C. cardunculus*). It has been cultivated as a vegetable in southern Europe since the 16th century and for its flowers since 1960.
CULTIVATION: All temperate and subtropical areas with outdoor cut-flower cultivation.
AVAILABILITY: The middle of August to the end of September.
CARE: Cut off a bit of the stem, use cut-flower food.
KEEPING PROPERTIES: Around 3 weeks.
USES: In decorations and in flower arrangement; to a limited extent, in a vase.
SCENT: None.

Dahlia

The first description of a dahlia comes from the Spanish doctor Francisco Hernandes, who reported on the plant and animal worlds of 'New Spain' (Mexico) in 1615. He called the plant by its Indian name: acoctli. It was nearly two centuries later that the plant once again appeared in the literature: in a report by the Frenchman N.J. Thierry de Neninville, describing a trip to Mexico in 1787. He made the trip to look for a certain sort of insect from which a red dye-stuff could be obtained. Two years later, in 1789, the director of the botanical gardens of Mexico, Vincent Cervot, sent several dahlia seeds to the royal gardens in Madrid. The director of the gardens, Abbé Cavanilles, named the plant after the Scandinavian botanist A. Dahl, a pupil of Linnaeus, but kept its existence a secret for ten years. Only then did he give a number of seeds to the wife of the ambassador to the Spanish court.
Not until the turn of the century did more dahlias come from Mexico to England, France and Germany. In 1805 they arrived in the Netherlands, where much work has since been done on the improvement of the plant, and many new forms and cultivars have been developed. The Netherlands is still prominent today in the international dahlia world.

Dahlia hybrids
Dahlia

NAME: The flower is named after A. Dahl (1751-1789), a Scandinavian author of botanic works.
DESCRIPTION: A perennial plant, 50-180 cm high, with long, bulbous roots. The leaf shape varies; the lower leaves are generally deeply cut, the upper ones single and serrate. The flower heads show a great diversity in shape, depending on the ancestors. The colours, too, are varied: from white to very deep purple and even two-coloured.
ORIGIN: Mexico.
CULTIVATION: All cut-flower cultivating areas of the world, with the exception of the tropics.
AVAILABILITY: July-October.
CARE: The lower leaves must not touch the water. Cut off a bit of the stem, use cut-flower food. When purchased, the flowers should be well open: immature flowers will droop and buds that are still closed will not open.
KEEPING PROPERTIES: 6-14 days, depending on the cultivar.
USES: In a vase and in decorative work.
SCENT: Fairly strong, spicy.

△ Dahlia hybrid, semi-cactus 'Bacchus'   ▽ Dahlia hybrid, pompom 'Silver Baby'

Doronicum orientale

Cultivars

Decorative dahlias A multiple-flowered type, the broad flower petals of which are curled up somewhat to the inside or outside lengthwise towards the centre. The tops of the petals are generally flat or somewhat fluted. Many cut-flower cultivars come from this group.

Semi-cactus dahlias Multiple-flowered cultivars, with generally pointed petals that are wide at the base, and are curled up to the middle of the length axis. They are straight or narrow towards the centre of the flower.

Globular dahlias The flowers of this group are multiple and are globular or somewhat flattened on the top. The tops of the petals are rounded or blunt. The petals are arranged in a spiral fashion and curled up towards the inside over more than half of the length axis. The flowers are smaller than those of the previous groups.

Pompom dahlias This type is smaller than the globular dahlias and the petals are rolled up along the entire length axis.

Collar dahlias This type of dahlia has a single row of ray flowers which encircles a dense group of tubular flowers (the centre). The centre must be closed. The highly ornamental flower form is very fragile.

Peony-flowered dahlias This type of dahlia has two or more rows of ray flowers which encircle an open centre of tubular flowers.

Doronicum orientale
Leopard's bane
NAME: *Doronicum* is thought to be a latinized Arabic name. *Orientale* means 'coming from the east'.
DESCRIPTION: A downy-haired perennial with a short and creeping rootstock, it grows up to 40-50 cm high. The leaves are heart-shaped, dentate and long-stemmed; the single yellow flower heads have a diameter of approx. 5 cm.
ORIGIN: South-east Europe and the Caucasus. The plant was first cultivated in Germany in 1808.
CULTIVATION: Temperate areas with outdoor cut-flower cultivation.
AVAILABILITY: April-May.
CARE: When purchased, the flower should be half open. Remove lower leaves, cut off a bit of the stem, use cut-flower food for herbaceous plants.
KEEPING PROPERTIES: Approx. 5 days.
USES: In mixed bouquets; in a vase.
SCENT: None.

Doronicum plantagineum
'Excelsum'
Leopard's bane
NAME: See also previous variety. *Plantagineum* means 'resembling plantain' and refers to the similarity of the leaf shape to that of plantain (*Plantago* species).
DESCRIPTION: Perennial plant with swollen and somewhat creeping rootstock; up to 80 cm high. The flower stems bear silky hairs at the tops. The elliptical, somewhat fluted leaves narrow to a winged stem. The flower heads, 6 cm across, are bright yellow and stand alone or in groups of three. The most frequently cultivated cultivar is 'Excelsum'.
ORIGIN: Central and southern Europe. The plant was first cultivated in England in 1570.
CULTIVATION: Temperate areas with outdoor cut-flower cultivation.
AVAILABILITY: April-May.
CARE: The flowers should be half open when purchased (two to three rows of tubular flowers should be open). Remove the lower leaves; cut off a bit of the stem and use cut-flower food for herbaceous plants.
KEEPING PROPERTIES: 7-10 days.
USES: In mixed bouquets and in a vase.
SCENT: None.

△ ▽ Echinacea purpurea, syn. Rudbeckia

Echinacea purpurea,
syn. *Rudbeckia*
Echinacea

NAME: *Echinacea* means 'resembling a sea urchin' and refers to the prickly chaffy scales of the receptacle. *Purpurea* stands for 'purple-red', the colour of the flower.
DESCRIPTION: A perennial plant with downy hair and stems of 60-80 cm. The leaves, 10-15 cm long, are oblong and elliptical, have 3-5 nerves and narrow abruptly into a small winged stem. The single flower heads with a diameter of 4 cm have dark brown centres with orange-yellow styles surrounded by 12-20 deep lavender pink ray flowers; as the flower matures, they will start to droop somewhat and are often picked off, leaving only the centre.
ORIGIN: The eastern United States. The plant was first cultivated in England in 1692.
CULTIVATION: Temperate areas with outdoor cut-flower cultivation.
AVAILABILITY: July-September.
CARE: Remove lower leaves, cut off a bit of the stem, use cut-flower food.
KEEPING PROPERTIES: Entire flowers 7-8 days; the centre alone 2-3 weeks.
USES: In flower arrangement and in mixed bouquets.
SCENT: None.

Echinops banaticus
Globe thistle

NAME: *Echinops* means 'sea-urchin' and refers to the prickly involucral bracts of the capitula. *Banaticus* indicates its origin: Banat, a region to the south of the Donau (Hungary).
DESCRIPTION: A 80-150 cm high perennial with greyish felt-like erect stems and cleft, prickly, wrinkled leaves. The upper sides of the leaves are downy, the undersides are matted grey. The lower leaves have stalks, the upper ones encircle the stem. The large, globular inflorescence is composed of numerous small, dark greyish-blue flowers. The most frequently cultivated cultivar, 'Taplow Blue', has deep blue flowers.
ORIGIN: Serbia. It has been under cultivation for centuries.
CULTIVATION: Temperate areas with outdoor cut-flower cultivation.
AVAILABILITY: July-September.

Echinops banaticus

CARE: When purchased, the flower should be two-thirds open; to dry them, they should be bought closed. Cut off a bit of the stem; use cut-flower food.
KEEPING PROPERTIES: 2-3 weeks (in a vase).
USES: In flower arrangement, in a vase, in mixed bouquets. As a dried flower, the globe thistle is sometimes dyed deep blue.
SCENT: None.

Echinops ritro
Globe thistle

NAME: See also previous sort. *Ritro* is derived from the Greek *rutros*, formerly the name for a horny or prickled plant.

DESCRIPTION: A perennial plant, 60-80 cm high, with round grey stalks and stiff, cleft leaves with prickly pointed tips. On the upper side the leaves are glabrous; on the underside they are a matted grey. The flower heads are 2-4 cm across; they have a flattened round shape and are light blue, at least originally. The cultivar 'Veitch's Blue', for example, is a deep steel-blue colour with greyish-green leaves. This cultivar is very branched and is regarded as the best globe thistle for cut-flower cultivation.

ORIGIN: South-eastern Europe and western Asia. The plant was first cultivated in Germany in 1542.

CULTIVATION: Temperate areas with outdoor cut-flower cultivation.

AVAILABILITY: July-September.

CARE: When purchased, the flowers should be two-thirds open; to be dried, they should still be closed. Cut off a bit of the stem; use cut-flower food.

KEEPING PROPERTIES: 2-3 weeks, in a vase.

USES: In a vase, in flower arrangement and in mixed and dried bouquets. The blossom is often dyed (blue).

SCENT: None.

Erigeron hybrid 'Dunkelste Aller'
Flesbane

NAME: *Erigeron* means 'greying young' and is derived from the Greek words *eri* (= early) and *geron* (= grey). The name refers to the grey pappus, which becomes visible after the bloom.

DESCRIPTION: The hybrid 'Dunkelste Aller' is one of the crossings of *E. speciosus* and *E. macranthus*, which chiefly differ in the shape of their leaves: the former is spatula-shaped, the latter elliptical. The flower heads, with a diameter of 4-5 cm, stand in sparsely flowered clusters; in the ancestors, they consist of yellow tubular flowers with a dense wreath of violet ray flowers. They are perennials with a height of around 50 cm. The various hybrid cultivars vary in colour: violet, pink, carmine and even white. 'Dunkelste Aller', the most frequently cultivated variety, is a very dark red.

ORIGIN: Western United States. The plant has been cultivated since 1832.

CULTIVATION: Temperate areas with outdoor cut-flower cultivation.

AVAILABILITY: End of May - mid-July.

CARE: When purchased, the flower head should be entirely open. Cut off a bit of the stem, remove lower leaves, use cut-flower food for herbaceous plants.

KEEPING PROPERTIES: 2-3 weeks.

USES: In a vase and in mixed bouquets.

SCENT: None.

Eupatorium purpureum
Hemp agrimony, Thoroughwort, Trumpetweed

NAME: The name is derived from *eupatoria*, the oldest Greek name for the plant. It was named after king Mithridates Eupator of Pontus (the Great) (132-63 B.C.), a great herb expert. The plant was regarded as a remedy for liver and venereal diseases. *Purpureum* means 'purplish red'; *atropurpureum* = dark purplish red.

DESCRIPTION: A perennial plant, growing up to 1.60 m high, with a sturdy, erect, hollow stem that is green to purple. The leaves stand in whorls of 3-6 around the stem. They are lanceolate and pointed, have short stalks and serrate margins. The small purplish red flower heads stand in pyramidal clusters. The many rows of involucral bracts are also tinged purple. The cultivar 'Atropurpureum' has very dark coloured flowers.

ORIGIN: The central and south-eastern United States. The plant was first cultivated in France in 1635.

CULTIVATION: Temperate areas with outdoor cut-flower cultivation.

AVAILABILITY: From July-end of August.

CARE: Cut off a bit of the stem, use cut-flower food.

KEEPING PROPERTIES: 10-16 days.

USES: In mixed bouquets and large decorative work.

SCENT: None.

Erigeron hybrid 'Dunkelste Aller'

Gaillardia hybrids
Blanket flower

NAME: The plant is named after Gaillard de Marenttonneau, a French botanist who lived near the end of the 18th century.

DESCRIPTION: A downy perennial plant with spatula-shaped leaves; the upper ones are cut, the lower ones have smooth margins. The stem is 60-70 cm long. The flower heads have a diameter of approx. 8 cm; depending on the cultivar, the ray flowers come in all shades of red or are two-coloured, for instance, golden yellow with red.

ORIGIN: The hybrid is a cross between *G. aristata* and *G. pulchella* and was discovered in Belgium in 1850. The ancestors came from the eastern and southern United States.

CULTIVATION: In temperate areas with outdoor cut-flower cultivation.

AVAILABILITY: From June until August.

CARE: Remove lower leaves, cut off a bit of the stem, use cut-flower food for herbaceous plants. Upon purchase, two or three of the flower wreaths should be open.

KEEPING PROPERTIES: 8-15 days.

USES: Primarily in mixed bouquets.

SCENT: None.

Gerbera jamesonii hybrids
Transvaal daisy

NAME: The flower is named after Traugott Gerber, a German doctor who collected many plants on the Danish peninsula and died there in 1742. *G. Jamesonii* is the most important ancestor of the present cultivars and was called after the plant collector, Jameson, who discovered the plant in Transvaal.

DESCRIPTION: A hairy perennial plant with root rosettes and numerous leaves of approx. 30 cm long. They are pinnate and have long stalks; the underside is somewhat woolly. The flower heads stand alone at the end of long, leafless stems. Their diameter is 12-16 cm, depending on the cultivar. There are many shades of red, orange, yellow, pink, cerise and white, sometimes with a centre of a different colour. The flowers of some cultivars are single, of others double. The assortment is classified according to the flower shape (see Cultivars).

ORIGIN: The ancestors are native to South Africa, chiefly the Transvaal and Cape Province. The first Transvaal daisies were cultivated in the United Kingdom in 1887. Later, refinement of the flower moved to the French Riviera; after 1950 the Netherlands gained in prominence.

CULTIVATION: Cut-flower cultivation areas throughout the world.

AVAILABILITY: Throughout the year, with a peak in spring.

CARE: The flowers are sold in boxes. For the single-flowered cultivars, 2-3 of the stamen whorls should be open; for the double-flowered sorts, the ray flowers in the centre should lie flat, while the stem should feel sturdy. The stem of the Transvaal daisy rapidly pollutes the water with bacteria, which makes the flower hard to keep. Florists use special agents and methods to prevent this pollution (including ultraviolet lamps). Tips for the consumer: clean the vase with a bleach solution, cut off a bit of the stem, use cut-flower food, change the water regularly, rinsing the stems and cutting off a bit more each time. The flowers cannot withstand temperatures lower than 5°C.

KEEPING PROPERTIES: 5-14 days, depending on the bacteria content of the water.

USES: In a vase, in floral work and sometimes in mixed bouquets.

SCENT: None.

△ Eupatorium purpureum   ▽ Gaillardia hybrid

Cultivars

Single-flowered cultivars

The largest group; they form approx. 63% of the total Transvaal daisy supply. The most important cultivars are 'Fleur' (cerise), 'Apple blossom' (pink), 'Clementine' (orange), 'Delphi' (white), 'Beatrix' (pale pink and with slightly pointed ray flowers) and 'Pimpernel' (red).

Double-flowered cultivars

This group forms approx. 23% of the supply. The centres of the flowers of these cultivars are filled with ray flowers. The most important cultivars in this group are 'Marleen' (yellow), 'Hildegarde' (pale pink), 'Bingo' (orange), 'Maria' (greenish white) and 'Amber' (carmine, with very pale margins and tubular flowers in the centre).

Black centre

These cultivars have single flowers with a dark centre of tubular flowers. They are the offspring of crossings with a small-flowered white cultivar with a black centre from South Africa. These crossings were made at the Testing Station for Floristry in Aalsmeer. The group forms some 6% of the Transvaal daisy supply. The most frequently cultivated cultivars are 'Fabio' (orange with a yellow ring at the base of the ray flowers), 'Kaukasus' (white), 'Calypso' (very pale creamy whitish-pink), 'Terre Parva' (yellow) and 'Rosetta' (pale pink).

Helenium hybrids
Sneezeweed

NAME: *Helenium* is the Latin translation of the Greek plant name *helenion*, formerly used for the plant which we now know as *Inula*.

DESCRIPTION: A perennial plant, 1-1.5 m high, with narrow, winged stems. The leaves have smooth or dentate margins; the upper ones are lanceolate, the lower ones spatula-shaped. The flower heads have a semi-globular or flat round disc of brownish-red disc flowers and a wreath of 10-15 ray flowers. A commonly cultivated cultivar is the copper red 'Moerkens Beauty'.

ORIGIN: *Helenium* hybrids are crossings of botanic sorts. The most important ancestors are *H. autumnale* and *H. nudiflorum*; they are native to the eastern United States and Canada. Most hybrid cultivars were raised in Germany and the Netherlands.

CULTIVATION: All temperate areas with outdoor cut-flower cultivation.

AVAILABILITY: Depending on the cultivar, between July and the end of October.

CARE: Remove lower leaves, cut off a bit of the stem, use cut-flower food.

KEEPING PROPERTIES: 10-12 days.

USES: In a vase and in mixed bouquets.

SCENT: None.

△ Helenium hybrid   ▽ Gerbera Jamesonii, single-flowered

Gerbera Jamesonii, double-flowered

Helianthus annuus

NAME: See also Common sunflower. *Debilis* means 'weak'; *cucumerifolius* = with leaves like the cucumber.

DESCRIPTION: An annual plant which greatly resembles *H. annuus* but, in contrast to this sort, shows branchings from the base. The somewhat triangular-elliptical leaves are much smaller, as are the long-stemmed flower heads (6-12 cm in diameter). The involucral bracts are unfringed. The most frequently cultivated cultivar is the golden yellow 'Stella'.

ORIGIN: Southern United States. The plant was first cultivated in Germany in 1876.

CULTIVATION: Temperate and subtropical areas with outdoor cut-flower cultivation.

AVAILABILITY: End of June - end of September.

CARE: The flowers should be well open when purchased. Put them in water straight away and definitely use cut-flower food.

KEEPING PROPERTIES: 9-12 days.

USES: In a vase and in mixed bouquets.

SCENT: None.

Helianthus annuus (Common) sunflower

NAME: *Helianthus* is derived from the Greek words *helios* (= sun) and *anthos* (= flower): the flower resembles a shining sun. *Annuus* means 'annual'.

DESCRIPTION: A bristly annual plant that can reach a height of 1-4 m or more. The stems are not branched (or branch only near the top) and bear large, elliptical or heart-shaped leaves standing apart; they are rough to the touch and stand on long stalks. The nodding flower heads have a diameter of 20-35 cm. They have a dark-coloured disc and numerous ray flowers, mostly yellow. The many involucral bracts are wide, oblong, rounded and fringed. Multiple-flowered cultivars are cultivated as well. The colours of the cultivated cultivars range from yellow to reddish-brown.

ORIGIN: The south and west of the United States. The plant was cultivated by the North American Indians for many years.

CULTIVATION: The entire world, although sometimes limited. In the warmer climates the sunflower is important for its seeds (cattle feed) and the oil which can be pressed from them (sunflower seed oil).

AVAILABILITY: From July until October.

CARE: When purchased, the flower must be well open. Cut off a bit of the stem; be sure to use cut-flower food for herbaceous plants, or else the flower will not keep well.

KEEPING PROPERTIES: 6-10 days.

USES: In a vase and in decorations.

SCENT: None.

Cultivars

Yellow Several yellow cultivars are cultivated as cut flowers. Examples: 'Sungold' (double-flowered), 'Primrose' (single-flowered, light yellow), 'Henry Wilde' or 'Golden Nigger' (golden yellow) and 'Schnittgold' (very large-flowered and with narrow ray flowers). All single-flowered cultivars have a dark to black centre.

Mixture This group is composed of the cultivars 'Avondzon', in various reddish-brown shades, and 'Modekleuren', a mixture of red, purple, yellow and bronze pastel shades.

Helianthus decapetalus

Helichrysum bracteatum

Helianthus decapetalus
Little sunflower

NAME: See also common sunflower. *Decapetalus* means 'having ten corona petals'.

DESCRIPTION: A perennial plant, 1-1.5 m high. The erect stems branch at the top, where they are sometimes a little bristly. The thin dark green leaves are elliptical and pointed with dentate or serrate margins. The leaf base flares into a small, winged stalk. The flower heads consist of 8-15 bright yellow ray flowers of 3 cm long with centres of dark yellow tubular flowers. The lanceolate involucral bracts, mostly glabrous, are fringed; they stand out and are higher than the disc.

ORIGIN: United States and Canada. The plant was first cultivated in Germany in 1588.

CULTIVATION: Temperate areas with outdoor cut-flower cultivation.

AVAILABILITY: August-September.

CARE: The flowers should be entirely open when purchased. Cut off a bit of the stem, remove lower leaves; definitely use cut-flower food.

KEEPING PROPERTIES: 11-15 days.

USES: In a vase and in mixed bouquets.

SCENT: None.

Helichrysum bracteatum
Strawflower

NAME: *Helichrysum* means 'sun gold' and is derived from the Greek words for sun (*helios*) and gold (*chrysos*). The name refers to the shiny golden flower heads of the ancestral form. *Bracteatum* means 'having clear bracts'.

DESCRIPTION: An almost glabrous perennial plant which is usually cultivated as an annual. The green lanceolate leaves are 7-10 cm long; the flower heads have a diameter of 4-5 cm and stand alone or in loose clusters. The flaring involucral bracts are curved inwards and resemble ray flowers; in the ancestral form, they are shiny yellow. Strawflowers are now cultivated in all kinds of shades of red, orange, yellow, pink, violet, salmon and white.

ORIGIN: Australia. The plant was first cultivated in France in 1799.

CULTIVATION: Temperate and subtropical areas.

AVAILABILITY: From July until early October.

CARE: For use as a fresh flower in a vase: cut off a bit of the stem, use cut-flower food for herbaceous plants. For use as a dried flower, the flower must be closed when purchased.

KEEPING PROPERTIES: 20-25 days (fresh flowers).

USES: Generally as dried flowers; sometimes as fresh flowers in a vase.

SCENT: None.

Heliopsis helianthoides var. scabra
Orange sunflower, Ox eye

NAME: *Heliopsis*, from the Greek words *helios* (= sun) and *opsis* (= appearance), means 'having an inflorescence resembling a sun'. *Helianthioides* = resembling a helianthus. *Scabra* = rough.

DESCRIPTION: A perennial reaching up to 1.5 m with rough hairs on the stems and leaves; the leaf shape is elliptical-lanceolate and pointed. The single flower heads are dark yellow and have a diameter of 5-8 cm. There are also double-flowered cultivars. The most frequently cultivated single-flowered cultivar is 'Karat', which is superior in flower size and in keeping properties.

ORIGIN: Northern and eastern United States. The plant was first cultivated in the United Kingdom in 1819.

CULTIVATION: Temperate areas with outdoor cut-flower cultivation.

AVAILABILITY: From July until September.

CARE: When purchased, the flowers should be half open and the stem neck should be firm. Cut off a bit of the stem, use cut-flower food.

KEEPING PROPERTIES: 12-16 days. Double-flowered cultivars keep less well.

USES: In a vase, in mixed bouquets and in floral work.

SCENT: None.

Helipterum humboldtianum

Heliopsis helianthoides, var. scabra

Helipterum humboldtianum
Everlasting

NAME: *Helipterum* is derived from the Greek; from *helios* = sun, and *pteron* = bird feather. The flower resembles a sun, the seed fuzz is feathery. The plant is also named after T.W.H. Alexander von Humboldt (1769-1859), a German mining engineer who studied the subterrestrial flora of the mineral rock near Freiburg and travelled to tropical America to collect plants in 1789.

DESCRIPTION: Annual plant, approx. 50 cm high with little branching stems and covered with cobweb-like hair. The lanceolate leaves are a matted white when they are young. The flower heads stand in dense, richly flowering clusters; they are yellow and have a diameter of 5-8 mm.

ORIGIN: Australia. The plant was first cultivated in the United Kingdom in 1860.

CULTIVATION: Temperate and subtropical areas.

AVAILABILITY: From end of June until early September.

CARE: The plant, which is only used as a dried flower, must be fairly dry when purchased and the buds should be closed. Dry with the buds hanging down.

USES: Only as dried flowers (with stem).

SCENT: None.

Helipterum manglesii

Liatris spicata 'Floristan Violet' and 'F. White'

Helipterum manglesii,
syn. *Rhodanthe manglesii*
Everlasting

NAME: See also previous sort. The
plant is named after the English
naval officer, James Mangles (1786-
1867), who brought the plant out
of Australia around 1830.
DESCRIPTION: A glabrous, rather
bluish-green annual plant, 30-50
cm high. The oblong-elliptical
leaves are 5-7 cm long and encircle
the stem. The nodding flower clusters stand on long stems. The individual flower heads have a diameter of 2-3 cm and are pink, with
dark veins. In addition to the original form, dark red and white
cultivars are cultivated as well. The
outer involucral bracts are fleshy
and silvery.
ORIGIN: Australia. The plant was
first cultivated in the United Kingdom in 1852.
CULTIVATION: Temperate and subtropical areas.
AVAILABILITY: From June until the
end of September.
CARE: The plant, which is used
only as a dried flower, must be
supplied fairly dry and the flower
should be still closed. To dry, hang
them in an airy place.
USES: Only as dried flowers.
SCENT: None.

Liatris spicata
Blazing star, Button snakeroot, Gay feather

NAME: The meaning of the genus
name is unknown. *Spicata* means
'spike-shaped' and refers to the
shape of the inflorescence.
DESCRIPTION: A perennial reaching
a height up to 1 m with broad,
lanceolate leaves growing close together. The spike-shaped inflorescence, which can be up to 40 cm in
length, is densely covered with
single tubular lavender-pink flowers. 'Floristan White' is a cultivar
with greyish white flowers. Ray
florets are sparse. The floral spike
blossoms from top to bottom, an
unusual phenomenon.
ORIGIN: Eastern United States. The
plant was first cultivated in the
United Kingdom in 1732.
CULTIVATION: Temperate and subtropical areas.
AVAILABILITY: Throughout the
year, from various cultivation
areas.
CARE: Cut off a bit of the stem, use
cut-flower food. When purchased,
the upper flowers of the spike
should be open.
KEEPING PROPERTIES: 12-15 days.
USES: In a vase and in flower arrangement.
SCENT: None.

Lonas annua
Lonas

NAME: *Lonas* is the Latin name of a
plant native to Algeria; *annua*
means 'annual'.
DESCRIPTION: Glabrous annual
plant, 30-40 cm high with spreading stalks. The pinnate leaves are
far apart; the lower ones are tripartite. The yellow flower heads stand
in clusters at the top of the stem;
ray flowers are lacking. ORIGIN:
The western part of the Mediterranean area. The plant was first cultivated in England in 1686.
CULTIVATION: Temperate and subtropical areas.
AVAILABILITY: Fresh in July and August. As a dried flower, throughout the year.

CARE: When purchased, all flowers
should be open. Dry them in an
airy place. To use as fresh flowers,
use cut-flower food.
KEEPING PROPERTIES: As fresh flowers, 10-12 days.
USES: Primarily as dried flowers, in
all sorts of floral work.
SCENT: None.

△ Lonas annua   ▽ Rudbeckia laciniata

Rudbeckia laciniata
Cone flower

NAME: The plant is named after the Swedish botanist and anatomist O. Rudbeck (1660-1740), a professor in Uppsala and mentor of Linnaeus. *Laciniata* means 'cut' or 'divided' and refers to the incisions on the leaves.

DESCRIPTION: Perennial plant growing up to 1.5 m with branched stalks and finely cut and divided leaves with 3-7 lobed or dentate tips. The upper leaves are elliptical and have smooth or serrate margins. The flower heads have a diameter of 10-12 cm; the disc is green, with 6-10 yellow ray flowers. The most frequently cultivated cultivars are multiple-flowered, such as 'Goldhugel'.

ORIGIN: Eastern United States. The plant was first cultivated in France in 1635.

CULTIVATION: Temperate areas with outdoor flower cultivation.

AVAILABILITY: From July until September.

CARE: When purchased, the floral disc should be formed and the first rows of tubular flowers open. Take care they do not dry out; keep them in water as much as possible and use cut-flower food for herbaceous plants.

KEEPING PROPERTIES: 15-18 days.

USES: In a vase, in mixed bouquets and in decorations.

SCENT: None.

Rudbeckia nitida
Cone flower

NAME: See previous sort. *Nitida* means 'shining'.

DESCRIPTION: Perennial plant, up to 2 m high, with branched stalks and elliptical-lanceolate leaves of which the lower ones stand on long stalks. The flower heads, with a diameter of 8-10 mm, have yellowish-green discs. The 6-10 yellow ray flowers fold back quickly upon maturing.

ORIGIN: South-eastern United States.

CULTIVATION: Temperate areas with outdoor cut-flower cultivation.

AVAILABILITY: From July until September.

CARE: See previous sort.

KEEPING PROPERTIES: 15-18 days.

USES: In a vase, in mixed bouquets and in decorations.

SCENT: None.

Rudbeckia nitida

65

X Solidaster luteus

X Solidaster luteus
(no popular name)
NAME: The name X Solidaster refers to the origins of this flower: a cross of a Solidago with Aster ptarmicoides. Luteus means 'sulphur yellow', the colour of the flower.
DESCRIPTION: A perennial plant covered with short hairs, approx. 80 cm high; the stalks are very branched near the top. The lanceolate leaves are quite hard and rough, approx. 8 cm long and somewhat dentate at the tips. The flower heads stand in dense plumes; the flowers have a diameter of 6-8 mm. The tubular flowers are bright yellow, the ray flowers pale yellow.
ORIGIN: This hybrid genus was raised in the French city of Lyons in 1909.
CULTIVATION: Temperate zones with outdoor cut-flower cultivation.
AVAILABILITY: From July until September.
CARE: Cut off a bit of the stem, use cut-flower food.
KEEPING PROPERTIES: 8-12 days.
USES: In a vase and in mixed bouquets.
SCENT: None.

Solidago hybrids
Goldenrod
NAME: The genus name is composed of the Latin words solidus (= sturdy) and agere (= to make) and in this case means 'healing'. The plant was formerly thought to have medicinal properties.
DESCRIPTION: A somewhat downy 60-200 cm high plant. The leaves are lanceolate with fine hairs on the underside. Except for the upper ones, they have somewhat serrate edges. The small yellow flower heads stand in large, broad pyramidal plumes which nod slightly. The tongue-shaped ray flowers stand out. The most frequently cultivated cultivars are 'Strahlenkrone' and 'Golden Mosa'.
ORIGIN: Most of the approx. 130 species are native to the United States. The hybrids are crossings; the most important ancestor is S. canadensis. Most of them came about in the United Kingdom, Germany and the United States.

CULTIVATION: In temperate areas with outdoor cut-flower cultivation.
AVAILABILITY: From July until October, depending on the cultivar.
CARE: Cut off a bit of the stem, use cut-flower food. When purchased, the flowers should be about half open.
KEEPING PROPERTIES: 7-10 days.
USES: In a vase and in mixed bouquets. Sometimes, too, as dried flowers.
SCENT: None.

Solidago hybrid

Tagetes erecta

Tagetes erecta
African marigold

NAME: The plant is named after the grandson of Jupiter, Tages or Tagetis, who was gifted with great wisdom. *Erecta* means 'erect' and refers to the manner of growth.

DESCRIPTION: A 60-80 cm high annual plant. The stalks are branched near the top; the light green leaves are finely cut and have dentate tips. The flower stems are quite swollen under the flower heads; the involucral bracts are fused at least half way. The flower heads have a diameter of 8-10 cm and can be creamy white, yellow, golden yellow or orange. Primarily the less strongly scented cultivars are used as cut flowers, such as 'Climax' and 'Lady F1 hybrid'.

ORIGIN: Mexico. The plant was first cultivated in Switzerland in 1561.

CULTIVATION: Flower cultivation areas all over the world.

AVAILABILITY: From April until September.

CARE: Use cut-flower food for herbaceous plants. The water rapidly becomes polluted; so first clean the vase well and change the water regularly. A weak point is the hollow and swollen flower stem under the blossom, which easily snaps.

KEEPING PROPERTIES: 6-8 days.

USES: In mixed bouquets, for instance, Biedermeier style and in decorations.

SCENT: Highly aromatic.

Venidium fastuosum
Namaqualand daisy, Cape daisy

NAME: *Venidium* is derived from the Latin *vena*, meaning 'vein'. The achenes of the plant have 3-5 sturdy veins, or ribs, on the back side. *Fastuosum* (from *fastus*) means: 'arrogant'.

DESCRIPTION: An annual plant growing up to 40 cm high, covered with a thin layer of cobweb-like hairs. The lyrate and finely cut leaves are 7-12 cm long and have short, blunt lobes; the lower ones encircle the stem. The single flower heads have dark brown tubular flowers; the ray flowers are bright orange but dark brown at the base. Unopened buds are covered with silvery grey hairs.

ORIGIN: South Africa. The plant was first cultivated in Austria in 1797.

CULTIVATION: Temperate and subtropical areas.

AVAILABILITY: July-September.

CARE: Remove lower leaves, cut off a bit of the stem, use cut-flower food for herbaceous plants.

KEEPING PROPERTIES: 6-8 days.

USES: In a vase, in mixed bouquets and in floral work.

SCENT: None.

△ Venidium fastuosum   ▽ Xeranthemum annuum

Xeranthemum annuum
Paper flower

NAME: *Xeranthemum* is derived from the Greek words *xeros* (= dry) and *anthos* (= flower): 'a plant with dry flowers'. *Annuum* means 'annual'.

DESCRIPTION: A greyish-white annual plant, 70-80 cm high. The leaves are oblong and pointed at the top; they have smooth margins. The flower heads stand on long stems; they are elliptical-globular and have a diameter of 3-4 cm. The outer involucral bracts are fleshy and stand out; they are white and they remain on the flower.

ORIGIN: Southern and eastern Europe, Asia Minor. The plant was first cultivated in England in 1570.

CULTIVATION: Temperate and subtropical areas.

AVAILABILITY: As a fresh flower, from June until September.

CARE: The plant is primarily used as a dried flower. The flowers should be closed when purchased, because an open centre easily turns grey in the drying process.

USES: Exclusively as a dried flower.

SCENT: None.

Zinnia elegans, large-flowered

Zinnia angustifolia

Zinnia elegans
Youth and old age
NAME: The flower is named after the German botanist, J.G. Zinn (1727-1759) of Göttingen. *Elegans* means elegant.

DESCRIPTION: An annual plant which will grow from 50 to 100 cm high, depending on the cultivar. The stems are stiff; stems and leaves feel rough. The stem neck directly under the flower is hollow, a weak point for a cut flower. The leaves are oval-elliptical and encircle the stem; the leaf margins are smooth. The involucre leaves are blunt. The single flower heads are 12 cm across in the larger cultivars and 3-5 cm in the smaller ones. The colour of the original flower was lilac, but nowadays it comes in shades of red, orange, yellow, pink, salmon, white and violet. The cultivars are available both by colour and as formula mixtures.

ORIGIN: Mexico. The plant was first cultivated in Austria in 1613.
CULTIVATION: Cultivating areas all over the world; especially in the United States.
AVAILABILITY: From April until October.
CARE: Remove lower leaves, cut a bit off the stem, use cut-flower food for herbaceous plants. To reinforce the hollow stem neck, you may stick a match through the centre of the flower.
KEEPING PROPERTIES: 6-10 days.
USES: In a vase and in mixed bouquets.
SCENT: None.

Cultivars
Large-flowered cultivars
The most frequently cultivated large-flowered cultivar groups are the Dahlia-flowered Giants, The Giants of California, the Burpee Super Giants (with tubular ray flowers) and the Yoga Formula mixture.

Lilliput or pompom mixture
Plants with many branchings, 40-50 cm high and with pompom-shaped flowers of 3-5 cm in diameter. They are almost always cultivated outdoors, sometimes by colour but generally as a mixture in the same colour assortment as the large-flowering cultivars.

Zinnia angustifolia,
syn. *Z. haageana*
(no popular name)
NAME: See also previous sort. *Angustifolia* means 'narrow leaved'.
DESCRIPTION: A zinnia variety with pointed, lanceolate leaves which do not encircle the stem. The flower stems, 20-25 cm long, are somewhat thicker at the top. The involucral bracts are blunt, and the tops stand out. The stray scutes are longer than the tubular flowers; they resemble ray flowers and are yellow with dark tops. The ray flowers themselves are straw-coloured. The 'Persian carpet mixture', with double and semi-double flowers in a mixture of yellow with red and reddish-brown, is commonly cultivated. The single-flowered cultivar 'Pascal' is red with a yellow edge.
ORIGIN: Mexico; the plant was first cultivated in Belgium in 1855.
CULTIVATION: See previous variety, but more limited.
AVAILABILITY: See previous variety.
CARE: See previous variety.
KEEPING PROPERTIES: See previous variety.
USES: In floral work, as in Biedermeier bouquets.
SCENT: None.

Crassulaceae

The succulent family (*Crassulaceae*) consists of 35 genera comprising some 1500 sorts of shrubs and herbaceous plants with thick (*crassus* = thick), fleshy leaves. Its representatives live all over the world, although the large majority live in Africa; they are very rare in Australia and South America.
A familiar variety is stonecrop (wall pepper, Sedum acre). Because they can store moisture in their leaves, the *Crassulaceae* do not need much water; many sorts grow in warm and dry regions where it may not rain for a long time. They are xerophytes: plants which survive lengthy drought or strong seasonal dehydration with few problems.
Most *Crassulaceae* are perennial herbs or soft woody shrubs. The generally fleshy leaves grow close together on the stem or in rosettes and have no stipules; the flowers, often small, are closely grouped in clusters and plumes. They are generally pentamerous, with one or two whorls of stamens. The ovary is superior; its carpels are fused at the foot. The fruit consists of a group of capsules with numerous, very tiny seeds. One gram of seed from *Kalanchoe blossfeldiana*, for example, contains 50,000 to 80,000 tiny seeds.
Protective characteristics were ascribed to a number of members of this family. In South-east Asia after a death the relatives set branches of Kalanchoë in the house of the deceased to repel evil spirits and to attract good ones. And in Western Europe, in our regions as well, people planted stonecrop and houseleek (*Sempervivum tectorum*) on their roofs as protection against thunderbolts.

Kalanchoë hybrids
(no popular name)
NAME: *Kalanchoë* is the Latin form of *kalan chau*, the Chinese popular name for *K. laciniata*.
DESCRIPTION: A plant with round, green stalks and fleshy leaves with fluted or lightly cut margins. The flowers stand in dense clusters on stems of 60-70 cm. That is too long for a pot-plant, so they are kept short by using growth inhibitors. This is not done for the cut-flower cultivars. Hybrid cultivars are available in shades of red, orange and yellow.
ORIGIN: The present hybrids are crossings of *K. blossfeldiana* with the sorts *K. flammea* (large-flowered, red), *K. velatina* (orange-yellow), *K. schumacheri* (red) and *K. pumila* (lilac). The ancestors of these crosses came from Madagascar and Africa.
CULTIVATION: Nearly the entire world, in areas with ornamental plant cultivation. Main areas: the United States, Germany, the Netherlands and Switzerland.

AVAILABILITY: Throughout the year, thanks to artificial daylight treatment.
CARE: Cut off a bit of the stem; use cut-flower food. When purchased, the first flower must be open.
KEEPING PROPERTIES: 17-24 days.
USES: In a vase and in ornamental floral work. The *Kalanchoë* hybrids are growing in popularity as a cut flower.
SCENT: None.

Kalanchoë hybrid

Sedum spectabile
Stonecrop

NAME: *Sedum* is derived from the Latin *sedere* (= seated) or from *sedare*, which means 'painkilling'. In the first case the name might refer to the manner of growth; in the latter, to the fact that the leaves were formerly used as a remedy for pain. *Spectabile* means 'lovely' or 'worth seeing'.

DESCRIPTION: A perennial plant around 60 cm high with bluish-green leaves that stand opposite or in whorls. They are 6-12 cm long. The lavender-pink flowers stand in many-flowered clusters approx. 20 cm wide. The stamens are striking in that they are twice as long as the corolla petals. The most frequently cultivated cut-flower cultivar is 'Brillant'.

ORIGIN: East Asia. The plant was first cultivated in the United Kingdom in 1868.

CULTIVATION: Temperate areas with outdoor cut-flower cultivation.

AVAILABILITY: August-September.

CARE: When purchased, the first flowers of the cluster should be open. Cut off a bit of the stem; use cut-flower food.

KEEPING PROPERTIES: 18-24 days.

USES: In a vase, in floral work and dried.

SCENT: None.

Sedum spectabile

Sedum telephium subsp. telephium
Stonecrop

NAME: See also *Stonecrop*. *Telephium* is the Latin translation of the Greek name for a thick-leaved plant. Legend has it that the plant is named after King Telephos of Musia, who used the leaves to heal wounds.

DESCRIPTION: Glabrous perennial plant, approx. 40 cm high, with inversely elliptical, bright green leaves. They have a small somewhat wedge-shaped cuneate base, except for the upper ones, which are narrower and have a rounded base. The flowers stand in globular clusters approx. 10 cm wide. The most frequently cultivated cultivar, 'Herbstfreude', grows up to 50-60 cm high and has purplish-red flowers. It is sometimes regarded as a cross between *S. telephium* and *S. spectabile*.

ORIGIN: Europe and North Asia. The plant was first cultivated in England in 1596.

CULTIVATION: In temperate areas with outdoor cut-flower cultivation.

AVAILABILITY: From July until October.

CARE: When purchased, the first flowers should be open. Cut off a bit of the stem, use cut-flower food.

KEEPING PROPERTIES: 18-24 days.

USES: In a vase, in flower arrangement and as a dried flower.

SCENT: None.

Sedum telephium, subsp. telephium

Cruciferae

The mustard family (*Cruciferae*) derives its economic significance primarily from its contribution to the world food supply. Among its members are all the cabbage sorts and several plants from which oil is pressed, including coleseed or colza. The family has some 380 genera and around 3000 varieties. They grow all over the world, but chiefly in the temperate zones of the northern hemisphere and in the Mediterranean area. The mustard family has produced a great many ornamental plants.

Most *Cruciferae* are annual or perennial herbs. The leaves are alternate and lack stipules. To establish the genus and variety, the type of hair is often of great importance.

The inflorescence is generally in the shape of a cluster or a plume without bracts. The flower is composed of four sepals, four petals placed crosswise, usually four long and four short stamens and an ovary with a parietal placenta. The ovary is superior; it consists of two fused carpels and is generally divided into two compartments by a membrane, which may be broad and shining, as in Honesty. The shape of the nectaries, at the foot of the stamens, is variable and is used for the classification of the family. The stigma is club-shaped and bilobate. The characteristic fruit is a capsule which springs open from the bottom into two valves. Such a fruit is called a silique.

Hesperis matronalis

Cheiranthus cheiri
Wallflower, Handflower
NAME: The name is composed of two words, the Greek word for flower (*anthos*), and, according to some, from the Arabic popular name for this flower: *kheiri*. Others, however, trace it back to the Greek word for hand: *cheir*: a flower to hold in the hand. The English name might indicate this; at English flower markets, the wallflower was formerly offered as a hand bouquet.
DESCRIPTION: Perennial plant but cultivated as a biennial, and reaching a height of 50-60 cm. The lanceolate leaves end in points, have slight stems and smooth margins. The flowers stand in bunches and reach a maximum diameter of 4 cm. The petals are veined. Other important colours, in addition to yellow, cream, orange and violet, are warm dark red and brownish-red shades.

ORIGIN: The Mediterranean area and West Asia. The plant was cultivated in ancient times.
CULTIVATION: In temperate areas · with outdoor cut-flower cultivation.
AVAILABILITY: March-May.
CARE: When purchased, two or three of the flowers should be open. Cut off a bit of the stem, use cut-flower food for herbaceous plants.
KEEPING PROPERTIES: 7-11 days.
USES: In a vase and in bouquets (especially for their scent).
SCENT: Very fragrant; a sweet, pleasant scent.

Hesperis matronalis
Sweet rocket
NAME: The Greek word *hespera* means 'of the evening'; the flowers smell the strongest in the evening. *Matronalis* is derived from the Latin word *matrone*, which means 'distinguished married woman'.
DESCRIPTION: Downy perennial plant, 40-60 cm high. The leaves can grow up to 10 cm long and are oblong and lanceolate, with pointed tips and a widely dentate edge. The flowers are lavender-pink; they stand in clusters approx. 2 cm across. The most frequently cultivated cultivar is the white 'Albiflora'.
ORIGIN: Southern Europe, north and west Asia. The plant was cultivated in ancient times.

CULTIVATION: Limited, in temperate areas with outdoor cut-flower cultivation.
AVAILABILITY: May-June.
CARE: When purchased, a few flowers in the cluster should be open. Cut off a bit of the stem, remove the lower leaves, use cut-flower food for herbaceous plants.
KEEPING PROPERTIES: 6-8 days.
USES: In bouquets and in floral work, especially for the scent.
SCENT: Very fragrant, especially in the evening.

Matthiola incana

Lunaria annua
Money plant, Honesty

NAME: *Lunaria* (from *luna* = moon) means 'moon-shaped' and refers to the round form of the fruit (the silique). *Annua* means annual.

DESCRIPTION: An annual plant. The heart-shaped leaves, 10 cm long, are dentate and fairly long-stemmed, except the upper ones, which have practically no stem at all. The fragrant violet flowers stand in loose clusters. More important, however, is the silver-coloured septum or partition of the capsule, which determines the decorative value of the plant as a dried flower.

ORIGIN: South-eastern Europe. The plant was first cultivated in Switzerland in 1830.

CULTIVATION: Temperate areas with outdoor flower cultivation.

AVAILABILITY: As dried flowers, throughout the year. The first dried branches from the new harvest come on the market in October/November.

CARE: Carefully hang the fresh branches in an airy place to dry. Moisture during the drying process causes them to turn black.

USES: Exclusively as dried flowers, alone or in dry bouquets.

SCENT: Fresh flower: pleasant. As dried flower: none.

Matthiola incana
Gillyflower

NAME: The plant is named after the personal physician to Emperor Maximilian of Austria, Dr. Matthiole (1527-1576), who wrote several medical and botanical works. *Incana* means 'grey' and refers to the hairs on the plant.

DESCRIPTION: This perennial plant, which is cultivated as an annual, is stiff and covered with grey hair. The leaves, 6-10 cm long, are oblong spatula-shaped and have smooth margins. The fairly large flowers stand in clusters and are generally white, although carmine red, pink, salmon, lilac and yellow shades are cultivated as well. Mostly double-flowered sorts are supplied as cut flowers; the single-flowered sorts are reserved for seed cultivation.

ORIGIN: The Mediterranean area and the Canary Islands. The plant was cultivated in ancient times.

CULTIVATION: Temperate areas, especially as hothouse flower.

AVAILABILITY: Throughout the year, with a large peak between March and May.

CARE: To prevent the production of ethylene, the flowers must be put in treated water immediately after they have been cut. Make sure of this when you buy them; ethylene is an ageing hormone in gaseous form which has an unfavourable effect on the keeping properties of all flowers in the vicinity. Without such treatment, the gillyflower should never be mixed with other flowers. When purchased, the first flowers on the branch should be open. If possible, use cut-flower food for carnations.

KEEPING PROPERTIES: 8-14 days, depending on the temperature. At high temperatures the flowers quickly fade and wilt.

USES: In a vase and in mixed bouquets.

SCENT: Very strong; 'pleasant' or 'unpleasant' is a matter of personal taste.

Lunaria annua

Dipsacaceae

The teasel family (*Dipsacaceae*), with its 11 genera and some 350 species, is among the smaller ones of the plant kingdom. Its range is limited, with the Mediterranean as the centre, and offshoots to central and southern Africa, eastern Asia and northern Europe.

The leaves of the dicotyledonous *Dipsacaceae* are opposite or grouped in whorls and have no stipules. They generally have flower heads which are surrounded by an involucre. The flowers are female or hermaphrodite and bilaterally symmetrical. Each flower is subtended by a secondary calyx composed of bracts. The small calyx is cup-shaped and consists of numerous teeth or bristles. The corolla has 4 or 5 unequal lobes or may be bilobate. The 2-4 stamens stand on the base of the corolla, alternated by the lobes of the corolla. The superior ovary is unilocular and contains one germ-cell (ovule). The dry fruit remains closed; it is enclosed in the secondary calyx and often bears the true calyx. Some varieties are pollinated by insects; others, such as the genus *Scabiosa*, are self-pollinating.

Formerly, when they had finished flowering, the prickly heads of one species of teasel were used in carding, or combing the tangled hairs of sheep wool before spinning. Nowadays the teasel is only important in dried flower arrangements. Other members of the family are cultivated as ornamental plants.

Scabiosa caucasica 'Miss Wilmott'

Scabiosa caucasica 'Clive Greaves'

Scabiosa atropurpurea
Scabious
NAME: *Scabiosa* is derived from *scabius* (= scabies). The name comes from the knautia (*Knautia arvensis*), which used to be included in the *Scabiosa* genus; it was long thought to be a remedy for the skin disease, scabies, which has now practically disappeared. *Atropurpurea* means 'dark crimson' and refers to the original colour of the flower.
DESCRIPTION: A downy annual plant, up to 80 cm high, with lyrate, roughly dentate leaves with lanceolate tips. The stems are quite weak. They bear semi-globular flowers with a diameter of approx. 5 cm which are generally cultivated in a colour mixture of blue, scarlet, pink, dark red and white.
ORIGIN: Southern Europe. First cultivated in England in 1588.
CULTIVATION: Temperate and subtropical areas.
AVAILABILITY: From July until September.
CARE: Cut off a bit of the stem, use cut-flower food for herbaceous plants.
KEEPING PROPERTIES: 6-10 days.
USE: In a vase and in mixed summer bouquets.
SCENT: Smells of musk.

Scabiosa caucasica
Scabious
NAME: See also previous variety. *Caucasica* refers to its origin: the Caucasus.
DESCRIPTION: A perennial with bluish-green leaves and a height of 80-90 cm. The leaves on the non-flowering stems are simple and have entire margins; those on the flowering stems are sometimes cleft, with (near the top of the stem) lanceolate tips. The flower heads, originally lavender-blue, are 7-10 cm wide. At present the most frequently cultivated cultivar is the bright blue 'Clive Greaves'.
ORIGIN: The Caucasus. The plant was first cultivated in France in 1803.
CULTIVATION: Temperate regions with outdoor flower cultivation.
AVAILABILITY: From July to early October.
CARE: When purchased, the flowers should be half open and their colour visible. Remove the lower leaves, cut off a bit of the stem, use cut-flower food for herbaceous plants.
KEEPING PROPERTIES: 10-12 days.
USE: In flower arrangement for the striking bright blue colour and the flower shape. Also in mixed bouquets and, to a limited extent, in a vase. Its weak stem is a drawback.
SCENT: None.

Dipsacus sativus
Fuller's teasel
NAME: *Dipsacus* is the Latin form of the Greek *dipsakos*, which means 'teasel'. *Sativus* indicates a cultivated plant.
DESCRIPTION: A stiff, rather prickly, bi-annual plant, around 1.5 m high and with elongated, blunt leaves, except for the top ones: they are narrower and taper to a point. Their margins are slightly prickled. The lilac-coloured flowers are grouped in dense, long and oval-cylindrical heads of 6-10 cm. The bracteoles have hooked tips and are nearly as long as the flowers. The involucres also have hooked tips but bear no prickles.

ORIGIN: Probably Asia Minor. The plant is no longer wild, but has been cultivated since ancient times.
CULTIVATION: On a limited scale, in areas with a temperate climate.
AVAILABILITY: From July until September.
CARE: For fresh flowers, use cut-flower food and change the water regularly.
KEEPING PROPERTIES: As a fresh flower, 3-4 weeks.
USE: In a vase, in mixed bouquets but chiefly as dried flowers.
SCENT: None.

Dipsacus sativus

Elaeagnaceae

Ericaceae

The small buckthorn family (*Elaeagnaceae*) has only three genera with a total of some fifty species. However, they are widely distributed over the steppes and coastal areas of North America, Europe, southern Asia and Australia. Most of them are small, thorny trees or shrubs.

The simple leathery leaves have smooth margins and are scattered or opposite. The stems are covered with silvery or gold, sometimes brown, hairs or scales. The flowers are solitary, in racemes and are unisexual or hermaphrodite. Petals are absent; the sepals are fused to form a tubular calyx. This tube has two or four lobes, with 4-8 stamens implanted in it. In some sorts, however, the stamens stand at the base of the tube. Each flower has a superior ovary with one cavity, one style and one stigma, as well as one anatropous (=inverted) ovule. The fruit is enclosed by a bulge at the bottom of the calyx.

The buckthorn family is closely related to the *Thymelaeaceae*, the daphne family, and to the *Rhamnaceae*, the buckthorn family. They differ in the structure of their flowers and fruits.

The large heath family (*Ericaceae*) - it has around 100 genera and approx. 3000 species - comprises familiar plants such as rhododendron and heather. Representatives of this family occur all over the world, except in Australia. They usually grow on acid soils and often live in symbiosis with certain fungi. Most heaths are shrubs, but there are also a few climbers among them. Their evergreen leaves are simple and generally scattered. Some species, including *Erica*, have needle-shaped leaves to protect them from dehydration.

The inflorescence varies from a single bloom to umbellate racemes or panicles. The flowers are hermaphrodite. The calyx consists of four or five sepals which are fused at the base. The corolla has four or five lobes, also fused at the base. Some rhododendrons have more corolla lobes. The number of stamens is often twice the number of petals; they generally stand on the receptacle. The fruit is a multilocular capsule, unless the ovary is inferior: then it is a berry. Many *Ericaceae*, including the rhododendrons, are poisonous.

Hippophaë rhamnoides
Sea buckthorn

NAME: *Hippophaë* is the Latin form of the Greek *hippophaes*, which means 'unknown'. It was originally the name for a thorny *Euphorbia* species; only later was it given to the Sea buckthorn. *Rhamnoides* means: resembling the plant genus *Rhamnus*, the buckthorn.
DESCRIPTION: A stout bush with very thorny, scaly twigs and golden brown buds. The linear silvery-grey leaves, 2-6 cm long, are also covered with scales. The yellowy-green dioecious flowers are grouped in bunches and develop into beautiful yellow or orange berries. They determine the ornamental value of the plant.
ORIGIN: Europe and Asia. The plant has been cultivated for a very long time.
CULTIVATION: The branches are usually cut from natural plantings, as in the dunes.
AVAILABILITY: From August until October.
CARE: Cut off the lower part of the stem, use cut-flower food for shrubs. Without it, they rapidly pollute the water.
KEEPING PROPERTIES: 2-3 weeks.
USE: In mixed bouquets and in floral work. The large, sharp thorns are a problem.
SCENT: None.

Hippophaë rhamnoides

Calluna vulgaris
Heather

NAME: *Calluna* is derived from the Greek word for cleaning (*kallunein*) and recalls the use of heather, or ling, for brooms and scrub brushes. *Vulgaris* means 'ordinary', 'widespread'.
DESCRIPTION: Small evergreen bushes with tiny, closely-packed overlapping leaves arranged in four ranks. There are both single and double-flowered cultivars in a range of colour from white to reddish purple. Generally, long-stemmed cultivars with double flowers are used as cut flowers.
ORIGIN: The northern hemisphere. The plant has long been under cultivation. Many new cultivars originated in the United Kingdom.
CULTIVATION: Chiefly western Europe.
AVAILABILITY: From July until October.
CARE: Cut off the dried end of the stem, use cut-flower food. Put the flowers in a light place to stop them fading.
KEEPING PROPERTIES: 2-3 weeks.
USE: Primarily in flower arrangement.
SCENT: None.

Pernettya mucronata
Pernettya

NAME: The flower is named after A. Perne (1716-1796; sometimes also spelled Pernet or Pernetty), a Benedictine monk who accompanied the French discoverer, De Bougainville, to the Falkland Islands. Later he left the order to become a follower of the Swedish mystic, Emanuel Swedenborg. *Mucronata* means 'having a spire' and refers to the shape of the leaf.
DESCRIPTION: An evergreen shrub with reddish-brown twigs and ovate, prickly pointed leaves of 5-15 mm. They are shiny green. The white flowers stand in groups of 2-3. In the male flowers, the stamens are longer than the ovary; in the female flowers, the style is as much as twice as long. The plant derives its ornamental value from the white, lilac or carmine red berries. The bloom is in May-June.
ORIGIN: Southern South America. The plant was first cultivated in the United Kingdom in 1828, where cultivars were selected by colour.
CULTIVATION: In western European tree nurseries, especially in the Netherlands.
AVAILABILITY: From September until January, with a peak in October/November.
CARE: Usually marketed as a plant, from which the florist cuts the berried branches. Put them in water with cut-flower food for shrubs.
KEEPING PROPERTIES: 4-5 weeks.
USE: Chiefly in flower arrangement.
SCENT: None.

Calluna vulgaris

Rhododendron hybrid, rose bays

Rhododendron hybrids
Rhododendron, Rose bay

NAME: *Rhododendron*, derived from the Greek words *rhodon* (= pink) and *dendron* (= tree) means 'tree with rose-red flowers'.

DESCRIPTION: An evergreen shrub with large, elongated-oval leaves which are shiny dark green on top and on the underside dull and somewhat lighter. The large flowers, which vary in colour from white to dark red, are grouped in profusely blooming short racemes.

ORIGIN: America, Asia. The hybrids are crosses of hardy species from the United States with splendidly coloured ones from Asia Minor and western China, but especially the Himalayas. The first crosses were made in the United Kingdom; later Dutch (Boskoop) and Belgian breeders also played a role in the crossbreeding, and fairly recently many new species have come from Germany and the United States.

CULTIVATION: Various flower cultivation areas around the world. Forced early flowering primarily takes place in the Netherlands.

AVAILABILITY: From February to the end of May.

CARE: Cut off the lower part of the stem, use cut-flower food for shrubs.

KEEPING PROPERTIES: 12-20 days, depending on the cultivar.

USE: Chiefly in floral work and decorations, sometimes in a vase.

SCENT: None.

Rhododendron 'Kirin'
Japanese azalea

NAME: See previous species. 'Kirin' is a Japanese name.

DESCRIPTION: Partly evergreen shrub with oval, spatula-shaped leaves that are sometimes a bit downy. The flowers, 2-3 cm in diameter, stand in groups of 3-5. The most important colours are pink, salmon and carmine red (in several shades).

ORIGIN: Japan. There are many other cultivars of Japanese origin.

CULTIVATION: Flower cultivating areas all around the world, with the exception of the tropics.

AVAILABILITY: From October until May.

CARE: Cut off a bit of the stem, use cut-flower food for shrubs.

KEEPING PROPERTIES: 14-20 days.

USE: In a vase and in modern floral work.

SCENT: None.

Rhododendron hybrids
Mollis azalea

NAME: See previous species.

DESCRIPTION: A profusely flowering deciduous azalea. It is typified by the great variety in flower colour: from golden yellow to many shades of light red and orange-red, often with a greenish or orange spot.

ORIGIN: See Rhododendron.

CULTIVATION: Chiefly in the Netherlands (forced flowering), on a limited scale in Germany.

AVAILABILITY: April-May or, forced in the hothouse, starting in February.

CARE: Cut off a bit of the twig; use cut-flower food for shrubs. To prevent the flowers from dropping off prematurely, they should still be fully closed when purchased. The flowers are sometimes stuck on with a drop of glue near the base.

KEEPING PROPERTIES: 12-15 days.

USE: In modern floral work and in a vase.

SCENT: Weak.

Pernettya mucronata

Euphorbiaceae

The spurge family or *Euphorbiaceae* (300 genera, over 5000 species) is very well represented in the tropics, although it also occurs in areas with a temperate climate. Several members of this dicotyledonous family are of economic importance: for example, the genera of *Hevea*, *Manihot* and *Ricinus*, which are suppliers of rubber, cassava and castor oil respectively. From some other species, such as *Croton tiglium*, emetics are made; fairly logical, because a number of spurge species contain poisonous milky juices.

In most cases, the leaves are alternate and have stipules. They are generally simple, palmate or oddly pinnate in a few species.

The flowers generally have one whorl of floral bracts; sometimes they are absent. In most species, the stamens have two anthers. The number of stamens ranges from one to many. The male flowers usually bear the remains of an ovary. The trilocular ovary has one or two seed cavities and free or fused styles. The fruit is sometimes a berry, but more often a tripartite capsule.

Characteristic of the family is the presence of nectaries. They are found on or near the flowers, on the stamens or at their base, at the base of the ovary or on the inflorescence.

Euphorbia polychroma

Euphorbia fulgens
Spurge

NAME: The plant is named after Euphorbes, court physician to the Numidian king Juba II, who is said to have discovered the poisonous but also medicinal effects of spurge shortly before the beginning of our era. *Fulgens* means 'beautiful' or 'shining' and refers to the flowers.
DESCRIPTION: A shrub with overhanging branches and approx. 10 cm long, narrow lanceolate leaves with pointed tips and smooth margins. The actual flowers are inconspicuous. The plants derives its ornamental value from its apparent flowers. They consist of brightly coloured, petal-like involucral leaves, which are sticky and give off nectar. The original colour was orange. Later mutants were developed with white, yellow, salmon-coloured and deep orange apparent flowers.
ORIGIN: Mexico. The plant was first cultivated in the United Kingdom in 1835.
CULTIVATION: All hothouse flower cultivating areas of the world.

AVAILABILITY: The year round, thanks to artificial daylight treatment. The peak supply is in October/November; the plant is scarcely found on the market in April/May.
CARE: Cut off a bit of the stem and stop the 'bleeding' by holding the stem in boiling water for a few seconds. Use water with a temperature of 20° C and add to it only half the concentration of cut-flower food solution, to prevent the leaf from searing. The foliage will keep better if put in water to which silver thiosulphate has been added.
KEEPING PROPERTIES: If well treated, 8-12 days.
USE: In a vase and in floral work.
SCENT: None.

Euphorbia polychroma
Spurge

NAME: See also previous species. *Polychroma* means 'many-coloured'.
DESCRIPTION: Perennial plant, approx. 40 cm high, with erect and pubescent stems. The leaves are elongated to inverted ovoid; they are also slightly pubescent and taper to a point on both ends. The margins are smooth. The flower umbels usually have five forked rays. The bright yellow, ovate bracts are somewhat scalloped. The marginal nectaries are waxy yellow. The fruits are smaller than 0.5 cm. In autumn, the entire plant turns a bronze-like orange.
ORIGIN: South-eastern Europe. The plant was first cultivated in Austria in 1805.
CULTIVATION: Temperate areas with outdoor flower cultivation.

AVAILABILITY: From May until July.
CARE: Cut off a bit of the stem and hold it briefly in boiling water (or in dry sand) to stop the 'bleeding'. Use lukewarm water, with half the concentration of cut-flower food.
KEEPING PROPERTIES: 20-25 days.
USE: Chiefly in modern floral arrangement.
SCENT: None.

Euphorbia pulcherrima

Euphorbia pulcherrima
Poinsettia

NAME: See also previous species. *Pulcherrima* is the superlative of the Latin *pulcher* = lovely.

DESCRIPTION: A robust, erect shrub with sturdy branches which, depending on the treatment, can reach lengths up to 100 cm. The large leaves are ovate and wavy edged. The leaves under the actual inflorescence turn bright red, pink or white, depending on the cultivar. It is these leaves that give the plant its ornamental value. The actual flowers are inconspicuous; they resemble those of *E. fulgens* but have no nectar glands.

ORIGIN: Mexico and tropical South America. The plant was first cultivated in the United States in 1828.

CULTIVATION: Nearly all over the world.

AVAILABILITY: In Europe, especially in November/December for use during Christmas; in the United States, the year round.

CARE: Hold the cut surfaces of the branch in boiling water a few seconds to stop the 'bleeding'. Use water with a temperature of 20° C in the vase, and half the concentration of cut-flower food. Room temperature should not be below 15° C. Lower water and air temperatures cause the leaves to droop.

KEEPING PROPERTIES: 7-15 days.

USE: In floral work and decorations, in mixed bouquets and in a vase.

SCENT: None.

Euphorbia griffithii 'Fireglow'
(no popular name)

NAME: See also previous species. The plant is further named after the Englishman W. Griffith (1810-1845). He served as a health officer in British India, and there and in Afghanistan he collected large quantities of plants. His botanical works were not published until after his death.

DESCRIPTION: A perennial plant, up to 60 cm high and with narrow, elongated and pointed leaves. The thin but sturdy stems are somewhat bronze in colour; the inflorescence is bright orange.

ORIGIN: Tibet and the eastern part of the Himalayas. The plant has only recently come under cultivation.

CULTIVATION: Temperate areas. The plant is not hardy in severe winters and hates wet soil.

AVAILABILITY: May-June.

CARE: Cut off a bit of the stem; hold the wound surface a moment in boiling water to stop the 'bleeding'. Use water with a temperature of 20° C in the vase and half the concentration of cut-flower food. Room temperature not below 15° C.

KEEPING PROPERTIES: 14-20 days.

USE: Modern floral work; also (sometimes) in a vase.

SCENT: None.

Euphorbia marginata
Spurge

NAME: See also previous species. *Marginata* means 'having margins' and refers to the white leaf margins.

DESCRIPTION: A pilose annual plant that can grow up to 50-70 cm high. The elongated oval leaves have smooth margins and are approx. 6 cm long. The upper ones have white margins or are even entirely white. The nectaries have large white, petal-like appendages.

ORIGIN: The south-eastern United States. The plant was first cultivated in the United Kingdom in 1811.

CULTIVATION: Temperate and subtropical areas with outdoor flower cultivation.

AVAILABILITY: The year round.

CARE: Cut off a bit of the stem; hold the wound surface briefly in boiling water to stop the 'bleeding'. Use lukewarm water and a low concentration of cut-flower food.

KEEPING PROPERTIES: 12-18 days.

USE: In colourful bouquets; as leafy material in flower arrangement.

SCENT: None.

Euphorbia marginata

Gentianaceae

The gentian family (*Gentianaceae*) is fairly small: some 80 genera comprise no more than around 900 species of annual and perennial dicotyledonous plants and a few shrubs. In spite of this, members of the gentians have spread nearly all over the world. Many of them grow in the mountains and form a leaf rosette.

Most *Gentianaceae* have a root-stock. The leaves are nearly always opposite or grow in a rosette; they have no stipules. The regular flowers are hermaphrodite. They have four or five sepals and the same number of petals fused in a bell or saucer shape. Each petal bears one stamen. The superior ovary consists of two fused carpels with a nectary-bearing disc at the base. The seed capsules contain many small seeds. Many species of this family live in symbiosis with a sort of fungus. Many gentians are cultivated for their ornamental value; some of them yield a dye or substances with medicinal effects.

Eustoma grandiflorum,
syn. *Lisianthus russelianus*
Lisianthus
NAME: *Eustoma* (from *eu* = good and *stoma* = mouth) literally means 'having a good mouth'; the name refers to the wide-open flowers. *Grandiflorum* = large-flowering.
DESCRIPTION: A biennial plant that, in the hothouse, can reach a height of 70-80 cm. It has erect branching stems and ovoid, pointed opposite leaves with smooth margins. The sepals are narrow and enclose the young buds; the four wide petals are dark purple, pale pink or white in colour. There is also a double-flowering form.
ORIGIN: United States and northern Mexico. The plant became popular as a cut flower in Europe via Japan and (later) the Netherlands.
CULTIVATION: Temperate and sub-tropical areas with hothouse flower cultivation.

AVAILABILITY: From May until December, with a peak from August until the end of October.
CARE: Cut off a bit of the stem, use cut-flower food for herbaceous plants.
KEEPING PROPERTIES: The first flowers on the stem wilt after 6-7 days, but the others will open gradually. The branch is therefore ornamental for 3-4 weeks.
USE: In a vase and in floral arrangement.
SCENT: None.

Gentiana makinoi 'Royal Blue'
Gentian
NAME: The plant is thought to be named after the Illyrian king Gentius (2nd century before our era), who is said to have discovered the medicinal effects of yellow gentian. *Makino* is the name of a Japanese botanist.
DESCRIPTION: A plant with sturdy stems that can reach a length of 160 cm. The opposite lanceolate leaves have smooth margins. The flower raceme can be 50 cm long and consists of 20-30 bright blue flowers.
ORIGIN: The plant is a selection of *G. makinoi*, native to Japan.
CULTIVATION: Temperate areas. The cultivation is no simple matter, probably because symbiosis with a fungus is involved in it.

AVAILABILITY: August.
CARE: When purchased, around three-fourths of the flower buds should be open. Remove the lower leaves, cut off a bit of the stem, use cut-flower food.
KEEPING PROPERTIES: 3-4 weeks.
USE: In exclusive bouquets and in floral arrangement. The flower is greatly valued for its unique colour and good keeping properties.
SCENT: None.

Eustoma grandiflorum

'Royal Blue'

Geraniaceae

The 11 genera of the geranium family (*Geraniaceae*) comprise a large number of species. The majority of them belong to the two most important genera: *Geranium* (375 species) and *Pelargonium* (250 species). The crane's bill is an example of the former genus native to our regions; the latter contains the familiar garden and house plants which are popularly known as 'geraniums', although the name 'pelargonium' is becoming more widely used.

Most members of the geranium family are annual or perennial herbaceous plants, although the family also has a few shrubs. They grow in all temperate and subtropical regions. Stems and leaves are often covered with glandular hairs which sometimes give off a strong odour.

The leaves are simple or compound and often have stipules. They are opposite or alternate. The flowers are hermaphrodite. They are simple blooms or grow in two-branched composite umbels. They generally have five sepals and the same number of petals. The stamens stand in one to three whorls which may or may not be fused; sometimes some are sterile. The filaments are generally fused at the base. At the base of the stamens there are often nectaries. The five superior carpels stand around a central axis, with two ovules in each cavity. Each of the five styles has its own stigma. The fruit, a schizocarp, is affixed at the top with styles; the carpels come loose at the base. The seeds contain little storage food.

Most *Geraniaceae* have ornamental value; geraniol, which is used in the perfume industry, is obtained from some *Pelargonium* species.

Pelargonium zonale hybrids
Zonal pelargonium

NAME: *Pelargonium* is the Latin form of the Greek *pelargos* (for 'stork' or 'long-beaked bird') and refers to the beak-shaped fruit. *Zonale* means 'having a band or zone' and refers to the marking on the leaves.

DESCRIPTION: A plant with thick, fleshy and pilose stems. The top side of the leaves shows a broad reddish-brown band. The flower umbels stand on long stems; the petals are red, orange, pink, lilac, salmon or white. There are both single and double-flowered cultivars. For cut flowers, chiefly double-flowered cultivars such as 'Sharrowel' (red) and 'Louis Pasteur' (pale pink) are used.

ORIGIN: The plant is a cross between *P. zonale* and *P. inquinans* and other South African species first described by the Dutch botanist Johannes Commelin (1629-1692), employed by the Amsterdam botanical gardens. The improvement work was primarily performed in England and Germany.

CULTIVATION: On a limited scale, in areas with hothouse flower cultivation.

AVAILABILITY: From May until the end of October.

CARE: When purchased, the flower should be at least half open. Cut off a bit of the stem; use cut-flower food.

KEEPING PROPERTIES: 10-14 days.

USE: In flower arrangements, such as Biedermeier bouquets.

SCENT: Strong and herb-like ('geranium smell') when touched.

Pelargonium Zonale hybrid

Gesneriaceae

In earlier publications, the family of the *Gesneriaceae* was sometimes erroneously called the gloxinia family. Together, the some 125 genera comprise more than 2000 species of herbaceous plants and shrubs, most of which are native to the tropics.

The leaves are alternate or opposite and, in some species, are basal. A number of *Gesneriaceae* form tubers.

The flowers are hermaphrodite; they stand alone, in a branching inflorescence. The five sepals are usually fused into a tube at the base; often they are fused with the petals as well. The unilocular ovary is inferior or superior and contains many ovules. The flower bears a single style with two stigma lobes or a mouth-like stigma. Between the base of the corolla and the ovary there is often a ring-shaped or lobed gland which produces nectar. The flowers have adapted their shapes to their pollinators: humming-birds, bats, butterflies, bees and flies.

The family is subdivided into Old World species, which have cotyledons of unequal length (as in *Saintpaulia* and *Streptocarpus*) and which are called *Cyrtandroideae*, and the America subfamily *Gesnerioideae*, with cotyledons of equal length (as in *Columnea* and *Sinningia*).

Saintpaulia Ionantha hybrid

Saintpaulia ionantha hybrids
African violet

NAME: The plant is named after Walter Baron de Tannaux von Saint Paul Illaire, a resident of the German colony of Tanga. He discovered the plant during a trip through the Usambarage mountains. *Ionantha* means 'having violet-like flowers'.

DESCRIPTION: A plant with a rosette of ovoid leaves, the margins of which are sometimes scalloped.
The flowers stand in clusters of 5-8 on stems in the leaf axils. Each flower is approx. 3 cm in diameter. The double-flowering species, with fringed flower margins, are used as cut flowers. They are available in blue, purple, violet, pink and white.

ORIGIN: The tropical rain forest of Tanzania. The present hybrids are crosses between *S. ionantha*, which was first described in 1892, and *S. confusa*, which was introduced three years later. Much of the improvement work was done in the country of origin.

CULTIVATION: Chiefly by potted plant breeders in the United States.
AVAILABILITY: All the year round.
CARE: Let the flowers absorb water in which cut-flower food is dissolved, and then arrange them, for example, in a tuft of damp cotton wool.
KEEPING PROPERTIES: 6-10 days.
USE: In flower arrangement, such as bridal bouquets, corsages and Biedermeier bouquets.
SCENT: None.

Bromus lanceolatus

Graminae

In economic terms, the grass family (*Graminae*) is the most important plant family in the world. It is a family of monocotyledonous plants with a place all its own. It yields all the grain sorts we know and, in the tropics, bamboo, still the universal provider of everything from food to building materials. Grasses occur all over the world and form around 20% of the earth's vegetation. There are around 650 genera, with over 9000 species.

Grasses have a fibrous root system which is sometimes supplemented with adventitious roots from the lowest stem buds. They form tussocks, or clumps, by means of subterranean root-stocks or stem shoots just above the ground. The stems are round and generally hollow.

The leaves are arranged in two rows along the stem. They consist of a stem-encircling sheath and a blade. The sheath supports the soft growth zone above each bud. Thanks to the changing speed of growth in the growth zone, grass rights itself again if it has been knocked down by rain or wind. The blade, which also has a growth zone at the base, has parallel veins.

The inflorescence of the grasses has no petals; it is branched and usually stands at the end of the stem as a plume, a spike or a raceme. The unisexual or hermaphrodite flowers are highly reduced, and generally have three stamens. They are pollinated by the wind. The ovary has a single seed compartment which bears two or three feather-shaped stigmata. The fruit is a caryopsis. The family is now classified into six subfamilies; however, as a result of modern research, change is expected in this.

Briza maxima
Quaking-grass

NAME: *Briza* was originally the Greek name for a grain species from Thrace. It is derived from *brizein*, which means 'sleepy' and might allude to the 'nodding' of the hanging spikes. *Maxima* means 'the largest', to distinguish it from a species with smaller spikes (*B. minima*).
DESCRIPTION: A hairless annual or biennial grass. The leaves are 1 cm wide; they have a widened base and are rough edged at the top. The oval spikelets, approx. 2 1/2 cm long, are grouped in sparsely-flowered racemes which can reach a length of 10 cm. The racemes nod. The membranous bracts are silvery-white; they are slightly hairy, with green veins.
ORIGIN: South Africa, Madagascar and the Mediterranean area. The plant was first cultivated in England in 1633.
CULTIVATION: Temperate and subtropical areas with outdoor cut-flower cultivation.
AVAILABILITY: As a fresh flower, August-September. Dried, the year round.
CARE: The dried grass must be kept quite dry, to prevent discolouration by mould.
KEEPING PROPERTIES: In dried form, 6-7 months.
USE: In floral work and dried bouquets.
SCENT: None.

Bromus lanceolatus,
syn. *B. macrostachys*
Brome-grass

NAME: *Bromus* is Greek for 'oats'; some species are reminiscent of the oat plant (*Avena*). *Lanceolatus* means 'lance-shaped' and refers to the spikelets.
DESCRIPTION: A somewhat hairy annual plant, 40-50 cm high. The spikes stand in long, narrow, squat plumes of 2-8 cm with spreading or arching branches.
ORIGIN: From the Mediterranean area to eastern Asia.
CULTIVATION: Temperate and subtropical areas with outdoor cut-flower cultivation.
AVAILABILITY: Fresh in August; dried the year round.
CARE: Keep the dried plant away from damp to prevent discolouration by moulds.
KEEPING PROPERTIES: As a dried flower, 7-8 months.
USE: In flower arrangements and in dried bouquets.
SCENT: None.

Briza minima

Briza maxima

Cortaderia selloana
Pampas grass

NAME: *Cortaderia* comes from the Argentine popular name, *cortadera*. In addition, the plant is named after German botanist F. Sello (1789-1831), who travelled a great deal through Brazil and Uruguay and left a collection of 12,500 dried plants.

DESCRIPTION: A perennial with large tussocks of long (1.5 m), narrow, nodding leaves which are folded in a V-shape and very sharply toothed. The spikes stand in long white plumes at the end of a tall stem. The male flowers are bare and stand in loose, silvery-white plumes; the female flowers have long, silky hairs but are less silvery.

ORIGIN: Southern Brazil and Argentina. The plant was first cultivated in the United Kingdom in 1848.

CULTIVATION: On a limited scale in temperate and subtropical areas with outdoor cut-flower cultivation.

AVAILABILITY: Fresh stalks, from August to October; dried, the year round.

CARE: When fresh, use cut-flower food.

KEEPING PROPERTIES: Dried, for a few years.

USE: In decorations, sometimes dyed in bright, bizarre colours.

SCENT: None.

Lagurus ovatus
Hare's tail

NAME: The name is derived from *lagos* (= hare) and *oura* (= tail) and refers to the colour and shape of the inflorescence. *Ovatus* means 'ovate' and also refers to the shape of the inflorescence.

DESCRIPTION: Annual grass with softly pubescent leaves of 20-40 cm long and 10-12 mm wide. They are wide at the stem end but narrow towards the top. The ligule bears short hairs. The flower spikelets stand in dense, fluffy oval plumes from which numerous soft longer hairs protrude. The spike plumes are white.

ORIGIN: The Mediterranean area and the Canary Islands. The plant was first cultivated in Belgium in 1588.

CULTIVATION: Temperate and subtropical areas with outdoor cut-flower cultivation.

AVAILABILITY: Fresh in July/August; dried the year round.

CARE: Protect dried branches against damp to prevent discolouration by mould.

KEEPING PROPERTIES: 6-7 months (dried).

USE: In dried bouquets and floral work.

SCENT: None.

Pennisetum setaceum
(no popular name)

NAME: The genus name is derived from the Latin words *penna* (= feather) and *seta* (= bristle); the spikes stand in a whorl of feathered bristles. *Setaceum* means also 'bristly'.

DESCRIPTION: A hairy perennial plant which is cultivated as an annual. The leaves are stiff and rough; they stand erect and are channelled. Their width is approx. 3 cm. The spikes, 4-6 mm long, stand in cylindrical plumes of 25 cm; they have obliquely spreading awns of 3-4 cm long.

ORIGIN: From Ethiopia to Saudi Arabia. The plant was first cultivated in Italy in 1892.

CULTIVATION: Temperate and subtropical areas with outdoor cut-flower cultivation.

AVAILABILITY: Fresh in August, dried the year round.

CARE: Avoid high humidity to prevent discolouration by mould.

KEEPING PROPERTIES: Dried, 10-12 months.

USE: Dried, in dried bouquets and floral work.

SCENT: None.

Phalaris canariensis
Canary grass

NAME: *Phalaris* is the Latinized form of the old Greek name for a certain grass sort. The word is derived from *phalanoi* (= shining) or from *phaleria* (= bearing white flowers). *Canariensis* means 'from the Canary Islands'.

DESCRIPTION: Non-hair bearing annual plant without shoots and around 50 cm high. The leaves, 5-8 mm wide, have no cross veins. The flowers stand in dense, ovate pale green spikes. The lower glumes are winged; they are white with green stripes.

ORIGIN: Southern Europe. The plant was first cultivated in England in 1596.

CULTIVATION: Temperate and subtropical areas with cut-flower cultivation.

AVAILABILITY: Fresh in July/August; dried the year round.

CARE: Avoid high humidity to prevent discolouration by mould.

KEEPING PROPERTIES: Dried, 7-8 months.

USE: As a dried flower, in dried bouquets and floral work.

SCENT: None.

Lagurus ovatus

Pennisetum setaceum

Phalaris canariensis

Guttiferae

The St. John's wort family (*Guttiferae*) comprises 40 genera with around one thousand sorts of dicotyledonous shrubs and herbaceous plants. Although it is spread all over the world, it is the most strongly represented in the tropics.

The simple leaves are opposite and have no stipules. The flowers, unisexual or hermaphrodite, stand alone, grow in two-branched composite umbels or in a bushy inflorescence.

The perianth consists of tetramerous or pentamerous whorls with distinct petals and sepals. The stamens are grouped in two whorls of five stamen bundles. The inner whorl is fused; the stamens in the outer whorl are often infertile. The ovary is superior and consists of 3-5 fused carpels, with one to many cavities, each with one (or more) ovules. There are as many stigmata as there are carpels. The styles are fused, stand free or are entirely absent. The fruit is a capsule or sometimes a berry or a stone fruit. A few *Guttiferae* genera have some economic significance because they yield durable wood, bark, dye, gum or resin or because the dried leaves are used. Some varieties are used as ornamental plants.

Hypericum androsaemum
St. John's wort, Tutsan

NAME: *Hypericum* is the Latin form of a Greek name composed of the words *hupo* (= to approach) and *ereika* (= heather): resembling heather. *Androsaemum* comes from the Greek *androsakos*. The meaning is unclear.

DESCRIPTION: Spreading deciduous shrub. The broad leaves are ovate, with a heart-shaped base; the underside is whitish. The shrub reaches approx. 80 cm in height. The flowers, 3 cm across, stand in groups of three or more. When they open, they are golden yellow; however, they fade rapidly. They blossom from June until September. The ornamental value lies primarily in the ovate berries, which are initially reddish-brown but quickly turn shiny black.

ORIGIN: Western Asia. The plant was cultivated as early as 1594 in the Netherlands.

CULTIVATION: Temperate areas with berrying shrub cultivation.

AVAILABILITY: From September until November.

CARE: The branches are marketed when the berry is still reddish-brown. Remove the leaves, cut off a bit of the stem, use cut-flower food for shrubs.

KEEPING PROPERTIES: 3-4 weeks.

USE: In flower arrangement.

SCENT: None.

Hypericum hookerianum
St. John's wort

NAME: See also previous variety. In addition, this species is named after the British botanist Sir William J. Hooker (1785-1865), director of the Kew Gardens.

DESCRIPTION: A semi-hardy shrub with round twigs. The golden yellow, saucer-shaped flowers have a diameter of 5 cm; they are grouped in bunches and bear short stamens. The plump fruits are first brownish-red and later turn shiny green. The shrub reaches a height of about 1 m. The most frequently cultivated cultivar is 'Hidcote', a hybrid with another species.

ORIGIN: The Himalayas and western China. The shrub was first cultivated in the United Kingdom in 1845.

CULTIVATION: Temperate areas with outdoor cut-flower cultivation.

AVAILABILITY: July-September.

CARE: When purchased, the first flower should be half open. Cut off a bit of the stem; use cut-flower food for shrubs.

KEEPING PROPERTIES: 7-12 days.

USE: In bouquets and floral work.

SCENT: None.

Hypericum inodorum

Haemodoraceae

Hamamelidaceae

The *Haemodoraceae* is a family of monocotyledonous herbaceous plants which are native to Australia, southern Africa and tropical America. It contains seventeen genera and around 100 species. The only genus of economic significance is *Anigozanthus*, the flowers of which have ornamental value.

The flowers of the *Haemodoraceae* are hermaphrodite and are usually grouped in racemes. The 3-6 stamens, the filaments of which stand free, are located on the inner perianth petals. The ovary is trilocular and may be either superior or inferior. The seeds have small kernels and contain much endosperm, a protein-containing nutritive tissue.

The family is subdivided into two groups: the *Haemodoreae* and the *Conostyleae*. The genera of the latter group, such as the kangaroo paw, have a single whorl of perianth petals, often with a long, crooked corolla base, and six stamens. The flowers are always woolly.

The number of varieties of the witch-hazel family (*Hamamelidaceae*) is limited: no more than 23 genera with a hundred species. Some yield satinwood or fragrant resins for the perfume industry (the genus *Liquidambar*, the sweet gum tree); the resins of others, such as *Hamamelis virginiana*, is used in creams which have a soothing effect on the skin and on superficial wounds.

The members of the family are trees or shrubs which grow in several temperate and subtropical areas. The leaves are alternate; their shape is simple or palmate. They have lobed stipules and, sometimes, hair formations.

The flowers are unisexual or hermaphrodite; the plants themselves monoecious or dioecious. The inflorescence is a flower head or a spike, sometimes surrounded by coloured ligulate bracts. The calyx consists of four or five fused sepals and an equal number of petals. The flower has 2-14 stamens; the ovary is semi-inferior or inferior, or superior, with two cavities and two styles. Each cavity contains at least one ovule. The outer layer of the fruit is woody, the inner layer generally horny. The seeds contain much storage food.

Anigozanthos flavidus
Kangaroo paw
NAME: *Anigozanthus* means 'plant with unusual flower'; *flavidus* = yellowish.
DESCRIPTION: Leafless branches of 1-1.70 cm are imported. They bear tubular, woolly flowers with a length of approx. 4 cm. In *A. flavidus* they are yellowy-green to reddish-brown; in the related *A. manglesii* they are somewhat larger and have red petals with green fringed margins.
ORIGIN: The subtropical areas of south-west (*A. flavidus*) and western (*A. manglesii*) Australia.
CULTIVATION: Flower cultivation areas with hothouse cultivation.
AVAILABILITY: From the hothouse, from May until August. Dried flowers are supplied from Australia chiefly in November/December for use in Christmas floral work.
CARE: The flowers should be open upon purchase. Cut off a bit of the stem; use cut-flower food.
KEEPING PROPERTIES: 3-4 weeks.
USE: Especially in floral work, both fresh and dried.
SCENT: None.

Hamamelis x intermedia
Witch hazel
NAME: The name *Hamamelis* is of Greek origin and is a contraction of the words *hama* (= at the same time as) and *melinis* (= apple). It belonged to a tree with edible fruits which blossomed at the same time as the apple tree. *Intermedia* indicates that it is a hybrid.
DESCRIPTION: A broad bush with pilose branches. The underside of the foliage is also pilose. The petals vary in colour from yellow to red, with many shades in between. The plants blossoms from the end of November until March. Frequently cultivated large-flowering cultivars are 'Jelena' (coppery-orange) and 'Ruby Glow' (dark purple-rose).
ORIGIN: The plant is a cross between *H. mollis* and *H. japonica* and was obtained in the Belgian arboretum, Kalmthout, in 1935.
CULTIVATION: Tree nurseries in temperate areas.
AVAILABILITY: End of November-March.
CARE: When purchased, the first flowers should be well open. Cut off a bit of the stem; use cut-flower food for woody plants.
KEEPING PROPERTIES: 10-14 days.
USE: In exclusive floral work.
SCENT: None.

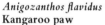

Anigozanthos flavidus

Iridaceae

Hamamelis mollis
Witch hazel

NAME: See also previous sort. *Mollis* means 'soft' and refers to the dense hairs on the underside of the leaf.

DESCRIPTION: Broad shrub with very hairy twigs. The ovate leaves are rough dentate with short points. Their undersides have a dense cover of grey hair. The flowers are grouped in clusters of 3-5. The petals are flat and linear; they are yellow, sometimes with a trace of red at the base.

ORIGIN: Eastern China. The plant was first cultivated in the United Kingdom in 1879.

CULTIVATION: Tree nurseries in temperate areas, although cultivated on a limited scale for cut twigs; the shrubs do not recover well after having been cut.

AVAILABILITY: From December until March.

CARE: When purchased, the first flowers should be open. Cut off a bit of the stem; use cut-flower food for woody plants.

KEEPING PROPERTIES: 8-12 days.

USE: In exclusive floral decorations.

SCENT: None.

Hamamelis x intermedia

The only representative of the flag family (*Iridaceae*) that grows wild in our regions is the yellow flag (*Iris pseudacorus*), an inhabitant of watersides and marshy grounds. The world over, however, this group contains more than 1800 varieties, classified into some 70 genera. Many are native to the Mediterranean area, South Africa and South and Central America. In general, they are perennial herbaceous plants which store food in bulbs, tubers, or root-stocks. The leaves are usually ensiform and stand in two rows; they grow from the bulb or tuber or stand on the root-stock. The plants have no stems; only a flower stem forms. The inflorescence is surrounded by a sheath. The perianth petals are grouped in two whorls which may or may not have the same shape. The hermaphrodite flowers are pollinated by insects. In some varieties, such as the iris, the insects are attracted by a spot on the perianth; they creep along the stamens to the nectar. These stamens stand opposite the outer perianth petals. The ovary is nearly always inferior and usually trilocular. The style is variable in form, but usually trichotomous, with terminal stigma surfaces. In the iris the styles, together with the perianth, form a protective tunnel for the stamens. The fruit is a capsule; the seeds have small kernels and contain much storage food.

The family is subdivided into 11 groups of genera which are related to one another as to flower shape and root type. It is a close relative of the *Amaryllidaceae* and the *Liliaceae*.

Many flags are of economic importance because of their role in flower cultivation. Well-known examples: the crocus, the gladiolus, the freesia and the iris.

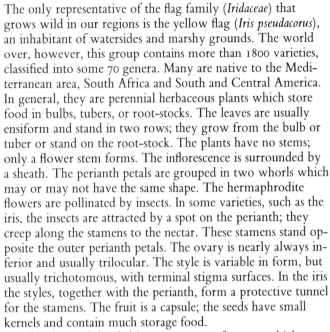

Acidanthera bicolor var. murielae,
syn. *Gladiolus callianthus*
Abyssinian gladiolus

NAME: *Acidanthera*, from the Greek words *akis* (= arrow point) and *anthos* (= flower), means 'having a flower like the point of an arrow'. *Bicolor* = two-coloured. The variety is named after Muriel, daughter of the plant's discoverer E.H. Wilson, who obtained it in 1920.

DESCRIPTION: A plant with flat, bulb-shaped corms, stems of approx. 50 cm in length and narrow, sword-shaped leaves. The flower spikes spring from the axils of the long bracts and bear 5-6 flowers. They are around 7 cm in diameter and are creamy white, with dark purple spots. They are shaped like bells, with long corolla bases. The axis of the inflorescence is arched.

ORIGIN: Ethiopia. The botanic sort was first cultivated in the United Kingdom in 1896; the variety *murielae* was first cultivated in 1920.

CULTIVATION: Temperate and subtropical aeas.

AVAILABILITY: Especially in July/August.

CARE: When purchased, the first flower should be open. Use cut-flower food for bulb plants.

KEEPING PROPERTIES: 6-9 days.

USE: In a vase and in flower arrangement.

SCENT: Fragrant.

Acidanthera bicolor, var. murielae

Crocosmia masonorum
(no popular name)

NAME: See also previous variety. In addition, the plant is named after the American botanist Herbert Louis Mason, who worked during the first half of this century.

DESCRIPTION: Stocky plant with sword-shaped leaves of 75 cm long and 5 cm wide. The flowers are larger than those of the previous variety, and the stems longer and heavier. The flower colour is bright orangish-red.

ORIGIN: Transvaal (South Africa).

CULTIVATION: Temperate and subtropical areas. The plant is not hardy.

AVAILABILITY: Early June - September.

CARE: When purchased, the lowest bud should be open. Use cut-flower food for bulb plants.

KEEPING PROPERTIES: 7-10 days.

USE: In a vase, in bouquets and in flower arrangement.

SCENT: None.

Crocus species
Crocus

NAME: *Crocus* comes from the Greek word for saffron (*krokos*), a colouring and flavouring agent which is obtained by drying or roasting the stigmata of *C. sativus*.

DESCRIPTION: A bulbous plant with a rosette of narrow leaves with parallel veins. The tubular, stemless flowers bear two whorls of three perianth petals. The genus has over 70 species with which many crosses have been performed. The modern assortment varies in colour from white to dark purple. Sometimes the flowers are striped; many have orange stigmata.

ORIGIN: The most important ancestor is *C. vernus*, a white crocus with purplish stripes from the Alps, Jura mountains, Carpathians, and Pyrenees.

CULTIVATION: Chiefly in the Netherlands.

AVAILABILITY: From November until the end of January.

CARE: The flowers are sold, tuber and all, in bunches of 10, and wrapped in paper to prevent dehydration. Set them in damp soil or moss.

KEEPING PROPERTIES: 6-14 days, depending on the temperature.

USE: In arrangements in small bowls or holders.

SCENT: None.

Cultivars

'**Remembrance**' is the most frequently cultivated crocus cultivar. The large round flowers are purple and very shiny. Another purple cultivar is 'Purpureus Grandiflorus', with oval flowers.

'**Jeanne d'Arc**' is a cultivar of beautiful, large, bright white flowers with dark purple bases and bright orange stamens.

'**Pickwick**' is one of the striped crocus cultivars. The background of the flower is pale pearl grey, with over it dark purple stripes. The base of the flower is dark purple.

Crocosmia x crocosmiiflora
Montbretia

NAME: *Crocosmia* is derived from the Greek words *krokos* (= saffron) and *osme* (= scent); a plant smelling of saffron. *Crocosmiiflora* means 'having the flowers of the crocosmia'.

DESCRIPTION: A plant with small flat tubers which are covered with brown membranes. The narrow, sword-shaped leaves are 1 cm wide; the flowers are around 5 cm long and stand in two rows along many-flowered spikes. The base of the corolla is somewhat curved; the slips are spreading and lanceolate. The flower colour ranges from yellow to orangish-red, depending on the cultivar. Frequently cultivated cultivars are 'Aurora', 'Fireking' and 'Emily MacKenzie'.

ORIGIN: This hybrid was obtained in France in 1880 by crossing the South African species *C. aurea* and *C. pottsii*.

CULTIVATION: Temperate areas, including the Netherlands and the United Kingdom.

AVAILABILITY: From June until the end of September.

CARE: When purchased, the lowest bud should be fully grown but preferably not yet open. Use cut-flower food for bulb plants.

KEEPING PROPERTIES: 7-10 days.

USE: In a vase, in bouquets and in floral work.

SCENT: None.

Crocosmia masonorum

'Blue Heaven'

Freesia hybrids
Freesia
NAME: The plant is named after a German physician, F.H.T. Freese, a fellow student of the discoverer of the genus.

DESCRIPTION: A bulbous plant with two rows of long, narrow, sword-shaped leaves. The stem is branched; the side branches are said to be 'hooked'. At the top, the flower stem becomes horizontal; on this 'comb' grow 8-14 flowers. They have two whorls of three perianth petals (more in double-flowering cultivars). The modern cultivars have large, open flowers and, in addition to white or yellow, may be red, pink, orange, cream, blue or purple. The orifice (mouth or throat) of the flowers has lovely markings and is a different shade.

ORIGIN: South Africa. The original botanic sorts were first cultivated in the United Kingdom in the course of the 19th century. The most important ancestors of the modern hybrid cultivars are *F. refracta* (especially the varieties *leichtlinii* and *odorata*) and *F. armstrongii*. Much improvement work took place in the Netherlands, France and the United Kingdom.

CULTIVATION: Nearly all over the world; much cultivated in the Netherlands.

AVAILABILITY: The year round, by controlling the temperature of the tubers and the ground. The planting times have been spread out in this way.

CARE: When purchased, the first bud should be fully grown but not yet open. Cut off a bit of the stem, add plain sugar to the water so that all the buds can mature. Regularly pinch off flowers which have finished blooming.

KEEPING PROPERTIES: 14-18 days. The first flowers of the comb finish blooming after 7 or 8 days.

USE: In a vase, often in flower arrangement.

SCENT: Pleasantly sweet; not too powerful.

Cultivars
'**Miranda**' is the most frequently cultivated white cultivar, with long, sturdy stems and a good comb, the flowers of which open very well. A white cultivar gaining in popularity is 'Athene'.

'**Blue Heaven**' is the most popular blue freesia; pretty bright blue flowers of a robust format and on a sturdy stem.

'**Moya**', a cultivar grown on a limited scale, is striking for its different colour, cream, and the very large flowers, which are will keep extra long. The stem is straight and strong.

'**Golden Wave**' is the best double-flowering yellow freesia, with remarkably fine and open flowers. The main stem has many side branches.

'**Fantasy**', pale yellow in colour, is the oldest double freesia. The flower meets high requirements, but the cultivar is somewhat difficult to grow, for one reason because the stem easily grows crooked.

'**Uchida**' is a multiple-flowering cultivar, with flowers that are dark purplish-blue on the outside. The buds, thick and round, are darker than the open flowers. Inside, the flowers have a brownish glow; the throat is white.

Gladiolus hybrids
Gladiolus, Sword lily
NAME: *Gladiolus* is the diminutive of the Latin *gladius*, which means 'sword'; the name refers to the leaf shape.

DESCRIPTION: A plant with large, flat tubers and broad, sword-shaped leaves. The flowers, with a diameter of 10-15 cm, are grouped in racemes on a stem of 80-120 cm long. The modern colour assortment is very large and contains all possible shades of the basic colours red, orange, yellow, pink, salmon, lilac and purple, often with lovely markings in the throat. Frequently cultivated cultivars are 'Hunting Song' (red), 'Peter Pears' (salmon pink), 'Nova Lux' (yellow), 'White Friendship' (white), 'Fidelio' (violet), 'Friendship' (pink), 'Nicole' (orangish-red) and 'Memorial Day' (purplish-blue).

ORIGIN: The wild species (more than 200) chiefly come from Africa. The most important ancestors of the modern cultivar assortment are *G. psittacinus* and *G. cardinalis*. The improvement work started in the vicinity of Ghent (Belgium) and later also took place in Germany. At present Dutch breeders take the most prominent place, although some new cultivars come from the United Kingdom as well.

CULTIVATION: Nearly all over the world.

AVAILABILITY: The year round, with a peak in July/August.

CARE: The best time to buy them is when the lowest bud shows colour. Sometimes the top is broken off the flower stem. Although the top buds are tiny and do not open, the absence of the top is ugly and docs not improve the keeping quality. Cut off a bit of the dried stem; use cut-flower food for bulbs. Remove flowers when they finish blossoming.

KEEPING PROPERTIES: 12-18 days. The gladiolus can withstand high temperatures very well.

USE: In a vase, in bouquets and in decorations.

SCENT: None.

'Hunting Song'

'Nymph'

Gladiolus x nanus
Sword lily

NAME: See also previous variety. *Nanus* means 'low'.

DESCRIPTION: The plant grows to a height of 70-80 cm and has a somewhat arched flower stem. The sword-shaped leaves are fairly narrow and the flowers have a diameter of approx. 5 cm. The colours vary. The most frequently cultivated cultivars are 'Nymph' (white with a red-edged cream coloured spot), 'Guernsey Glory' (salmon), 'Peach Blossom' (pink) and 'Spitfire' (red).

ORIGIN: The bulb grower Van Tubbergen in Haarlem, Holland, brought about this cross in 1900 from the varieties *G. cardinalis*, *G. cuspidatus*, *G. alatus* and *G. blandus*.

CULTIVATION: Nearly all over the world.

AVAILABILITY: From the hothouse, in April/May; from outdoor cultivation, in June/July.

CARE: When purchased, the bottom bud should show some colour. Cut off a bit of the stem; use cut-flower food for bulb flowers. Remove flowers when they finish blooming.

KEEPING PROPERTIES: 16-24 days.

USE: In a vase, in bouquets and in floral work.

SCENT: None.

Gladiolus colvillei hybrids
Sword lily

NAME: See also *G. hybrids*. The plant is also named after the British plant importer James Colvill (1795-1825).

DESCRIPTION: A small-flowering gladiolus, with flowers that are more erect than those of *G. x nanus* and a stem that is somewhat less arched. The most important cultivars are 'Albus' and 'The Bride', both white.

ORIGIN: A cross of *G. tristrix* and *G. cardinalis*, obtained in the United Kingdom in 1814. The ancestors come from South Africa.

CULTIVATION: Countries with hothouse and outdoor cut-flower cultivation.

AVAILABILITY: April/May from the hothouse; June/July from outdoor cultivation.

CARE: When purchased, the lowest bud should already show colour. Cut off a bit of the dried stem; use cut-flower food for bulb flowers. Remove flowers when they finish blooming.

KEEPING PROPERTIES: 16-24 days.

USE: In a vase, in bouquets and floral work.

SCENT: None.

Gladiolus x nanus 'Peach Blossom'   Gladiolus x nanus 'Guernsey Glory'

'White Wedgewood'

'Blue Magic'

Gladiolus x ramosus
Sword lily

NAME: See also *G. hybrids. Ramosus* means 'branched' and refers to the shape of the inflorescence.

DESCRIPTION: A small-flowering gladiolus, with stems of 1 m or longer and which are branched at the top. The flowers are fairly large and somewhat star-shaped. The cultivar 'Robinette', dark red in colour with a cream-coloured marking, is the only one which is cultivated as a cut flower.

ORIGIN: The ancestors come from South Africa; the origin of the cross is not known.

CULTIVATION: Areas with hothouse and outdoor flower cultivation.

AVAILABILITY: June-July.

CARE: When purchased, the lowest bud should show some colour. Cut off a bit of the stem; use cut-flower food for bulb flowers. Remove flowers when they finish blooming.

KEEPING PROPERTIES: 16-24 days.

USE: In a vase, in bouquets and in flower arrangement.

SCENT: None.

Iris x hollandica hybrids
Dutch iris

NAME: In Greek mythology, *Iris* (= rainbow) is the lovely and quick-footed messenger of the gods. Perhaps the name refers to the wealth of colour of this flower sort. *Hollandica* = from the Netherlands, where the cross was obtained.

DESCRIPTION: A bulb plant with narrow, pointed leaves that are almost as long as the 50-60 cm stem. It bears a single bloom, the three outer petals of which are folded back. The comb is a different colour from the rest of the flower (it is generally yellow). Most cultivars are blue; there are also yellow, white and two-coloured sorts. The style of the flower has three wide spreading coloured branches which hang over the pistil and stamens.

ORIGIN: This iris hybrid was obtained in the Netherlands in 1891, a cross of *I. xiphium* from Southern France, Spain and Portugal with *I. tingitana* from Morocco.

CULTIVATION: Almost solely cultivated in the Netherlands.

AVAILABILITY: All the year round, because by controlling the temperature of the bulbs, the planting times can be spread. 'Stunted' irises (especially blue) are chiefly sold between September and December; the largest assortment is available from March to May.

CARE: When purchased, the flowers should show around 1 cm of colour (more in some cultivars). Cut off a bit of the dried stem; use very clean water with cut-flower food for bulb flowers.

KEEPING PROPERTIES: 4-12 days, depending on the temperature.

USE: In a vase, in mixed bouquets and in floral arrangements.

SCENT: None.

Cultivars

'**Ideal**' is the most popular and most frequently cultivated cultivar, primarily because it lends itself very well to early and spring blossoming. Its colour is blue. Another familiar bright blue cultivar is 'Prof. Blaauw'. 'Ripe' buds of this cultivar should show a stripe of colour of 1 1/2 cm (in autumn as much as 4-5 cm).

'**White Wedgewood**' is a white mutant of one of the oldest iris cultivars, 'Wedgewood'. The white flowers show a hint of purplish-blue. The cultivar is gaining ground on two other white sorts, 'White Excelsior' and 'White Superior'.

'**Yellow Queen**' is an old cultivar with fairly small yellow flowers. It is exclusively supplied in spring. A new yellow cultivar gaining in popularity is 'Golden Harvest'.

Iris Hollandica hybrid 'Ideal'

Iris reticulata
(no popular name)

NAME: See also Dutch iris. *Reticulata* means 'having net-like venation' and refers to the skin of the bulb: thin fibres give it net-shaped markings.

DESCRIPTION: A small iris variety, 10-15 cm high and with dark green tubular leaves ending in points. The leaf cross-section is square; the leaves protrude above the flower. The simple, blue or purple, flower has a short stem. The outer slips are darker in colour and bear an orangish-yellow stripe. The inner slips are longer and stand erect.

ORIGIN: The Caucasus. The plant was first cultivated in the United Kingdom in 1829.

CULTIVATION: Bulb breeding companies in temperate regions.

AVAILABILITY: End of January - early March.

CARE: When purchased, the flower should just be open. The flowers are sold in bunches of 10 with bulb and all; they are wrapped in paper to prevent dehydration. Do not detach the bulbs; put them in water and use cut-flower food.

KEEPING PROPERTIES: 8-10 days. High temperatures and little light shorten their lifespan.

USE: In flower arrangement, especially in Biedermeier work.

SCENT: Fragrant.

Ixia hybrids
African corn lily

NAME: *Ixia* is the old Greek name for several plants which have nothing to do with the present ixia. Linnaeus fairly arbitrarily gave the name to this South African variety of iris.

DESCRIPTION: A bulb plant with narrow leaves and a long, thin, but very strong flower stem. The flower consists of two whorls of perianth segments and its cross-section is shiny and star-shaped; seen from the side, it has the shape of an open bell. The flowers are grouped in sparsely flowered racemes. The base of the petals is dark in hue, sometimes with a different coloured stripe. The assortment has numerous cultivars and colours. The most frequently cultivated cultivar is 'Castor' (red); other familiar sorts are 'Blauwe Vogel' (white with a violet centre) and 'Hogarth' (cream-coloured).

ORIGIN: South Africa. First cultivated in the United Kingdom around 1788 and much improvement work was done there.

CULTIVATION: Temperate areas; in the hothouse and (on a limited scale) outdoors.

AVAILABILITY: From March until September.

CARE: The lowest flowers should show good colour when purchased. Use cut-flower food for bulb flowers.

KEEPING PROPERTIES: 10-12 days.

USE: In a vase and in flower arrangement.

SCENT: None.

Watsonia hybrids
Watsonia, Southern bugle lily

NAME: The plant is named after English doctor, apothecary and author of scientific works Sir William Watson (1715-1787).

DESCRIPTION: A tuber plant, approx. 1 m high, which resembles a gladiolus in growth and shape. Around 14 of the wide open flowers are found on the long stem. The most common colour is pink.

ORIGIN: The ancestors of this 18th-century hybrid, which was obtained in the United Kingdom, were *W. pyramidata* (pink), *W. humilis* (pale pink), *W. coccinea* (carmine red), and *W. arderneri* (white). They all come from South Africa.

CULTIVATION: South Africa, and in the hothouse in Western Europe.

AVAILABILITY: From the hothouse, in spring; from the southern hemisphere in autumn.

CARE: The lowest 2-4 buds should show good colour when purchased. Cut off a bit of the stem; use cut-flower food for bulb flowers.

KEEPING PROPERTIES: 8-12 days.

USE: In a vase and in floral work.

SCENT: None.

Ixia hybrid   Watsonia hybrid

Labiatae

Although the mint family (*Labiatae*) is found all over the world, its members (there are some 3000, classified into approx. 200 genera) chiefly play a role in the flora of the Mediterranean area. Many genera of *Labiatae* contain terpenes, or aromatic flavouring substances, often in such abundance that they even end up in the honey of bees which collect nectar on these plants.

The labiates are primarily dicotyledonous herbaceous plants or semi-shrubs. They owe their family name to the fact that many genera have flowers which very clearly show a lower and an upper lip. The *Labiatae* are among the most highly developed plants.

The simple leaves stand opposite or in whorls on - frequently - square stems. They have no stipules. Within the family, there are large differences in the shape of the corolla and the location of the stamens. Some genera have a bilobate, sometimes hood-shaped upper lip and a trilobate lower lip. The tropical genera, however, have four-lobed upper lips and single-lobed lower lips, from which the stamens protrude. Sometimes the upper lip is entirely absent and the lower lip is five-lobed; in this case, the stamens stand free. The shape of the corolla tube varies; the nectar at the bottom of the tube is protected by a contracted throat or by a whorl of hairs. The ovary has four cavities, with a single style.

The composition of the flowers is adapted to pollination by flies and other hymenoptera. A very singular pollination mechanism can be found in the sage species (*Salvia*). When an insect creeps into the flowers, it presses against the end of the connective. This causes the lobes of the anther, at the other end, to strike the insect's abdomen. This is possible because the connective is hinged and is joined to the filament.

The flowers of the *Labiatae* are hermaphrodite; sometimes the stamens are infertile or the female flowers are insignificant.

Molucella laevis
Bells of Ireland

NAME: The name is derived from *molucca*. In the description of this genus, it was erroneously assumed that it came from the Moluccas (the Spice Islands). *Laevis* means 'balder' or 'less hairy'.
DESCRIPTION: Annual plant, 60-100 cm high with stemmed leaves of 10-15 cm long and crenate margins. The flowers are grouped above one another in verticillasters. The corolla is small and white; the plant derives its ornamental value from the large green calyx.
ORIGIN: The eastern part of the Mediterranean area. The plant, which used to be eaten as a vegetable, was first cultivated in Belgium in 1570.
CULTIVATION: In temperate and subtropical regions with outdoor cut-flower cultivation.
AVAILABILITY: All the year round, with a peak which starts in August and increases until November/December.
CARE: When purchased, the white corolla flowers of the lowest whorl should be open. Cut off a bit of the stem, remove lower leaves and use cut-flower food.
KEEPING PROPERTIES: 12-18 days.
USE: In floral work and mixed bouquets. Also sold as a dried flower.
SCENT: The leaf is slightly aromatic.

Monarda hybrids
Bergamot

NAME: The plant is named after Spanish physician N. Monardes, who wrote several works on medicinal herbs from the West Indies.
DESCRIPTION: A strong-scented perennial plant, up to 1 m high and with round or oval leaves which bear bristly hairs on the underside, especially along the veins. The leaf margins are serrate. The flowers are grouped in verticillasters and have red, brownish-red, pink or lilac-rose bracts. The corolla is long and narrow and is the same colour as the bracts.
ORIGIN: Central and eastern United States. The plant was first cultivated in the Netherlands in 1737. The old cultivars are of British origin; the newer ones were obtained in West Germany in the 1950s.
CULTIVATION: In temperate areas with outdoor cut-flower cultivation.
AVAILABILITY: From July until September.
CARE: The flowers should be half open when purchased. Cut off a bit of the stem; use cut-flower food for herbaceous plants.
KEEPING PROPERTIES: 8-11 days.
USE: In a vase and in mixed bouquets.
SCENT: Highly aromatic.

Moluccella laevis

Monarda hybrid 'Cambridge Scarlet'

Phlomis samia
Woolly sage

NAME: *Phlomis* (from *phlogmos* = inflammation) is the old Greek name for a *Verbascum* species. The dried woolly leaves of this plant were used as lamp wicks. *Samia* means 'from Samos', an island in the Greek archipelago.

DESCRIPTION: A plant of 60-90 cm high, with silvery-grey pilose leaves and golden yellow flowers. They are grouped in densely filled verticillasters which stand at some distance from one another and form long floral spikes.

ORIGIN: The island of Samos, off the coast of Asia Minor.

CULTIVATION: Temperate areas with outdoor cut-flower cultivation. The plant is gaining popularity as a cut flower in the Netherlands and Germany.

AVAILABILITY: July/August.

CARE: When purchased, the lowest whorl of flowers should be open. Remove the lower leaves, cut off a bit of the stem, use cut-flower food for herbaceous plants.

KEEPING PROPERTIES: 8-10 days.

USE: In a vase, in mixed bouquets and in flower arrangement.

SCENT: Slightly aromatic.

Physostegia virginiana 'Summer Snow'
False dragonhead

NAME: The name is a contraction of the Greek words *phuson* (= to blow up or inflate) and *stege* (= roof or cover). It refers to the calyx, which surrounds the inflated fruits after the flowering. *Virginiana* = from the American state of Virginia.

DESCRIPTION: A perennial plant with a creeping root-stock. The thin, straight, square stem can reach a length of 80-120 cm. The leaves are lanceolate: the lower ones are stemmed, the upper ones are sessile. Their margins are sharply serrate. The flowers, 2-3 cm long, are grouped in 20-30 long, pyramidal pseudo-spikes; they hinge around the axis. The original colour was pink. The grown cultivars are pale pink, purple-pink or white.

ORIGIN: The eastern United States. The plant was first cultivated in the United Kindom in 1683.

CULTIVATION: Temperate areas with outdoor cut-flower cultivation.

AVAILABILITY: June-September.

CARE: When purchased, the first flower should be fully grown. Remove lower leaves, cut off a bit of the stem, use cut-flower food for herbaceous plants.

KEEPING PROPERTIES: 15-18 days.

USE: In a vase, in bouquets and in flower arrangement. Sometimes the flowers are dyed in shades of yellow, green, blue or red.

SCENT: None.

Salvia x superba
Sage

NAME: The plant is named after Italian botanist G. Salvi (1769-1844), director of the botanical gardens of Pisa and author of the 'Flora of Pisa'. *Superba* means 'proud', 'excellent', 'beautiful'.

DESCRIPTION: A slightly pilose perennial plant, 60-70 cm high, with square stems which are somewhat purplish at the tops. The ovate-lanceolate leaves, 4-8 cm long, have short points and somewhat wrinkled; they have finely crenulate margins. The purplish-blue flowers have purple bracts and are grouped in long pseudo-spikes.

ORIGIN: The ancestors were native to south-eastern Europe and south-western Asia. Some say that the cross was obtained in the United Kindom in 1913: *S. nemorosa* x *S. villicaulis*. Others consider the plant to be a cultivar of *S. nemorosa*.

CULTIVATION: Temperate areas with outdoor cut-flower cultivation.

AVAILABILITY: June/July.

CARE: Cut off a bit of the stem; use cut-flower food for herbaceous plants.

KEEPING PROPERTIES: 7-10 days.

USE: In mixed bouquets, in floral arrangement and limited in a vase.

SCENT: Aromatic.

Phlomis samia

'Summer Snow'

Leguminosae

Salvia x superba

The legume family (*Leguminosae*), classified into some 600 genera, contains around 14,000 species of dicotyledonous herbaceous plants, shrubs and trees. Although its members grow all over the world, the family is most clearly represented in areas with a temperate climate. In addition to a number of ornamental plants, many important food plants such as beans and peas are found among the legumes.

The composite leaves are alternate and generally have stipules. There are also genera with simple leaves, and in some varieties, such as the acacia, the leaves have turned into thorns. The leaves of some species react in rather remarkable ways to changes in their environment. The mimosa, for example, closes its feathery leaves when evening falls; when touched, the sensitive plant (*Mimosa pudica*) folds its leaves closed and lets its leaf stems droop.

Some sorts, such as the sweet pea, can climb using leaf tendrils. Many legumes have root-tubers in which bacteria live that can turn the nitrogen in the air into nitrogen compounds important for the plant's nutrition. These sorts (including lupins) are sometimes cultivated on poor, sandy soils to fertilize them.

The inflorescence of most legumes is a cultivarme. The flowers are unisexual or hermaphrodite. The five sepals are more or less fused; the calyx has two or four lips; the arrangement of the petals varies per subfamily. The ovary is free-standing; the one-celled fruit is a legume; the seeds usually have hard skins and contain large kernels.

The *Leguminosae* are divided into three subfamilies. The *Caesalpiniaceae* exhibit *zygomorphism*: the flower is bilaterally symmetrical and can be divided into two equal halves by only one plane. The stamens (with a maximum of ten) are free-standing. The *Papilionaceae* have one large posterior petal (the vexillum), while two petals grow sideways (the wings or alae) and the two anterior petals are fused, forming a keel (carina). Lathyrus is a good example of this petal arrangement. In the subfamily of the *Mimosaceae*, the numerous stamens are partly fused with the filaments.

Salvia farinacea
Silver sage
NAME: See also previous sort. *Farinacea* is derived from *farina* (= flour or meal): the plant has a slightly powdery appearance.
DESCRIPTION: A grey felty perennial which is cultivated as an annual; it reaches a height of 60-70 cm. The leaves are lanceolate-linear and have entire or slightly fluted margins. Their upper sides are greener than the undersides. The lower lips of the blue flowers, which are 2 cm long, are longer than the upper lips.
ORIGIN: Texas, United States. The plant was first cultivated in Germany in 1847.

CULTIVATION: Temperate and subtropical areas.
AVAILABILITY: From early June until September, depending on when it is sown.
CARE: Remove the lower leaves, cut off a bit of the stem; use cut-flower food for herbaceous plants.
KEEPING PROPERTIES: 7-11 days.
USE: In a vase, in mixed bouquets and in floral work.
SCENT: None.

Acacia Dealbata hybrid

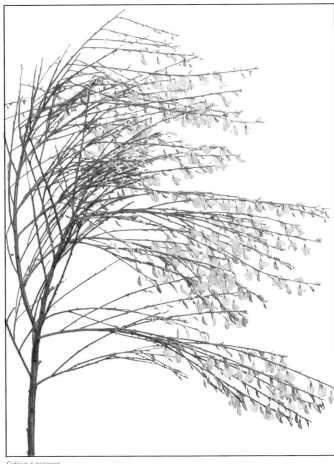

Cytisus x praecox

Acacia dealbata hybrids
Green wattle

NAME: The family name is derived from the Greek *akakio* (= prickly tree). *Dealbata* means 'to white' or 'to plaster' and refers to the colour of the leaves.
DESCRIPTION: Tree, 10-12 m high, with bipinnate, slightly pilose linear leaves. The large plumes bear a large number of yellow flower heads from the end of December until March. The ancestors of this hybrid are *A. decurrens* and *A. baileyana*. Frequently cultivated cultivars are 'Mirandole' (with small flowers), 'Fournaire' and 'Gaulois'.
ORIGIN: Australia, New Zealand and Tasmania.
CULTIVATION: Especially on the calcium-poor and silica-rich soils of the French Riviera.

AVAILABILITY: December to March.
CARE: The flower-bearing branches are usually wrapped in plastic foil. As soon as possible after purchase, cut off a bit of the dried stems and put the branches, still wrapped, in water of 50-55° C; add cut-flower food for mimosa or shrubs. When the branches and flowers have absorbed plenty of water, remove the wrapping.
KEEPING PROPERTIES: Around 2 weeks.
USE: In a vase and in decorations.
SCENT: Sharp fragrance.

Cytisus x praecox
Broom, Warminster broom

NAME: The genus name *Cytisus* was taken from the old Greek name *kytisos* for a plant that grew on Cynthus (or Kynthos), one of the Cyclades. *Praecox* means 'early-flowering'.
DESCRIPTION: A broad, dense shrub, 1.20-1.80 m high, with branches that bend downwards slightly at the ends. The young twigs are round or have shallow grooves; the simple linear spatula-shaped leaves have a length of 1-2 cm. During the blossoming period, the entire shrub is covered with large, creamy-white flowers, 1 cm across, which are spread over a large part of the branches, singly or in pairs.
ORIGIN: The plant is a cross of *C. multiflorus* and *C. purgans*; it was obtained by the Wheeler nursery in Warminster, England.
CULTIVATION: Italian and French Riviera, southern Germany.
AVAILABILITY: From February until the end of April.

CARE: The branches are sold when the first flowers are open. Cut off a bit of the branch if necessary; use cut-flower food for shrubs.
KEEPING PROPERTIES: 6-8 days.
USE: In bouquets and decorations. In a vase, only to a limited extent, because of their odour.
SCENT: Unplesasant.

Lathyrus odoratus
Sweet pea

NAME: *Lathyrus* is the Latin form of the Greek plant name *lathuris*, which was used for a spurge (*Euphorbia*). *Odoratus* means 'well-scented'.

DESCRIPTION: Annual climbing plant with leaf tendrils; it can reach up to 3 m high. The stems are winged; the elongated oval and pointed leaves have two stipules. The flower stems are located in the leaf axils; they are 25-50 cm long and they each bear 2-4 flowers (5-7 in the 'Galaxy' and 'Semi-Multiflora' cultivars). The original colour was lilac; the modern large-flowering cultivars can be white, cream and - from very pale to very dark - red, orange, salmon, pink, blue, lilac and purple. The perennial *L. latifolius* is also cultivated in white and carmine red, though on a limited scale. The stem of this sort is shorter, the flower smaller; besides, it has no scent.

ORIGIN: Italy (Sicily); first cultivated in 1699.

CULTIVATION: In temperate areas, both in the hothouse and outdoors.

AVAILABILITY: From March (from the hothouse) until August.

CARE: The bottom flower should be open when purchased. After they are cut, the flowers are left in treated water for 3-6 hours. At home, place in water with cut-flower food. The stem should stand around 5 cm deep in the water.

KEEPING PROPERTIES: 6-10 days.

USE: In a vase and in flower arrangement.

SCENT: Very fragrant.

Cultivars

'**Spencer Praecox**' is the collective name for early-flowering cultivars for cultivation in the hothouse. They were obtained in the United States in 1906 from the 'Spencer' cultivars. They are mostly cultivated in pale shades of pink, salmon, lilac and white. Well-known cultivars: 'Memory' (lavender), 'Cascade' (white), 'Daphne' (salmon pink), 'Shirley Temple' (pale pink) and 'American Beauty' (bright carmine red).

'**Spencer**' Collective name for a number of very large-flowering cultivars, with a beautiful posterior petal (vexillum) and a very wide range of colours. They are especially suited to cultivation in the open air. The first 'Spencer' culti-

var was obtained in the United Kindom in 1901.

The 'Royal Family', the 'Galaxy' and the 'Semi-Multiflora' cultivars are also used for outdoor cultivation. The number of cultivars and colours in these groups is much more limited than in the 'Spencer' cultivars.

Another group is the 'Old English' or 'Grandiflora' cultivars. They have short-stemmed small flowers, but are very highly scented.

Lupinus Polyphyllus hybrids
Lupine

NAME: The genus name is derived from the Latin word for wolf (*lupus*) and literally means 'wolf bean'. In a figurative sense: an inferior, unpalatable bean. *Polyphyllus* means 'with many leaves'.

DESCRIPTION: A herbaceous perennial plant, up to 1 m high, with 7-11 lanceolate leaves which have short hairs on the upper sides and silky hairs on the undersides. The flowers are grouped in dense racemes of 40-50 cm. The original flower colour was violet-blue. After the Russell hybrids were obtained in the United Kindom in 1936, a great variety of colours came about in shades such as red, salmon, pink, yellow and white. There are also bi-coloured and large flowering cultivars; all modern cultivars are large-flowering.

ORIGIN: California and south-western Canada. The plant was first cultivated in the United Kindom in 1826. It is now found in the wild in very many places.

CULTIVATION: Temperate areas with outdoor cut-flower cultivation.

AVAILABILITY: Chiefly in May-June.

CARE: When purchased, the lower flowers should be open. Immediately after cutting, the flowers are set in a cool place for at least an hour to keep them from drooping. They cannot withstand long journeys. Use cut-flower food for herbaceous plants.

KEEPING PROPERTIES: Around 5 days. If cut straight from the plant: 8-10 days.

USE: In mixed bouquets and in a vase.

SCENT: None.

△ Lathyrus odoratus 'Spencer'   ▽ Lupinus Polyphyllus hybrid

Liliaceae

Representatives of the lily family (*Liliaceae*) are spread all over the world. It is divided into some 250 genera with around 3500 species. Nearly all of them are monocotyledonous herbaceous plants; many are bulb and tuber plants. One species, the onion (*Allium cepa*), is of world-wide importance as a vegetable. The family as a whole, however, derives its economic value chiefly from its ornamental value. For example, many flower bulbs are members of the lily family.

The leaf arrangement and leaf shape of the *Liliaceae* is quite varied, although all of them have parallel venation. The flower composition is regular. The flowers are hermaphrodite. Often they form racemes, but sometimes also single flowers, as in the tulip. The flower usually has two whorls of three petals and generally two whorls of three stamens as well. The anthers have two pouches; the superior ovary is generally trilocular. The fruit is a capsule or a berry.

There is no agreement about how the family should be subdivided; the number of genera ranges from 12 to 28. There is fair consensus about the groups *Tulipae* (with plants such as the tulip and the lily) and *Scillae* (with such genera as *Eucomis*, *Muscari* and *Ornithogalum*). The genus *Allium*, along with *Brodiaea*, *Agapanthus* and *Triteleia*, has been considered a separate family, that of the *Alliaceae*. Most members of this group are ornamental plants, while the asparagus and the onion are its most important vegetables.

An alkaloid, colchicine, is obtained from sap of the poisonous autumn crocus; it is used in modern plant refinement techniques to double the number of chromosomes in the cell nucleus.

△ Agapanthus praecox   ▽ Allium aflatunense 'Purple Sensation'

Agapanthus praecox
'Blue Triumphator'
African lily

NAME: The genus name is a contraction of the Greek words *agape* (= love) and *anthos* (= flower): 'flower of love'. *Praecox* means early-blossoming.

DESCRIPTION: The blue or white funnel-shaped flowers are 4-5 cm long and stand in profusely blossoming umbels on the flower stems which are more than 1 m long. The spreading corolla segments are fairly narrow, but they are around three times as long as the flower tube. The leaves, approx. 3 cm wide, have a length of 50-60 cm and are grouped in rosettes.

ORIGIN: South Africa. The flower was first cultivated in the Netherlands in 1687.

CULTIVATION: In subtropical and temperate areas with outdoor cut-flower cultivation. The plant is moderately hardy.

AVAILABILITY: From April until September.

CARE: When purchased, the first flowers of the cultivarme should be open. Use cut-flower food. The flowers naturally 'drop'; the cultivar 'Blue Triumphator' does not drop, nor does 'Blue Globe'. The cultivars 'Goliath' and 'Blue Perfection' are somewhat more susceptible to it. All cultivars will drop if they are kept too long in cold storage.

KEEPING PROPERTIES: 2-3 weeks, sometimes even longer.

USE: In flower arrangement, for decorations and in bouquets.

SCENT: None.

Allium aflatunense
Onion

NAME: *Allium* is the Latin name for onion or garlic. *Aflatunense* refers to the origin, Aflatun-Tien Chan, a mountain range in Central Asia.
DESCRIPTION: The bluish-green leaves are long and slender and sometimes slightly bent back; they are always longer than 30 cm. The broad inflorescence stands on a lilac-coloured stalk of around 1.5 m in length. The most common cultivar is 'Purple Sensation', with dark lilac flowers.
ORIGIN: Central Asia.
CULTIVATION: Temperate areas; in the Netherlands, often in combination with flower bulb cultivation.
AVAILABILITY: May-June.
CARE: When purchased, one-third of the flowers should be open. Use cut-flower food for bulb flowers.
KEEPING PROPERTIES: 12-20 days.
USE: In a vase and in flower arrangement.
SCENT: Onion smell.

Allium moly

Allium moly
(no popular name)

NAME: See *A. aflatunense*. *Moly* is the Latin form of the Greek *molu*, used for a plant with white flowers and jet-black roots which were difficult to dig up. The god Hermes gave the plant to Odysseus so that he could protect himself from the spell of the nymph, Circe.
DESCRIPTION: The lanceolate leaves, up to 3 cm wide, stand alone or in pairs. The yellow flowers are grouped in umbels of 15 flowers; the flower involucres are bipartite.
ORIGIN: South-western Europe and the Pyrenees. The plant was first cultivated in England in 1596.
CULTIVATION: In temperate areas, often in combination with flower bulb cultivation.
AVAILABILITY: From April until June.
CARE: When purchased, around one-third of the flowers should be open. Use cut-flower food for bulb flowers.
KEEPING PROPERTIES: Around 14 days.
USE: In flower arrangement and in mixed bouquets.
SCENT: Weak onion smell.

Allium caeruleum
Onion

NAME: See *A. aflatunense*. *Caeruleum* means 'azure'.
DESCRIPTION: The linear leaves, ± 25 cm long, have sharp keels, which give them a triangular appearance; they dry out while the plant is flowering. The hollow flower stalk is 40-80 cm long and bears a globular raceme of bright blue flowers, the stamens of which are just as long as the flower petals.
ORIGIN: Turkestan, Siberia; first cultivated in 1830.
CULTIVATION: Temperate areas.
AVAILABILITY: May-July.
CARE: Put the flowers in water with cut-flower food for bulb flowers.
KEEPING PROPERTIES: 10-15 days.
USE: Especially in flower arrangement.
SCENT: Onion smell.

Allium giganteum
Garlic, Onion

NAME: See *A. aflatunense*. *Giganteum* = giant; it refers to the flower size.
DESCRIPTION: The flower stalk is smooth or somewhat ribbed and can reach a height of 1.5 m. The greyish-green lanceolate leaves are around 10 cm wide and lie partly on the ground; the underside has a keel and rough hairs. The dark lilac-rose flowers are grouped in wide umbels which can be up to 20 cm across. The bulb is elongated, with a long neck.
ORIGIN: Himalayas; first cultivated in 1883.
CULTIVATION: In temperate areas, often in combination with the cultivation of flower bulbs.
AVAILABILITY: July-August.
CARE: When purchased, nearly all flowers should be open. Use cut-flower food for bulb flowers.
KEEPING PROPERTIES: Around 20 days.
USE: In large floral work and in bouquets. The flower can also be dried.
SCENT: Onion smell.

Allium karataviense
(no popular name)

NAME: See *A. aflatunense*. *Karataviense* refers to the origin of the sort, the Karatau mountains in the Soviet Union.
DESCRIPTION: The two tongue-shaped leaves, 30 cm long and 10 cm wide, are arched; they are shiny grey with red margins. On the flower stalk, 20-25 cm long, the pale pink to nearly ashen white inflorescence unfolds; it can be up to 12 cm wide.
ORIGIN: Turkestan; under cultivation since 1876.
CULTIVATION: Flower bulb growers in temperate areas.
AVAILABILITY: From April until June.
CARE: When purchased, the flowers should be almost entirely open. Use cut-flower food for bulb flowers.
KEEPING PROPERTIES: 18-21 days.
USE: In floral work and as a dried flower.
SCENT: Onion smell.

Allium neapolitanum
(no popular name)

NAME: See *A. aflatunense*. *Neapolitanum*, from *neo* (= new) and *politus* (= to make smooth, polish), refers to the sheen of the flower.
DESCRIPTION: The leaves, 2 cm wide, have a weak keel on the underside. The bright white flowers are grouped in a semi-globular inflorescence, on stemlets which are twice as high as the flower. The corolla lobes are around 1 cm long.
ORIGIN: Mediterranean area.
CULTIVATION: Temperate areas.
AVAILABILITY: April-June.
CARE: When purchased, the flower should be one-third of the way open. Use cut-flower food for bulb flowers.
KEEPING PROPERTIES: 12-14 days.
USE: Chiefly in flower arrangement, such as bridal work.
SCENT: Onion smell.

Allium sphaerocephalum
(no popular name)

NAME: See *A. aflatunense*. *Sphaerocephalum* means 'having a globular head'.

DESCRIPTION: The flower stalks of this bulb plant are 50-80 cm long, much longer in any case than leaves, which wither early and, in cross-section, are semi-circular. The purplish-red flowers are grouped in many-flowered globular umbels. The stamens are longer than the petals.

ORIGIN: Central Europe and the Mediterranean area. First cultivated in the Netherlands in 1594.

CULTIVATION: In temperate areas, often in combination with flower bulb cultivation.

AVAILABILITY: From June until August.

CARE: When purchased, the flower should be half open. Use cut-flower food for bulb flowers.

KEEPING PROPERTIES: 15-20 days.

USE: In a vase, in mixed bouquets and in flower arrangement.

SCENT: Onion smell.

Convallaria majalis

Allium sphaerocephalon

Asparagus setaceus
Asparagus 'fern'

NAME: *Asparagus* is the Latin form of the Greek *asparagos*, which means 'asparagus-like plant'. *Setaceus* comes from *seta* (= bristle) and refers to the shape of the leaves.

DESCRIPTION: In the adult stage, a woody climbing plant; until then, it is herbaceous. The leaves have been reduced to needle-shaped scales and stand on stem branchings, forming decorative horizontal and feathery surfaces. They are bright green in colour. The branches that do not twine or climb are called 'feathers'; the climbing shoots can reach several metres in length. In cultivation, they are shortened, or topped.

ORIGIN: South Africa; first cultivated in the United Kingdom in 1875.

CULTIVATION: All over the world, but chiefly in Denmark and the Netherlands.

AVAILABILITY: All the year round.

CARE: When purchased, all scales at the end of the branches should be fully grown, otherwise they will droop. Cut off the white lower ends of the branches; use cut-flower food.

KEEPING PROPERTIES: 2-3 weeks.

USE: As greenery in bouquets - for example, with pinks and freesias - and in floral work. The use of the asparagus fern is rapidly declining.

SCENT: None.

Convallaria majalis
Lily of the valley

NAME: *Convallis* is Latin for 'deep valley'; *majalis* means 'flowering in May', the natural blossoming time of the plant.

DESCRIPTION: Perennial plant with creeping root-stock. The oval, bright green leaves are radical and stand in pairs. The flower stalk is 15-20 cm long. At its end stand the somewhat pendulous flower racemes with 4-10 nodding white flowers shaped like open-mouthed bells.

ORIGIN: Northern hemisphere; first cultivated in 1420.

CULTIVATION: Temperate areas. The plant material is often cultivated in West Germany and brought to blossom in the Netherlands.

AVAILABILITY: All the year round. The natural flowering falls in May; the plant, however, can be brought to blossom at any desired moment by storing the plant material below freezing point.

CARE: When purchased, the lowest flower of the raceme should be open. To stop them from wilting, the flower stalks are sold with roots and all. The flowers should always be put in water with cut-flower food.

KEEPING PROPERTIES: 4-6 days.

USE: Especially in flower arrangement, such as in bridal bouquets.

SCENT: Very pleasant scent.

Eremurus stenophyllus subsp. stenophyllus,
syn. *E.s. bungei*
Foxtail lily

NAME: Composed of the Greek words *eromos* (= desert or steppe) and *oura* (= tail); steppe plant with tail-shaped inflorescence. *Stenophyllus* means 'narrow-leaved'.

DESCRIPTION: A perennial plant with 5-9 basal linear leaves. The flowers are grouped in racemes which can grow to be 40 cm long, at the end of the 80-100 cm stalks. The flower has a diameter of about 2 cm and a wide bell shape. The petals have dark central veins.

ORIGIN: Iran, Afghanistan and Turkestan. The plant was first cultivated in the United Kingdom in 1875.

CULTIVATION: Temperate and subtropical areas, especially in Western Europe.

AVAILABILITY: June-early July.

CARE: When purchased, one-fourth of the flower raceme should be open. Cut off the lower end of the stem and repeat this every so often. Use cut-flower food.

KEEPING PROPERTIES: 10-18 days.

USE: In a vase, in mixed bouquets and in flower arrangement. The stalks are heavy.

SCENT: None.

Eremurus Ruiter hybrids
(no popular name)

NAME: See *E. stenophyllus*. In addition, it is named after the firm that obtained the hybrid: Ruiter in Heemskerk, the Netherlands.

DESCRIPTION: A plant of approx. 1.50 m high, outwardly resembling *E. stenophyllus* and cultivated in the colours yellow, orange, reddish-brown and white.

ORIGIN: See *E. stenophyllus*. Ruiter hybrid is a cross of this sort and *E. olgae*.

CULTIVATION: See *E. stenophyllus*.

AVAILABILITY: Mostly in June.

CARE: See *E. stenophyllus*.

KEEPING PROPERTIES: 15-18 days.

USE: In flower arrangement.

SCENT: None.

Eremurus robustus
(no popular name)

NAME: See *E. stenophyllus*. *Robustus* = powerful, robust.

DESCRIPTION: The leaves, approx. 5 cm wide, are bluish-green. The flower stalk reaches a length of around 2 m, the flower cultivarme 70-80 cm. The flowers, which have a diameter of about 4 cm, are bell-shaped at first, and later become rotate. In the bud they are pink, later they fade to nearly white. The flower petals have a brown spot at the base and a brown central vein.

ORIGIN: Turkestan. First cultivated in 1871. CULTIVATION: Temperate and subtropical areas.

AVAILABILITY: June-July.

CARE: See *E. stenophyllus*.

KEEPING PROPERTIES: 10-18 days.

USE: In a vase, in decorations and in flower arrangement.

SCENT: None.

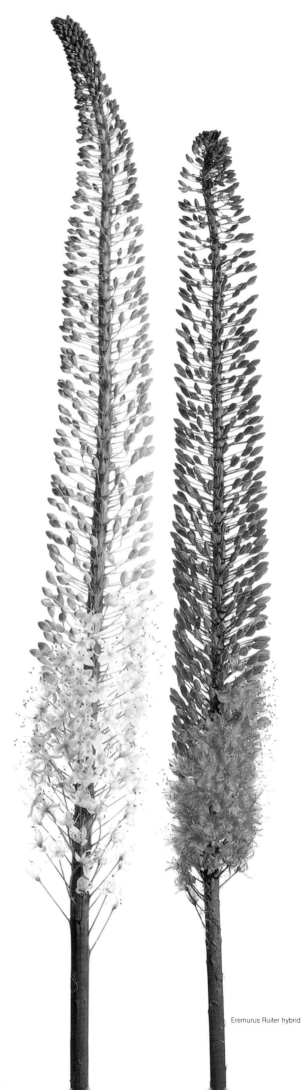

Eremurus Ruiter hybrid

Eucomis bicolor

Eucomis bicolor
(no popular name)

NAME: The genus name is of Greek origin and means 'with a lovely crest' (flower shape). *Bicolor* = two-coloured.

DESCRIPTION: A bulb plant with elongated ovate, basal leaves which can be up to 10 cm wide. Their margins are finely fluted. The greenish flowers have lilac-red margins and a crest of 15-20 green leaves. In addition to *E. bicolor*, *E. comosa* is also cultivated; it has pleasantly scented greenish-white flowers.

ORIGIN: South Africa; first cultivated in the United Kingdom in 1878.

CULTIVATION: In temperate and subtropical areas; quite a lot in the Netherlands.

AVAILABILITY: July-August.

CARE: When purchased, the first flowers of the inflorescence should be open. Cut off the dried end of the stem and, if necessary, repeat this now and then. Use cut-flower food for bulb flowers.

KEEPING PROPERTIES: 14-18 days.

USE: In a vase and in flower arrangement.

SCENT: None.

Galtonia candicans

Galtonia candicans
Cape hyacinth

NAME: The plant is named after Sir F. Galton (1822-1911), who spent time in South Africa as an explorer. He was the founder of dactyloscopy (the study of fingerprints).

DESCRIPTION: A bulb plant with stalks of approx. 1 m long and 4-5 leaves in a rosette shape; they are linear and about 8 cm wide. The white, pleasantly scented flowers are 4-5 cm long and somewhat pendulous; they are grouped in long, many-flowered racemes.

ORIGIN: Natal (South Africa); first cultivated in the United Kingdom in 1870. CULTIVATION: As a cut flower, on a limited scale in temperate and subtropical areas.

AVAILABILITY: July-August. From the southern hemisphere: January-March.

CARE: When purchased, the first flower should be open. Cut off a bit of the stem; use cut-flower food for bulb flowers.

KEEPING PROPERTIES: 12-14 days.

USE: In a vase, in mixed bouquets and in flower arrangement.

SCENT: Pleasant scent.

Gloriosa rothschildiana
Glory lily

NAME: *Gloriosa* from the Latin *gloria* = honour, fame. The plant is also named after Z.W. Baron de Rothschild, an authority on birds, who entered this *Gloriosa* species at a flower exhibition of the English Royal Horticultural Society at the beginning of this century.

DESCRIPTION: Plant with a tuberous root and a herbaceous stem several metres in length. The shiny green leaves have a tendril at the top which the plant uses to attach itself. The simple flowers stand at the end of a 12-15 cm long stem. They are bright orangish-red with a yellow spot and stand in the leaf axils. The petals are arched and somewhat fluted.

ORIGIN: Tropical Africa; first cultivated in the United Kingdom in 1902.

CULTIVATION: Primarily in the Netherlands, as a hothouse cut flower.

AVAILABILITY: End of April-end of October; there is also a limited supply from the tropics.

CARE: When purchased, the perianth segments should be arched and the stamens should lean away from the stigma. The flowers are sold in inflated foil bags to avoid damage. Use cut-flower food. Put drooping flowers under water for 8-12 hours so that they can absorb plenty of water.

KEEPING PROPERTIES: 10-12 days.

USE: Flowers with short stems and without leaves, in a vase and in flower arrangement. Long stems from the top of the plant, with leaves and flowers in the axils, for decorations and in flower arrangement.

SCENT: None.

△ 'Carnegie'

'Blue Jacket'

Gloriosa rothschildiana

Hyacinthus orientalis
Hyacinth

NAME: *Hyacinthus* is the Latin form
of the Greek *Huakinthos*, the name
of a young man who was loved by
Apollo and was fatally struck at a
discus-throwing event. From his
blood sprang a flower which Apollo named after his friend. *Orientalis*
= from the east.

DESCRIPTION: A bulb plant with a
flower stalk of approx. 25 cm and
6-8 basal, canaliculate and erect
leaves. The 8-14 funnel-shaped
flowers have recurved segments
and stand in racemes. The original
colour was violet-blue.

ORIGIN: Western Asia; introduced
into Austria around 1560.

CULTIVATION: Practically 90 per
cent of this is in the Netherlands.

AVAILABILITY: From the end of November until April.

CARE: When purchased, the first
flowers of the raceme should be
open. Cut off a bit of the stem; use
cut-flower food for bulb flowers.

KEEPING PROPERTIES: 12-16 days.

USE: In a vase and in Biedermeier
bouquets. The individual florets
are also used in corsages and bridal
work, for example. For cut flow-

ers, the lighter bulbs are generally
used, otherwise the flower stalks
become too heavy.

SCENT: Very pleasant.

Cultivars

'**Carnegie**'. The most frequently
cultivated white hyacinth, it is
usually brought to blossom before
Christmas. The florets are widely
used in bridal work.

'**Anna Marie**' is the most frequently cultivated pink hyacinth; pink is, after white, the
most popular colour. 'Anna
Marie' can be brought to blossom
throughout the bulb season.

'**Fürst Bismarck**' is one of the
loveliest blue hyacinths. This cultivar is not generally used with
other blue flowers, but more often
in bouquets of a mixture of
colours. 'Blue Jacket' is a new blue
cultivar which is gaining in popularity.

'Royal Standard'

Lilium auratum

Kniphofia hybrids
'Royal Standard'
Torch lily, Red-hot poker

NAME: The plant is named after the German physician J.H. Kniphof (1704-1763). He was a professor in Erfurt (now in East Germany) and published a number of botanical treatises.
DESCRIPTION: Perennial plant with numerous linear basal leaves. The flower stalks are longer than the leaves; the flowers are arranged in long spikes on a strong, solid stem. The flowers are yellow, orange or orangy-red in colour; there are also two-coloured cultivars. 'Royal Standard', the best cut-flower cultivar, is sulphur yellow with red flowers.
ORIGIN: South Africa. The hybrid is a complex cross involving *K.* *uvaria, K. pauciflora, K. macowanii, K. nelsonii* and perhaps some other species.
CULTIVATION: Temperate areas with outdoor cut-flower cultivation.
AVAILABILITY: From mid-May until October, depending on the cultivar.
CARE: When purchased, the lowest flower of the spike should be open; the plants should always be kept upright, for otherwise the buds will turn and the spike will become crooked. Cut off a bit of the stem; use cut-flower food. The heavy stems contain much silica, which will rapidly blunt the knife used in cutting.
KEEPING PROPERTIES: 10-14 days.
USE: In large mixed bouquets and for decorations.
SCENT: None.

Lilium auratum
Gold rayed lily

NAME: *Lilium* is the old Latin name for the lily; *auratum* comes from *aurea* (= gold) and refers to the golden-coloured centre stripe on the perianth petals of this lily sort.
DESCRIPTION: A lily with saucer-shaped, somewhat pendulous flowers. They are white, with golden-yellow bands over the middle of the perianth petals, and carmine red spots. The flowers are grouped in racemes with ten flowers each. The bluish-green stem often has a faint red blush.
ORIGIN: The Japanese island of Honshu. First cultivated in the United Kingdom in 1860.
CULTIVATION: The bulbs are cultivated in Japan and brought to blossom at hothouse cut-flower growers in the temperate regions.
AVAILABILITY: Practically the year round, with the exception of February-March. The peak supply starts in September and ends in December.
CARE: When purchased, the lowest flowers should be open. Cut off a bit of the stem; use cut-flower food.
KEEPING PROPERTIES: 8-14 days.
USE: Especially in flower arrangement, as in decorations.
SCENT: Heavy, very fragrant.

Lilium longiflorum
Easter lily

NAME: See *L. auratum. Longiflorum* means 'having long flowers'.
DESCRIPTION: A lily with a stalk as tall as 1.50 m. The three- to five-veined leaves are close together. The trumpet-shaped flower is pure white and is nearly horizontal on the stem. The pollen is yellow; the base of the stamens and the nectary bear no hairs. There are also crosses with *L. formosanum*.
ORIGIN: Japan. This frequently cultivated lily was introduced in the United Kingdom in 1819.
CULTIVATION: Many bulbs are imported from Japan. The cultivation of this lily is greatly on the rise in the Netherlands, with new cultivars from the Institute for the Refinement of Horticultural Plants in Wageningen. Some frequently cultivated selections are 'Eruba', 'Croft' and 'White Europe'.
AVAILABILITY: The year round, with a peak in March and April.
CARE: When purchased, the buds should show colour but still be closed. The flowers are sold in vials (most lily sorts are sold by the stalk). Cut off a bit of the stem; use cut-flower food. Remove the anthers from the stamens; the pollen makes troublesome stains on clothing, etc.
KEEPING PROPERTIES: 8-10 days.
USE: In flower arrangement, such as mourning work and church decorations. In the United States, it is much used as a potted lily at Easter.
SCENT: Heavy fragrance.

Lilium Mid-Century hybrids (no popular name)

NAME: See *L. auratum*. 'Mid-Century' refers to the year these crosses were introduced: 1949. They are now termed 'Asian hybrids'.

DESCRIPTION: A lily with erect flowers in all kinds of shades of orange, in yellow and (to a limited extent) also in white. The flowers have somewhat dark segments. The stem is about 1 m long; leaf and flower shape vary with cultivar. The assortment is large. Frequently grown cultivars are 'Connecticut King' (yellow) and 'Enchantment' (orange).

ORIGIN: The first cultivars of this hybrid group were introduced at the Oregon Bulb Farms in the United States by the Dutchman Jan de Graaff. He obtained them by crossing Umbtig hybrids (*L. hollandicum* hybrids x *L. tigrinum*) with *L. maculatum*. Later cultivars such as 'Connecticut King' (yellow) and 'Enchantment' (orange) were developed from this. The Mid-Century group today comprises some 60 per cent of all cultivated lilies. Because of the many crosses, the distinction between Mid-Century, Tigrinum and Hollandicum hybrids has become obscure. This is why all lilies with erect flowers are often referred to as Asian hybrids.

CULTIVATION: All temperate areas with cut-flower cultivation; particularly popular in the Netherlands and the United States.

AVAILABILITY: The year round, by varying planting times and by freezing the bulbs.

CARE: When purchased, the lowest three buds should show colour but should not be open. The keeping time is lengthened if they are treated straight away after they are cut. Cut off a bit of the stem; use cut-flower food.

KEEPING PROPERTIES: 10-14 days.

USE: In a vase, in mixed bouquets and in floral work.

SCENT: Slight.

'Star Gazer'

Lilium Oriental hybrids
Empress hybrid lily

NAME: See *L. auratum*.

DESCRIPTION: Lilies with conspicuous flowers, in the basic colours of white and pink. Each leaf has lovely markings. Well-known cultivars are 'Star Gazer', 'Journey's End' and 'Casablanca'. The group is still expanding.

ORIGIN: Chiefly from crosses from the United States, originally of *L. auratum*, later again crossed with *L. japonicum* and *L. rubellum*.

CULTIVATION: The bulbs are often cultivated in the Netherlands and the United States and brought to blossom by cut-flower growers all over the world; however, mainly in the Netherlands.

AVAILABILITY: Practically all the year round, with a peak in October-November and a minimum in January-February.

CARE: These lilies are sold by vial, in bouquets of 20. When purchased, the buds should just barely have opened. The flowers should be treated after being cut. Cut off a bit of the stem; use cut-flower food.

KEEPING PROPERTIES: 10-15 days.

USE: In flower arrangement and for large decorations.

SCENT: Heavy and fragrant.

Lillium Mid-Century hybrid 'Connecticut King'

Muscari armeniacum
Grape hyacinth

NAME: *Muscari* is derived from musk, after the scent of the flower. *Armeniacum* comes from the Latin word for apricot and refers to the shape or scent of the flower.

DESCRIPTION: A bulbous plant with a rosette of 6-8 leaves that are longer than the flower stems in the wild. In cultivation, the leaf may not protrude above the stem. The dark violet-blue ovate flowers are 5-7 mm across and are grouped in flower racemes of 7-8 cm long.

ORIGIN: The Balkans, Greece, Asia Minor.

CULTIVATION: Chiefly in the Netherlands.

AVAILABILITY: From early December until April.

CARE: When purchased, the lowest flowers should be open. Cut off a bit of the stem; use cut-flower food for bulb flowers.

KEEPING PROPERTIES: 6-10 days.

USE: In a vase, in flower arrangement, such as corsages, and in mixed Biedermeier bouquets.

SCENT: Weak musk scent.

Muscari botryoides var. botryoides
Grape hyacinth

NAME: See *M. armeniacum*. *Botryoides* from the Greek *botrus* = grape or bunch.

DESCRIPTION: Bulbous plant with flower stems of about 15 cm, and 3-4 leaves of the same length, arranged in a rosette. The flowers, which spread somewhat from the stem and tend to point down, are grouped in dense, profusely flowering racemes. They are violet-blue and have white edges which are curled over. The flowers are about 4 mm across.

ORIGIN: Europe and Asia Minor; under cultivation since 1576.

CULTIVATION: The flowers are brought to blossom by bulb flower growers all round the world, but chiefly in the Netherlands.

AVAILABILITY: Late February-early May.

CARE: The flowers are sold in bouquets with their leaves. The leaves should not protrude above the flower stem; when purchased, the lowest flowers should be open. Cut off a bit of the stem; use cut-flower food for bulb flowers.

KEEPING PROPERTIES: 6-10 days.

USE: In a vase, in flower arrangement, such as corsages, and in Biedermeier bouquets.

SCENT: Weak musk scent.

Ornithogalum arabicum

Ornithogalum arabicum
(no popular name)

NAME: *Ornithogalum*, from the Greek words *ornithos* (= bird) and *gala* (= milk), literally means 'bird milk'. *Arabicum* = from Arabia.

DESCRIPTION: Bulbous plant with stems of 60 cm and narrow lanceolate leaves. The flowers, 5-6 cm across, are creamy white and have a black ovary. They grow in racemes of 10-12.

ORIGIN: Mediterranean area; first cultivated in Austria in 1574.

CULTIVATION: The year round, with a peak in late summer and autumn.

AVAILABILITY: In the hothouse, in areas with a temperate climate; in the subtropics, in the open air. Important cultivating areas are Israel and South Africa.

CARE: When purchased, the first flowers of the raceme should be open. Cut off a bit of the stem. Use very clean water and add cut-flower food to it.

KEEPING PROPERTIES: 2-3 weeks.

USE: It has been gaining popularity as a modern cut flower in recent years. Used in a vase to a limited extent; chiefly used in flower arrangement.

SCENT: None.

Muscari armeniacum

Ornithogalum thyrsoides
Chincherinchee, Star of Bethlehem

NAME: See *O. arabicum*. *Thyrsoides* = plume-shaped.

DESCRIPTION: Bulbous plant with a stem length of 30-35 cm and fairly wide leaves. The 20-30 flowers are grouped in a pyramidal raceme; they are white, with a yellow-edged olive-green spot. The ovary is green.

ORIGIN: South Africa; first cultivated in the Netherlands in 1605. After 1950, its importance as a cut flower increased.

CULTIVATION: Cut-flower growers in temperate and subtropical areas.

AVAILABILITY: All the year round, with a peak in late summer and autumn.

CARE: When purchased, the first flower should just be opening. Cut off a bit of the stem; use cut-flower food.

KEEPING PROPERTIES: 3-4 weeks. A strong flower which withstands transport very well.

USE: In a vase and in mixed bouquets. The flowers are sometimes dyed in many shades of red, orange, yellow, blue and green.

SCENT: None.

Ruscus hypoglossum
Butcher's broom

NAME: *Ruscus* is the ancient Latin name for an allied species; *hypoglossum* means 'bearing a tongue', a reference to the small bract by each flower cluster.

DESCRIPTION: Evergreen shrub with leaf-like flattened stems (cladodes). They are 3-5 cm long, ovate and soft-textured. Clusters of small greenish-white flowers are borne in the centre of the cladodes - often on the underside.

ORIGIN: South-western Europe; first cultivated in England in 1594.

CULTIVATION: Mostly in Israel, to a lesser extent in southwestern Europe.

AVAILABILITY: All the year round, but especially between October and April.

CARE: Cut off the bottom of the stem; use cut-flower food.

KEEPING PROPERTIES: If it has not dried out, 4-6 weeks.

USE: Chiefly because of the ornamental value of the foliage, it is used with *Cymbidiums*, for example, to fill them out.

SCENT: None.

Tricyrtis hirta
Toad lily

NAME: The genus name is derived from the Greek words *tri* (= three) and *kurlos* (= crooked or humped). The name refers to the three outer perianth petals which have a bulge, a 'hump'. *Hirta* means 'having short hairs'.

DESCRIPTION: Perennial plant with creeping root-stock with hairy green stems which are branched at the top. The leaves are elongated, pointed and downy; the bases of the upper ones embrace the stem. The flowers, 2.5-3 cm wide, grow in short racemes and stand out somewhat; they show red spots on a pink to white background. The perianth petals are straight, except the three outer ones, which have a spur-like bulge at the base.

ORIGIN: Japan; first cultivated in the Netherlands in 1860.

CULTIVATION: In temperate areas with outdoor cut-flower cultivation.

AVAILABILITY: August-October.

CARE: When purchased, the first flowers should be open. Cut off a bit of the stem; use cut-flower food for herbaceous plants.

KEEPING PROPERTIES: 6-12 days.

USE: *Tricyrtis* has been gaining in popularity as a cut-flower in recent years. It is chiefly used in flower arrangement and in mixed bouquets.

SCENT: None.

Ruscus hypoglossum

Tricyrtis hirta

Triteleia 'Queen Fabiola'
Brodiaea

NAME: *Triteleia* is a contraction of the Greek words *tri* (= three) and *teleios* (= perfect) and refers to the three stigmas in which the style of the flower ends.
DESCRIPTION: Bulbous plant with linear leaves and a long flower stem (50-60 cm). At the end of it stands a large umbel of deep blue flowers, 3 cm long; they have triangular stamens. 'Queen Fabiola' is the most frequently grown cultivar.
ORIGIN: California; first cultivated in the United Kingdom in 1888. The cultivar 'Queen Fabiola' was raised in the Netherlands.
CULTIVATION: Temperate areas with bulb flower cultivation.
AVAILABILITY: April-late June.
CARE: When purchased, three flowers of the umbel should be open. Cut off a bit of the stem; use cut-flower food for bulb flowers.
KEEPING PROPERTIES: 15-20 days.
USE: In a vase, in mixed bouquets and in flower arrangement.
SCENT: Slight.

Triteleia laxa
Brodiaea

NAME: See *T*. 'Queen Fabiola'. *Laxa* means 'loose' or 'thin'.
DESCRIPTION: Bulbous plant with narrow, linear leaves and a thin but strong flower stem, 30-45 cm long. At the end of it stands an umbel of 10 dark blue flowers. The perianth segments are just as long or somewhat shorter than the flower tube; the thread-like stamens stand in two rows of three.
ORIGIN: United States, from California to Oregon. The plant was first cultivated in the United Kingdom at the beginning of the last century.
CULTIVATION: Temperate areas with bulb flower cultivation, especially the Netherlands.
AVAILABILITY: April-early July.
CARE: When purchased, three flowers should be open. Cut off a bit of the stem; use cut-flower food for bulb flowers.
KEEPING PROPERTIES: 12-18 days.
USE: In a vase, in mixed bouquets and in flower arrangement.
SCENT: Slight.

Tulipa
Tulip

NAME: The genus name may be derived from the word 'turban', a head covering in Turkey and Iran. It refers to the shape of the flower.
DESCRIPTION: The tulip is a bulbous plant with a single flower stem which, at least in the tulips used as cut flowers, bears one flower. It is composed of two whorls of three petals, two whorls of three stamens and a stigma with a superior ovary. All present cultivars, and there are thousands, were obtained from crosses of a few species: they are often still recognizable in the various cultivar groups. The colour assortment is very large and consists of all shades of red, pink, salmon, lilac, purple and yellow; in addition, there are white and bi-coloured or multi-coloured cultivars.
ORIGIN: The genus comprises over 100 species: they are native to Turkey, Asia Minor, Iran, Turkestan and Syria. One of the most important ancestors of the present cultivated tulips was *T. gesneriana*, which was cultivated before 1559. The development of the modern assortment took place for the most part in the Netherlands; which has been the most important tulip country in the world for several hundred years.
CULTIVATION: The western part of the Netherlands, chiefly the provinces of North and South Holland and the IJsselmeer Polders.
AVAILABILITY: Thanks to temperature treatment of the bulbs, tulips can be brought to blossom the year round. There is little demand during the summer months, however. The supply in September, October and November consists chiefly of 'iced tulips'. These are the flowers of bulbs which are kept below freezing point and whose bloom (normally in spring) can thus be postponed until autumn.
CARE: In some cultivars, the buds should show some colour when purchased; in others, the flower should be entirely coloured, but not yet open. Add special cut-flower food for tulips to the water.
KEEPING PROPERTIES: 5-8 days (average).
USE: Especially in a vase, in mixed spring bouquets and in flower arrangements. Tulips combine well with daffodils; in this case, you may also use special cut-flower food for tulips.
SCENT: Generally none; some old-fashioned early-flowering cultivars such as the orange tulip 'Generaal de Wet' are scented.

Cultivars
The large number of tulip cultivars, by now many thousands, can be classified according to the original blossoming time in early-blooming, mid-season-blooming and late-blooming cultivars - although nowadays it is possible to get them to blossom at any time of the year. All kinds of shapes and types are represented in the classification into the blossoming period. Naturally, we can only give a small selection here.

Early-blooming cultivars
A few early tulips
These are crosses of *T. gesneriana* from Iran and *T. suaveolens* from Asia Minor. They are among the oldest cultivar groups. Originally they were of great significance because they could be brought to blossom early. Their economic importance has decreased because now other cultivar groups can also be brought to blossom early by controlling the temperature.
'**Christmas Marvel**' is a cherry-red single early tulip which is often used for early blossoming. It keeps a long time, and is in sixth place in the top ten of the tulip assortment.
'**Brilliant Star**', the 'Christmas tulip', has bright red flowers and is sold with bulb and all, usually around mid-December.

Double early tulips
These tulips have been under cultivation since 1613, but still form only 4 per cent of the acreage. In the hothouse, they blossom as early as February/March; outdoors, they are among the earliest flowering cultivars.
'**Monte Carlo**' is the most frequently cultivated double early tulip and fifth in the top ten. The flower is bright yellow and beautifully filled; the stem is rather short.

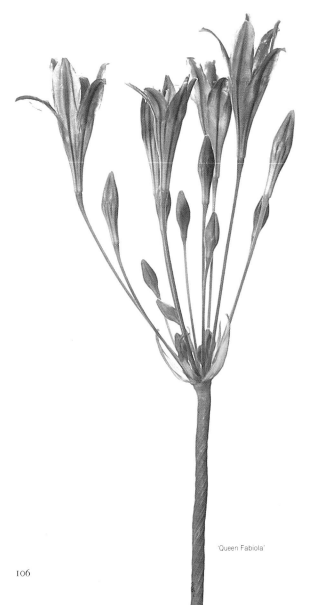

'Queen Fabiola'

'White Dream'

Mid-season-blooming cultivars

This, largest, cultivar group of the tulip assortment is classified into several types:

Mendel tulips

This tulip type is a cross between the very early blossoming, low and small-flowered 'Duc van Tol' tulips with the long-stemmed, large-flowered and late blossoming Darwin tulips (see below). The object of the cross, obtained in 1921 by Haarlem resident Krelage, was an early-blooming tulip with a long stem and a large flower. This type has by now lost much of its significance. The most frequently marketed cultivar is the apricot-coloured tulip '**Apricot Beauty**'.

Triumph tulips

This cross, too, was obtained by Krelage, with the same object as with the Mendel tulips. Triumph tulips are crosses of a few early tulips with late-blossoming Darwin, Breeder and Cottage tulips. The first Triumph tulips were traded in 1918; they are more substantial of build than the Mendel tulips. Some cultivars are two-coloured, such as '**Lustige Witwe**', deep red with white margins and no. 3 in the top ten of the tulip assortment. Number 2 on the list: the bright red Triumph tulip '**Prominence**'. '**Kees Nelis**' is an excellent Triumph tulip which will keep a long time. The flower is red-flamed on a yellow background.

Darwin hybrids

This group of very large-flowering and long-stemmed tulips came about from a cross of Darwin tulips (see below) with the very early-blossoming flame-coloured *T. fosteriana*. This group contains the two most popular tulips of the present assortment:

'**Apeldoorn**', a frequently cultivated tulip for cutting (4th in the top ten), is bright red and has a black receptacle. When purchased, its buds should show good colour. If this is not the case, the tulip was harvested too early and its keeping quality (which is barely sufficient anyway) is poor. Disadvantages of the cultivar: large and distracting coarse leaves, and flower stems which definitely hang from the vase.

'**Golden Apeldoorn**' is a golden yellow Darwin hybrid, also with a black receptacle. This cultivar, first in the top ten, comprises 8-9 per cent of the total cut tulip supply. The characteristics are the same as those of the 'Apeldoorn'.

Late-blooming cultivars

In this category there are numerous cultivar groups of which we will discuss only a few here.

A few late or Cottage tulips

A group of large-flowering tulips with long stems; they are less suitable for early blossoming.

'**White Dream**' is the most important of this group. The flower is white and can blossom as early as the end of December, although the main supply comes in February.

'**Queen of the Night**' has nearly black blooms; it is cultivated only on a limited scale.

Lily-flowering tulips

The flower shape of this type was already known in 1613. They are crosses of Darwin tulips with *T. retroflexa*. Despite the long stems and the lovely flower shapes, these tulips make up only 1.5 per cent of the acreage. They are not suited to early blossoming. Well-known cultivars are '**Aladdin**' (red with orange-red margins), '**West Point**' (yellow) and '**Queen of Sheba**' (red with yellow margins). The best-known lily-flowering tulip, however, is '**China Pink**', pink and with a long sturdy stem. The leaves are not too large and it keeps very well.

Darwin tulips

The Darwin tulips were first traded in Flanders (Belgium) in 1889. They are lovely, long-stemmed tulips with large, shiny and somewhat angular flowers. They keep particularly long, but have become less important economically because of the slow growth and the ensuing high production costs.

Fringed tulips

A fairly new group of cultivars, the supply of which is limited. They are extremely lovely tulips, the petal margins of which are covered with crystal-like fringe.

Viridiflora tulips

The perianth petals of these tulips are partially green and the rest is red, pink or yellow. This gives a bizarre and frivolous colour play, which is chiefly valued in modern flower arrangement.

Rembrandt tulips

Rembrandt tulips have red, white or yellow flowers with conspicuous bronze, black, purple, red or pink striped markings. The most frequently cultivated of this type is '**Cordell Hull**' with a carmine-coloured flower and creamy white markings.

Parakeet tulips

A groups of cultivars of limited cultivation; the flowers are so large that the stems can scarcely hold them up when they flower. The most striking aspects of the parakeet tulips are the irregularly cut and gaily shaped perianth petals and the streaky two-toned colouring of the flower. The best-known cultivars are '**Erna Lindgreen**' (red) and '**Karel Doorman**' (cherry red with yellow). '**Estella Rijnveld**' is a coming cultivar.

Double late tulips

Because of the filled-out flower shape, the group is sometimes called the peony-flowering tulips. They are cultivated on a very limited scale. The best known cultivar is '**Bonanza**': it has large, beautifully filled red with yellow flowers.

'Aladdin'   'Cordell Hull'   'Bonanza'   'Estella Rijnveld'

Loranthaceae

Lythraceae

The scientific name of the mistletoe family (*Laranthaceae*) is taken from that of the genus *Loranthus* (literally, 'belt flower') and refers to the shape of the perianth segments in the species of this genus. The family contains around 35 genera and some 1300 species, most of which grow in the tropics. They are dicotyledonous evergreen plants and live as semi-parasites on their host, usually a tree. Their strongly branched roots penetrate into the host and remove water and minerals from its tissue. Although they also make their own food (by assimilating carbon dioxide through their leathery green leaves) they can cause great damage, especially in the tropics, on citrus plantations, for example. The flowers are unisexual or hermaphrodite; the fruits are mostly berries or stone fruits and issue from the unilocular ovary. The seed has a sticky coating which sticks to the beaks of the birds that eat the fruits. This is how the seeds are spread.

The loosestrife family (*Lythraceae*) is mostly tropical of origin, although some of the 450 species come from temperate climate zones. The approximately 20 genera include herbaceous plants as well as trees and shrubs. They are dicotyledonous plants with simple and smooth-margined leaves which are opposite in most species, but sometimes arranged in whorls. The flowers, usually regular, are grouped in racemes or in compound umbels. They have four or six sepals and petals and eight or twelve stamens. The petals, wrinkled in the bud, are free-standing on the edge of the base of the calyx. The stamens stand at varying heights in the base of the corolla. The ovary is superior and has two to six cavities.

The family is subdivided into two groups of genera, the *Lythreae* and the *Nessaeae*. The former is the more important for cut-flower cultivation.

Viscum album
Mistletoe

NAME: *Viscum* means 'sticky' and refers to the sticky coating of the seeds. *Album* = white; the colour of the berries.
DESCRIPTION: A semi-parasitic plant on trees, preferably apple and poplar, but also on the mountain ash or rowan tree, and the hawthorn or may tree. The plant is evergreen and has forked branches; it blooms in February/March. The flowers have no ornamental value. The male ones are inconspicuous and consist only of four yellowish-green scales, each with a single stamen; the female ones have an inferior ovary with a sessile stigma. Mistletoe derives its ornamental value from the single-seeded, shiny white berries which develop from this ovary. They contain *viscotoxin*, a potentially dangerous substance, and should be kept away from children.
ORIGIN: North Africa and parts of Europe where the winters are not too severe; also in the Netherlands and Belgium.
CULTIVATION: Mistletoe is not cultivated but collected in the wild, chiefly in France.

AVAILABILITY: November-December.
CARE: The branches will keep well in or out of water. If in water, use cut-flower food for shrubs.
KEEPING PROPERTIES: 4-6 weeks.
USE: In flower arrangement. In the United Kingdom, mistletoe is primarily associated with Christmas decorations.
SCENT: None.

Viscum album

Lythrum salicaria
Purple loosestrife

NAME: The genus name is derived from the Greek *luthron* (= clotted blood) and refers to the flower's colour. *Salicaria* = resembling the willow; it refers to the leaf shape.
DESCRIPTION: Perennial, 1 to 1.20 m high and with ovate-lanceolate, somewhat pilose leaves. The dark red flowers, with a diameter of 1-1.5 cm, stand in verticillasters all along the spike-shaped inflorescence. The calyx teeth vary in length. There are several *Lythrum* cultivars, all of them rose-red shades.
ORIGIN: Northern hemisphere. The plant was first cultivated in England in 1596.
CULTIVATION: Temperate areas with outdoor cut-flower cultivation.
AVAILABILITY: From June until September.
CARE: When purchased, around one-fourth of the flowers on the stem should be open. Remove lower leaves, cut off a bit of the stem, use cut-flower food for herbaceous plants.
KEEPING PROPERTIES: 12-16 days.
USE: In a vase and in mixed bouquets.
SCENT: None.

Malvaceae

The mallow family (*Malvaceae*) is divided into around 80 genera and more than 1000 species. One of them, the cotton plant (*Gossypium* sp.), is of great economic importance. The *Hibiscus* genus (China rose or rose mallow) is very important to flower cultivation; it has around 300 species. The *Malvaceae* can be found all over the world, although most of them grow in South America. They are all dicotyledonous shrubs, trees or herbaceous plants. The leaves are alternate; they have stipules, and often hair formations as well. The regular flowers are hermaphrodite and pentamerous. The sepals, sometimes fused, are often surrounded by a secondary calyx. The flower has five free-standing petals, and the numerous stamens are fused into a long tube. The anther has a lobe. The ovary consists of five or more carpels; the fruit is a capsule or a schizocarp, and the seeds often bear hairs. Opinions are divided on the sub-classification of this family.

Lythrum salicaria

'Else Heugh'

Sidalcea malviflora
Prairie mallow

NAME: *Sidalcea* is a contraction of the names of two other plant genera to which *S. malviflora* bears a resemblance, *Sida* and *Alcea* (obsolete name for the genus of *Malva*). *Malviflora* means 'having flowers like the mallow'.

DESCRIPTION: Perennial, 80-100 cm high, with kidney-shaped leaves. The lower ones are deeply dentate; the upper ones have five linear lobes. The flowers, 4-5 cm wide, are arranged in spike-shaped racemes; in the frequently cultivated cultivar 'Else Heugh', they are a pale pink. There are also rose red, carmine red and white prairie mallows.

ORIGIN: The western United States.

CULTIVATION: Temperate areas with outdoor cut-flower cultivation.

AVAILABILITY: July-early September.

CARE: When purchased, the first flower should be open. Remove lower leaves, cut off a bit of the stem, use cut-flower food for herbaceous plants: the buds on the side branches will then flower as well.

KEEPING PROPERTIES: 10-16 days.

USE: In a vase, in mixed bouquets and in flower arrangement.

SCENT: None.

Marantaceae

Musaceae

The *Marantaceae*, a family of monocotyledonous herbaceous plants, are related to the banana family (*Musaceae*), the ginger family (*Zingiberacea*) and the canna family (*Cannaceae*). Most of them are native to tropical America; they also have representatives in Africa and Asia, however.

The *Marantaceae* all have underground root-stocks or radical tubers. The leaves, which stand in two rows, have a spathe-like leaf stem which is sometimes winged and almost always swollen at the transition to the leaf blade. The veins are pinnate and run parallel to the central vein. The inflorescence, a spike or a plume, is partly encircled by a bract. The flowers themselves are rather inconspicuous, having two whorls of three perianth petals. The stamens, on the base of the corolla, consist of one fertile stamen with one anther and several distorted infertile ones. The ovary is inferior, has one style and three cavities, one or two of which do not mature. The fruit is fleshy; the seeds have a coloured appendage.

The genera *Calathea*, *Ctenanthe*, *Maranta* and *Stromanthe* are cultivated for the ornamental value of the leaves. Only the first genus plays a role in cut-flower cultivation.

Calathea lancifolia, syn. *C. insignis* **Rattlesnake plant**

NAME: *Calathea* is derived from the Greek word *kalathos*; it means 'basket' and refers to the shape of the inflorescence. *Lancifolia* = having lanceolate leaves.

DESCRIPTION: The plant, which can grow up to 1 m high, has long lanceolate leaves. They bear dark green oval spots which decrease in size from the central vein towards the side veins. The largest ones extend to the leaf margin. The underside of the leaf is pale purple. This leaf gives the plant its ornamental value.

ORIGIN: Brazil. The plant was first cultivated in the United Kingdom in 1905.

CULTIVATION: On a limited scale, in hothouse cultivation.

AVAILABILITY: The year round.

CARE: The leaf should be fully grown when purchased. Cut off a bit of the stem; use very clean water.

KEEPING PROPERTIES: 12-15 days.

USE: In flower arrangement.

SCENT: None.

Calathea makoyana **Peacock plant**

NAME: See *C. lancifolia*. The sort is named after the Liège (Belgium) florist, Jacob Makoy. This company was started in the 19th century by Lambert Jacob (1790-1873), one of the founding fathers of Belgian and European flower cultivation.

DESCRIPTION: A foliage plant with elongated oval leaves which are sometimes even 60 cm long. On the upper side, along the central vein, they bear dark spots of varying size. The leaf margins are dark green; the rest of the leaf, in between the spots, is pale green and translucent. The underside is purple and the markings of the upper side vaguely show through. The brown petiole is around 30 cm long. The flowers are grouped in spikes and have white-edged bracts.

ORIGIN: Eastern Brazil; introduced in Belgium in 1871.

CULTIVATION: On a limited scale, in the hothouse, as a foliage plant. Quite a lot in the Netherlands.

AVAILABILITY: All the year round.

CARE: When purchased, the leaves should be fully grown. Cut off a bit of the stem; use very clean water.

KEEPING PROPERTIES: 12-15 days.

USE: In flower arrangement, for the ornamental value of the leaf.

SCENT: None

The *Musaceae* or banana family are a small family of herbaceous plants which are classified into six genera and around 95 species. They grow in West and South Africa, South America and, in Asia, from India to Indonesia. The 'stem' consists of closely connected leaf spathes. The leaves are opposite or alternate; they have a thick central vein and numerous feathery side veins.

The irregular and usually unisexual flowers are composed of two whorls of petal-like perianth petals, five stamens and one fused infertile stamen. The pollen is sticky. The pollination of some species is performed by bats.

The ovary is inferior and has three cavities with three fused carpels. The fruit is a fleshy berry with a large number of seeds. The genera *Strelizia* and *Heliconia*, both of importance in cut-flower cultivation, are sometimes considered a separate family, the *Strelitziaceae*. They have hermaphrodite flowers on a long-stemmed inflorescence which is encircled by a boat-shaped bract. The perianth consists of two whorls of three petals. The petals of the outer whorl are more or less the same shape; the inner whorl consists of two unequal parts and an elongated perianth petal which is folded around the style. The flower has five stamens. The trilocular ovary is inferior; the seeds sometimes have a coloured appendage.

Calathea makoyana

Heliconia rostrata
Hanging lobster claw
NAME: See *H. humilis. Rostrata* from the Latin *rostrum* = beak; the flower has the shape of a beak.
DESCRIPTION: A plant, up to 3 m high, with banana-like leaves. The inflorescence is located on a long, pendulous stem and contains 25 or more boat-shaped flowers. The bracts are scarlet, with yellow points.
ORIGIN: Peru.
CULTIVATION: In the tropics, in Africa and a great deal in Central America.
AVAILABILITY: Chiefly summer and late summer.
CARE: Cut off a bit of the stem; use cut-flower food.
KEEPING PROPERTIES: 3-4 weeks.
USE: In flower arrangement, in decorations.
SCENT: None.

Strelitzia reginae
Bird of paradise flower
NAME: Named after Charlotte Sophia von Mecklenburg-Strelitz, who married King George III of England in 1761.
DESCRIPTION: Herbaceous plant with large basal and arched leaves, bluish-green in colour and with somewhat frilled edges. The leaf stem is around three times as long as the leaf itself. The flower stems are nearly as long as the leaves. At the end of the stems is a horizontal boat-shaped bract which encircles 4-6 erect flowers, which are orange with blue.
ORIGIN: South Africa; first cultivated in the United Kingdom in 1773.
CULTIVATION: Much on the French and Italian Riviera; also elsewhere, in the hothouse.
AVAILABILITY: When purchased, the first flower should be open. Cut off a bit of the stem; use cut-flower food.
CARE: From the end of August until March, with a peak in November.
KEEPING PROPERTIES: 12-18 days.
USE: Primarily in flower arrangement and in decorations.
SCENT: None.

Heliconia psittacorum
Parrot flower
NAME: See *H. humilis. Psittacorum* means 'visited by parrots'.
DESCRIPTION: Perennial plant, up to 1.50 m high and with lanceolate, leathery leaves. The flower stems are 1-1.50 m long. The actual flowers are greenish-yellow, but the plant primarily derives its ornamental value from the 6-10 cm long bracts. Depending on the cultivar, they can exhibit various colour combinations: for example, orange with a red top, or cream with a yellow top. The cultivars 'Helena' (orange) and 'Rosea' (pink with cream-coloured top) are the most frequently cultivated.
ORIGIN: From the coast of Guyana to inland Brazil.
CULTIVATION: All areas with hothouse flower cultivation.
AVAILABILITY: Chiefly from June until October.
CARE: When purchased, the lower two bracts should protrude. Cut off a bit of the stem; use cut-flower food.
KEEPING PROPERTIES: 8-14 days.
USE: In a vase and in flower arrangement.
SCENT: None.

Heliconia bihai
Firebird, Wild plantain
NAME: See *H. humilis. Bihai* is the original Indian popular name.
DESCRIPTION: Elongated oval erect leaves with a leaf stem of around 2 m. The flower spike is borne on a long stem and is ± 60 cm long. The flower itself is orangish-red in colour; the bracts are red and yellow.
ORIGIN: From Central America to Brazil; first cultivated in England in 1786.
CULTIVATION: Tropical Africa (Ivory Coast, Kenya) and tropical South America.
AVAILABILITY: Nearly the year round, with a peak in September-October; little supply between the end of December and June.
CARE: Cut off a bit of the stem; use cut-flower food.
KEEPING PROPERTIES: 3-4 weeks.
USE: Especially in flower arrangement.
SCENT: Generally none; sometimes an odour of decay between the bracts.

Heliconia psittacorum

Strelitzia reginae

Myrtaceae

A large family of dicotyledonous evergreen shrubs and trees from the tropics and subtropics, chiefly America and Australia, the *Myrtaceae* include around 100 genera and 3000 species. The leathery leaves have smooth margins and are opposite or alternate.

The regular formed flowers are hermaphrodite and are usually grouped in an inflorescence. The four or five sepals are generally free-standing, or form a hood which falls off before the bloom. Sometimes they are underdeveloped or even absent. The four or five small, round petals are usually free-standing. In the eucalyptus sorts, however, they are somewhat fused and fall off as a whole. The numerous stamens frequently stand in bundles opposite the leaves. The connective often has a glandular top. The ovary is generally inferior; the style is long and has a club-shaped stigma. In most cases, the fruit is a fleshy berry or a nut.

Eucalyptus globulus

Eucalyptus cinerea
Silver dollar tree

NAME: The genus name is composed of the Greek words *eu* (= good) and *kalyptos* (= covered) and refers to the fused petals which cover the stigma and stamens before the flowering. *Cinerea*, from the Latin *cinis*, means 'ashen grey' and refers to the colour of the plant.
DESCRIPTION: An elegantly shaped tree, 5-7 m high and with round, silvery-grey leaves (which give it its name). The stem and branches are dark brownish-red. The leaves that are used in flower arrangement come from the juvenile form. Adult trees often have elongated oval leaves with a yellow central vein.
ORIGIN: Australia, especially New South Wales and Victoria. First cultivated in the United Kingdom around 1815.
CULTIVATION: United States, Israel.
AVAILABILITY: The year round.
CARE: Cut off the lower bit of the stem, use cut-flower food for shrubs. beanches. The branches are sometimes very dirty with dust etc. Always change the water when it becomes cloudy. The leafy branches are sometimes treated with glycerine to make them keep longer.
KEEPING PROPERTIES: Approx. 3 weeks.
USE: In bouquets and floral work.
SCENT: Aromatic.

Eucalyptus globulus
Southern blue gum, Tasmanian blue gum

NAME: See *E. cinerea*. *Globulus* = sphere and refers to the shape of the flower buds.
DESCRIPTION: A large tree with thick leathery leaves which smell of eucalyptus oil when bruised. In young plants they are heart-shaped. The simple flowers grow out of the leaf axils. The silver-coloured receptacle and the cover are angular, and covered with warts. The red flower only becomes visible when the cover opens.
ORIGIN: South Australia, Tasmania; first cultivated in the United Kingdom around 1820.
CULTIVATION: Chiefly on the French and Italian Riviera.
AVAILABILITY: November-December.
CARE: See *E. cinerea*.
KEEPING PROPERTIES: 3-4 weeks.
USE: Chiefly in floral work for Christmas.
SCENT: Highly aromatic.

Chamelaucium uncinatum
Geraldton waxplant

NAME: The genus name is derived from the Latin *chamae*, which means 'remaining low'. *Uncinatum* = having hooks, hook-shaped.
DESCRIPTION: Semi-shrub of 1.50-2 m high, with thin, narrow, leathery leaves. In the leaf axils grow tiny lilac-rose or red flowers (about 6 mm). There is also a white form.
ORIGIN: Western Australia.
CULTIVATION: Subtropical areas, especially Israel.
AVAILABILITY: From October until May, with a peak between the end of December and the end of February.
CARE: Cut off a bit of the branch, put them in water of approx. 40° C and use cut-flower food for shrubs.
KEEPING PROPERTIES: 12-18 days.

USE: In bouquets and in flower arrangement.
SCENT: The leaves are sweetly aromatic when bruised.

Eucalyptus cinera

Nepenthaceae

Nephrolepidaceae

The pitcher plant family (*Nepenthaceae*) has only one genus (*Nepenthes*) which contains around 70 species. All of them are epiphytes (= living on other plants but not parasitic) and they feed themselves with insects which they catch in their pitchers. They are native to the tropical areas of the Old World, with Borneo as the centre.

The alternate leaves have no clear leaf stem. The central vein extends into a tendril, which grows out to a pitcher with lid; this opens when the pitcher is fully grown. The edge of the pitcher is curved inward. Insects are attracted by the red and shiny green colours of the beaker as well as by nectaries at the entrance to the pitcher. Below these nectaries, the pitcher's walls are quite slippery. Insects cannot get a hold on it, and fall into the water at the bottom of the pitcher. There they drown and are digested, after which the plant absorbs the dissolved nutrients. The pitchers can reach a length of 15 cm and may even contain up to 2 litres of water.

The flowers (usually white, but in some sorts green, yellow or red) are dioecious and arranged in a spike-shaped inflorescence. The perianth consists of 3-4 sepals. In the male flowers, the filaments of the 4-24 stamens are fused to form a pillar. The female flowers have one disc-shaped stigma on a short style. The ovary has four cavities. The light seeds have hair-like appendages and are encased in a capsule.

The *Nephrolepidaceae* family, which has only one genus (*Nephrolepis*), belongs to the very extensive class of the *Polypodinae*, the fern tribe. This class contains some 11,500 different ferns in all.

The ferns are among the lower plants; they do not reproduce themselves by means of seeds, but with spores. The subclassification of the *Polypodinae* takes place based on the shape and the location of these spores.

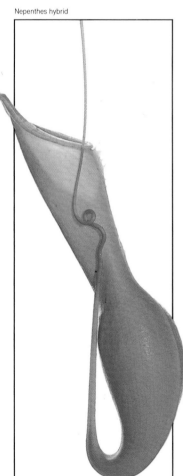

Nepenthes hybrid

Nepenthes hybrids
Pitcher plant
NAME: The genus name is composed of the Greek words *ne* (= deny, negate) and *penthos* (= sadness, sorrow). It is derived from the name of a magic potion which made a person forget all suffering. The name alludes to the water in the pitcher, which is clear and potable as long as the lid is closed.
DESCRIPTION: The foliage of this epiphytic plant consists of a leaf-like, widened, somewhat pendulous stem with at the top an erect pitcher with a cover. The upper edge of the pitcher is curved inwards. The colour of the pitcher is green; it is 10-20 cm long.
ORIGIN: Tropical rain forests of Asia (Borneo, New Guinea, Sumatra). The Nepenthes hybrids were chiefly obtained before 1914 from crosses of sorts such as *N. psitticina*, *N. hookeriana*, *N. mirabilis* and many others.
CULTIVATION: Much in the United States; elsewhere on a limited scale in the hothouse.
AVAILABILITY: The year round.
CARE: Put them in very clean water.
KEEPING PROPERTIES: Several weeks.
USE: Modern flower arrangement, for exclusive work.
SCENT: None.

Nephrolepis exaltata
Sword fern, Boston fern
NAME: *Nephrolepis* means 'kidney-shaped scale' and refers to the scale-shaped membranes over the spores. *Exaltata* = very high, and refers to the long leaves.
DESCRIPTION: Fern with shoots. The leaves can reach a length of 1 m and are 6-15 cm wide; they stand on green, slightly pilose stems. The leaflets of which the leaf is composed are close together along the shiny, dark stem. The spores are on the underside, near the leaf margins. Frequently cultivated cultivars are, in addition to the species 'Maassii', 'Teddy Junior' and 'Rooseveltii Plumosa'.
ORIGIN: All tropical areas. First described in the United Kingdom in 1793.

CULTIVATION: United States and in areas with hothouse plant cultivation.
AVAILABILITY: The year round.
CARE: Upon purchase, the top of the leaf should be fully grown. Use cut-flower food in half the usual concentration; cut off a bit of the stem.
KEEPING PROPERTIES: 12-15 days.
USE: As leafy material in bouquets and in flower arrangement.
SCENT: None.

Nephrolepis exaltata

Nymphaeaceae

Oleaceae

The water lily family (*Nymphaeaceae*) has representatives all over the world, although it has only nine genera and a little over 90 species. They are all dicotyledonous perennial water plants with root-stocks. The simple flowers have three to six stamens and three or even many more petals; in some genera, these petals turn into numerous stamens. Water lilies have 5-35 carpels; they are superior or inferior, and sometimes fused. The flowers, often lovely, are generally pollinated by beetles or flies. The fruit is a spongy berry which springs open when its slimy contents swell. The seeds often have a coloured appendage.
The genus *Nelumbo* is sometimes considered to be a separate family.

Nelumbo nucifera
East Indian lotus
NAME: *Nelumbo* is the original Ceylonese name of the plant. *Nucifera* means 'bearing nuts'.
DESCRIPTION: Water plant with creeping root-stock and fairly large, round leaves which generally protrude a little above the water. The fragrant pink flowers have white centres. After pollination, the receptacle, with numerous seeds, is formed. It is this receptacle that is used, dried, in flower arrangement.

ORIGIN: Tropical and subtropical Asia; the plant has been under cultivation since ancient times.
CULTIVATION: Harvested in the wild, in Egypt and in the Far East and elsewhere.
AVAILABILITY: The year round (dried).
CARE: Not applicable.
KEEPING PROPERTIES: Very long.
USE: For decoration in flower arrangement.
SCENT: None.

Nelumbo nucifera

The olive family (*Oleaceae*) is a group of dicotyledonous trees, shrubs and climbing plants which are found all over the world but are the most numerous in South-east Asia and Australia. Some species are evergreen, others lose their leaves. Some members of the olive family are covered with scaly or ordinary hairs, which give them a greyish or silver-coloured appearance. The leaves are generally opposite and have no stipules; they can be simple, pinnate or ternate. The inflorescence is often a two-branched compound umbel of which both side axes are filled out; it looks like a raceme or plume. The flowers are nearly always hermaphrodite. They usually have four, sometimes six or twelve petals; they are free-standing or are fused to form a tube. The two or four stamens have short filaments and are attached to the petals. The superior ovary consists of two fused carpels and has two cavities. The style has a two-lobed or bifurcated stigma. The shape of the fruit varies.
The olive family is divided into two subfamilies, the *Forsythieae* and the *Jasminoideae*.

Forsythia x intermedia
Golden bell
NAME: The genus is named after the Scot, W. Forsyth (1737-1804), director of the Royal Gardens in Kensington and author of a number of works on fruit trees. *Intermedia* means 'midway between' and refers to a combination of ancestral characteristics in this hybrid.
DESCRIPTION: A shrub with branches up to 2.5 m long, yellowish-green in colour and having a laddered pith. The leaves are elongated ovate and serrate. The yellow flowers, which appear earlier than the leaves, are arranged in groups; their calyx slips are shorter than the corolla.
ORIGIN: *F. x intermedia*, obtained in 1889, is a German cross of *F. suspensa* (long, weak branches and beautiful flowers) and *F. viridissima* (sturdy, straight branches, inconspicuous flowers). The hybrid combines the branches of the latter with the flowers of the former.
CULTIVATION: Especially in the Netherlands: shrub hothouses in the vicinity of Aalsmeer.
AVAILABILITY: From the end of November until March. If the branches are cooled, they can be made to flower the year round.
CARE: Cut off a bit of the stem; use cut-flower food for woody plants; constantly keep the water clean.
KEEPING PROPERTIES: 10-14 days.
USE: In a vase and for decorations; the lighter branches also in mixed bouquets.
SCENT: None.

Cultivars
'**Spectabilis**' is a selection from 1906 by German tree nurseryman Spaeth. The large flowers are golden yellow, the flower petals are pointed and form a sort of tube. The style is short. This cultivar, the only one for years, has been losing popularity recently.
'**Lynwood**' or '**Lynwood Hold**' is a cultivar which originated in the United Kingdom around 1940; nothing more is known about its origin. The bright yellow flowers have a flat bell shape and bear wide, blunt flower slips. The short shoots on which the flowers grow are more regular in form than those of 'Spectabilis'. The twigs of this cultivar are hollow, the pith on the buds is smoother and the leaf margins are entire.

Forsythia x intermedia

'Andenken an Ludwig Späth'

Syringa vulgaris
Lilac

NAME: The genus name is derived from *seringa*, the popular name for this flower on the island of Crete in the second half of the 16th century. *Vulgaris* (= common) refers to the general occurrence of the variety in the area where it originated.

DESCRIPTION: Long, leafless branches with two or four flower panicles per branch; they are termed 'heads' in florist jargon, which also speaks of two and four-headers. The white, purple or lilac flower panicles are composed of a large number of small flowers, the 'flower nails'.

ORIGIN: Southern Europe.

CULTIVATION: Netherlands, primarily Aalsmeer.

AVAILABILITY: White lilacs (95 per cent of the supply) from October to April; coloured cultivars especially in February/March.

CARE: When purchased, only the very first flower should be open; the rest of the raceme should still be greenish. Cut off a bit of the stem; use cut-flower food for shrubs and water with a temperature of 13-15° C. Regularly add water with cut-flower food. Coloured cultivars will fade if they were brought to blossom early.

KEEPING PROPERTIES: 10-15 days; longer in a cool, light place.

USE: In a vase, in church decorations, in mourning work and in mixed bouquets.

SCENT: Very fragrant, especially the coloured cultivars.

'Madame Florent Stepman'

△ 'Lavaliensis'   ▽ 'Hugo Koster'

Onagraceae

Representatives of the evening primrose family (*Onagraceae*) are found all over the world, but the variety in this family of dicotyledonous herbaceous plants and shrubs is certainly the largest in the United States and Mexico. The family has 18 genera and around 640 species.

The simple leaves are opposite or alternate; they generally have no stipules. The flowers, unisexual and dioecious or hermaphrodite, stand only in the leaf axils, or are grouped in plumes. Their form is regular and they usually have a differently coloured hollow outgrowth on the receptacle. The flower has two, four or five free-standing sepals and petals. There are usually eight stamens which are grouped in two whorls. The ovary is inferior and usually bilocular; the style is smooth or four-lobed. The flowers are frequently pollinated by butterflies. The fruit is generally a capsule.

Cultivars

'Madame Florent Stepman'
forms over 90 per cent of the total lilac supply. It is a cross of two cultivars from the last century, 'Dr. Lindley' (1859) and 'Marie Legraye' (1879), and was brought on the market in 1908 by the Brussels flower grower Stepman-Messemacher. The cultivar has coarse, bright white florets and straight, not too heavy, branches.
'Andenken an Ludwig Späth'
('Souvenir of Louis Späth') is a lovely dark purple lilac which was obtained in Germany in 1833. The cultivar is exclusively suited to late cultivation (which is highly labour intensive; the flowers are not cheap) and has a strongly scent.

'Lavaliensis' is a lilac-rose lilac; of all present cultivars, this one has the strongest scent. It dates back to 1865. The main supply takes place in February/March.
'Herman Eilers' is a cultivar with large, coarse florets in large panicles. The number of 'heads' per branch is usually not more than two.
'Hugo Koster' is a purple cultivar, suited for early forced blossoming. Demand for it is rapidly increasing; the same is true of a deeper coloured mutant of it.

Clarkia unguiculata,
syn. *C. elegans*
Clarkia, Satin flower
NAME: The genus is named after the American army officer William Clark (1770-1838). He and Meriwether Lewis, private secretary to President Jefferson, crossed North America on horseback (the famous Lewis and Clark expedition), bringing back an important collection of plants, with among them the Clarkia. *Unguiculata* is the diminutive of the Latin *unguis* (= nail) and refers to the shape of the flower. *Elegans* = elegant, decorative.
DESCRIPTION: Annual plant, to 80 cm high and with ovoid lanceolate leaves which are somewhat dentate. The simple flowers grow from the leaf axils. The petals are smooth or slightly dentate; the flowers are not dentate. The flower has eight fertile stamens. Its original colour was lilac-rose. Presumably by crosses with the pink-flowering *C. pulchella*, the colour assortment now includes all shades of pink, salmon and lilac.
ORIGIN: California; first cultivated in the United Kingdom in 1832.
CULTIVATION: Temperate and subtropical areas with outdoor cut flower cultivation.
AVAILABILITY: June-September.
CARE: When purchased, the lowest flower of the raceme should be open. Remove lower leaves, cut off a bit of the stem, use cut flower food for herbaceous plants.
KEEPING PROPERTIES: 6-10 days.
USE: In a vase and in mixed bouquets.
SCENT: None.

Godetia hybrids
Farewell to spring (U.S.A.)
NAME: The genus is named after the Swiss education inspector, C.H. Godet (1797-1879) who published a number of botanical works, including a flora of the Jura.
DESCRIPTION: Annual herbaceous plant, 50-70 cm high, with smooth-margined, ovate lanceolate leaves. The simple blooms grow out of the leaf axils; they have no stems and are pink, lilac, orange or red. The sepals remain attached or fused after it blooms.
ORIGIN: California. This hybrid, first cultivated in the United Kingdom in 1870, is a cross between *G. amoena* and *G. grandiflora*. The latter predominates. These species are now often included in the genus *Clarkia*.
CULTIVATION: Temperate and subtropical areas with outdoor cut-flower cultivation.
AVAILABILITY: July-late September.
CARE: Cut off a bit of the stem; use cut-flower food for herbaceous plants. Farewell to spring is treated before being offered for sale. They are cut when the lower buds are fully grown and show good colour. Then all the leaves are nipped off and the sepals are peeled back, so that the coloured buds become visible.
KEEPING PROPERTIES: 14-18 days.
USE: In a vase; limited in bouquets and in flower arrangement.
SCENT: None.

Orchidaceae

After the composites, the orchids (*Orchidaceae*) are the largest family of the plant kingdom, with around 750 genera, over 20,000 species and a very large number of hybrids and cultivars obtained by crosses. The name of the family is derived from the Greek word for 'testicle' and is based on the root shape of the genus Orchis: two tubers growing in close proximity, of which the old one is drained by the new one that forms on it.

Orchids occur all over the world, with the exception of the polar regions and the deserts. The genera important to cutflower cultivation originally come from Asia (*Cymbidium, Paphiopedilum, Phalaenopsis, Dendrobium, Vanda, Arachnis*) or from South and Central America (*Cattleya* and related genera such as *Laeila* and *Brassavola*; *Odontoglossum, Cochlioda, Miltonia* and *Oncidium*). Orchids from the other continents, such as the European genus *Orchis*, have no importance for flower growing.

Orchids naturally grow *terrestrially* (in the earth) or *epiphytally*, that is, on trees and rocks. The epiphytic varieties have aerial roots which are covered with a tissue layer of dead cells, the *velamen*. They absorb moisture from the air with this membrane. No distinction is made between the two manners of growth in cultivated orchids; all orchids are raised on a uniform soil mixture on the basis of peat, mineral wool and tree bark.

An orchid flower consists of two whorls of three perianth petals, as in so many monocotyledons. The inner whorl, the corolla petals, all have different shapes; the central petal has grown out into a lip, or 'slipper'. The lip generally exhibits beautiful colours and markings. Characteristic of the flower is its stigma column, an organ in which stamens and pistils are fused together. The classification of the family is largely based on the structure of this column. The lobes of the anthers at its tip contain the pollen, which is not powdery in orchids, but lumpy. Below the lobes of the anther is the stigma. In nature they are pollinated by bees, bumblebees, and humming-birds. The seeds are very tiny, consisting of an embryo of only a few cells. One fruit may contain a hundred thousand of these seeds, sometimes even more than a million. The seeds naturally germinate only in symbiosis with a mould, which produces several substances needed by the orchid for germination and growth.

Because it took a very long time for flower growers to unveil the secret of this symbiotic form of cohabitation, and because the development from seed to flowering plant takes a very long time (from three to eight years, depending on the genus), orchid cultivation was long a difficult and very costly affair. This did not change until the development of *in vitro* cultivation on an artificial culture medium. Because all the necessary elements can be added to this culture medium, the presence of the mould is no longer necessary for *in vitro* cultivation. The problem of the variations in seedings was solved after 1960, when tissue culture *in vitro* became possible: the asexual and sterile propagation of orchids from very small bits of plant material.

The genera of the orchids have a remarkable capacity to cross with one another. This makes it possible to breed countless sexual hybrids, such as X *Vuylstekeara*, X *Wilsonara* and X *Odontioda* (X before a genus name means: 'crossbreeding'). Often they are crosses of three or four genera. Orchid species are often crossed as well, resulting in a large number of hybrids and cultivars. Thanks to the great many crosses, the colour variation in the orchid assortment has become very large. Much of the crossing work was and is done by amateurs. The origins of orchid growing lie in the United Kingdom. A very important role was played by the firm Sanders, which sent hundreds of 'orchid hunters' into the jungles of South and

'Arcadian Sunrise Golden Fleece'

Central America and tropical Asia to look for unknown sorts in the 19th century. British amateurs bought up the specimens which survived the long journey to the United Kingdom for their own collections, often at very high prices. Later orchid growing spread to Belgium, the Netherlands and France. Nowadays, in addition to the United Kingdom and the Netherlands, many orchids are cultivated in the United States, Singapore, Thailand and Australia. There are close contacts between amateurs and breeders in all parts of the world; in flower cultivation, orchid growing is a world in itself. All orchid crosses from all over the world are registered in the United Kingdom by the Royal Horticultural Society (RHS) in Sanders List of Orchids.

X Aranda 'Wendy Scott'

NAME: *Aranda* is a compound name derived from the parental genera, *Arachnis* and *Vanda*.
DESCRIPTION: The build of this plant is the same as that of *Vanda*. The flower is a mixture of *Arachnis* and *Vanda*; the appearance of the latter dominates.
ORIGIN: The Aranda is an English cross of *Arachnis flos-aëris* with *Vanda* hybrids whose ancestors are native to Malaysia, Indonesia (including Java) , Thailand and Burma. In addition to 'Wendy Scott', the most frequently grown cultivar is 'Christine'.
CULTIVATION: Chiefly in Thailand. The cultivation requires a great deal of warmth and takes a long time; it is therefore cheaper to import them for the European and American markets than to cultivate them locally in the hothouse.
AVAILABILITY: All the year round.
CARE: After they are cut, the flowers are put in treated water to prevent them from drooping, which is caused by the aging hormone, ethylene. After purchase, put them in water with cut-flower food.
KEEPING PROPERTIES: 18-24 days, if the temperature does not go below 15°C.
USE: In a vase and in flower arrangement.
SCENT: Lightly fragrant.

Arachnis flos-aëris
Scorpion orchid

NAME: The genus name is derived from the Greek word *arachnis*, which means 'spider' and alludes to the shape of the flower. *Flos-aëris* means 'flower of the air' and refers to its manner of growth, high in the trees.
DESCRIPTION: A climbing plant with stems up to 4.5 m and numerous stem-encircling, lanceolate leaves. The flowers, yellow to reddish-brown and with purple spots, are grouped in single or branched, profusely flowering racemes. The petals are narrow and curve downward; the lip is short.
ORIGIN: Nearly all the year round.
CULTIVATION: Malaysia, Indonesia.
AVAILABILITY: Thailand, Malacca, Singapore.
CARE: These flowers are treated before they are sold. After purchase, put them in water with cut-flower food.
KEEPING PROPERTIES: 7-9 days, depending on the quality.
USE: In a vase and in flower arrangement.
SCENT: A pleasant musk scent.

Calanthe hybrid
(no popular name)

NAME: *Calanthe*, from the Greek, means 'with lovely flowers'.
DESCRIPTION: A terrestrial (= growing on the ground) deciduous orchid; the old leaves fall before the flower stems appear. The plant has large ovoid pseudo-bulbs and three or four folded leaves. The stems, 50-60 cm long, bear 8-10 blooms which have a diameter of ±6 cm. All perianth segments have the same shape and are overlapping. The lip is split and the spur is thread-like or crooked. Colours: white, pink or carmine red, with red, orange or yellow markings.
ORIGIN: The ancestors are native to Burma and Vietnam and were first cultivated in the United Kingdom around 1850. This hybrid is a cross between *C. vestita* (white flowers) and *C. rosea* (rose-flowering); the latter sort predominates in the cross.
CULTIVATION: On a limited scale, all over the world.
AVAILABILITY: From autumn until February.
CARE: The flowers are sold in vials with water and food; put this in the vase as well.
KEEPING PROPERTIES: 10-14 days.
USE: In a vase and in flower arrangement.
SCENT: None.

Arachnis flos-aëris

X Aranda 'Christine'

X Laeliocattleya hybrid

Calanthe hybrid

Cattleya hybrids
Cattleya

NAME: The genus was named in 1824 after the wealthy British merchant William Cattley. He was a member of the Royal Horticultural Society, possessed a large collection of exotic plants and a collection of rare plant drawings, and published writings on botanical topics.

DESCRIPTION: An orchid with pseudo-bulbs (20-25 cm) which bear two to four flowers in the large-flowering cultivars, sometimes with a diameter of 20 cm or more. The small-flowering cultivars bear eight or more flowers on each stalk. Colour of the flowers: lilac, yellow, orange and white, generally with a dark lilac lip which has lovely markings in the throat.

ORIGIN: Central and South America. Ancestors of these hybrids were *C. labiata, C. dowiana, C. gigas, C. mossiae, C. trianae* and *C. gaskelliana.*

CULTIVATION: All over the world, chiefly in the United States.

AVAILABILITY: All the year round. Using artificial light arrangements, growers try to induce a sort of peak around Christmas and other important holidays.

CARE: In order for them to keep well, the flowers should have been open for six or seven days when purchased. Use cut-flower food. The flower is sensitive to temperatures below 15° C.

KEEPING PROPERTIES: 7-10 days.

USE: In a vase, in bridal work and in corsages. Also for funerals.

SCENT: Slight.

X *Laeliocattleya hybrids*

NAME: *Laelia* is the name of one of the ancestors of this hybrid (the other was *Cattleya*). When Lindley described this genus in 1831, he gave no explanation of its name. Some think that the genus is named after the Roman field marshall Laelius; others presume it comes from the name of a woman important to Lindley.

DESCRIPTION: The build of this plant is the same as that of *Cattleya*, only it blossoms somewhat more profusely: 3-4 blooms per branch. There are a great many cultivars in all shades of lilac, yellow, orange and white, mostly with a dark lip with lovely markings.

ORIGIN: The older cultivars come from the United Kingdom and, to a lesser extent, from Belgium and France, the newer ones from the United States.

CULTIVATION: See *Cattleya*.

AVAILABILITY: See *Cattleya*.

CARE: See *Cattleya*.

KEEPING PROPERTIES: See *Cattleya*.

USE: See *Cattleya*.

SCENT: See *Cattleya*.

X *Brassolaeliocattleya hybrids*

NAME: See *Laeliocattleya* and *Cattleya*.

DESCRIPTION: The same build as *Cattleya*, but the whole is somewhat coarser. Although there are fewer blooms per branch, they are somewhat larger. The large lip is beautifully fringed and is usually dark lilac, with a lovely yellow marking in the throat. The most frequent colour is lilac; in addition, there are cultivars with yellow, white and orange flowers.

ORIGIN: See *Cattleya*. The first cross, between the genera *Brassavola, Laelia* and *Cattleya*, was obtained in the United Kingdom in 1897; from that country, and from Belgium, come the older hybrids. The modern cultivars come primarily from the United States.

CULTIVATION: See *Cattleya*.

AVAILABILITY: See *Cattleya*.

CARE: See *Cattleya*.

KEEPING PROPERTIES: 6-8 days.

USE: See *Cattleya*.

SCENT: Very fragrant.

'California Cascade'

'Isle Magic'

Cymbidium hybrids
Cymbidium

NAME: *Cymbidium* is the Latin translation of the Greek *kumbidion*, the diminutive of *kumbe* (= little boat). The name alludes to the shape of the flower lip.

DESCRIPTION: Long or short branches with a fairly large number of somewhat waxy flowers in many colours and colour combinations, always with a lip remarkable for shape or colour. The flower consists of two whorls of three petals; on the inner whorl, the centre petal has developed into a lip. The 'stem' with which the flowers are attached to the branch is in fact the inferior ovary. There are large and small-flowering culti-vars (the latter are known as mini-cymbidiums), with early, medium and later-flowering sorts in both categories. For flowers from the northern hemisphere, this means September-December, January-March and April-June respectively. Depending on the cultivar, cymbidiums are sold by the branch or flower.

ORIGIN: Asia (Nepal, Burma, India, Sikkim, China, Sri Lanka) and Australia.

CULTIVATION: United States, Western Europe, South Africa, Australia, New Zealand.

AVAILABILITY: From Western Europe and the United States, in autumn and late autumn. Outside of this period, they are imported from the southern hemisphere.

CARE: If you purchase individual flowers, remove the vial in which they are sold. If you buy them as branches, cut off a bit of the stem. Use lukewarm water and cut-flower food. Do not put them in the sun; do not touch the underside of the stigma column (to prevent pollination and, as a result, rapid wilting).

KEEPING PROPERTIES: 2-5 weeks; medium and late-flowering cultivars will keep the longest. To keep them best, the minimum temperature is 8° C.

USE: In a vase (individual flowers or branches), usually with a branch of *Ruscus* as filling. Also in corsages, bridal bouquets, funeral wreaths and small arrangements.

SCENT: None.

Cultivars

The number of cymbidium cultivars is particularly large and still growing. A number of the best-known and most frequently cultivated:

'Amesbury Willows'. A small-flowering cultivar with very pale pink flowers; the outer petals are purplish on the backs. The lip has red markings. The flowers are closely grouped on the branch. The cultivar is sold as early as October and, for an early bloomer, it keeps very well.

Arcadian 'Sunrise Golden Fleece'. The flowers of this large-flowering cultivar are yellow and have a lip with red markings. Because of the lovely flowers and the branch composition, it is much in demand; it is sold from October to December.

Barcelona 'Magic Wand'. The yellowish-green flowers of this large-flowering cultivar are spread rather irregularly over the branch. The flowering period is between February and mid-May.

Beauty 'Fred' is an early-flowering cultivar (November-January) with large, predominantly white flowers and somewhat reddish markings on the lip. Some selections have been made of this cultivar, such as 'Beauty Fred Marionne' (with rather clearer lip

'Beauty Fred Nieske'

'Eliot Rogers' C 290

markings) and 'Beauty Fred Nieske' (with a somewhat less dense branch composition and more obscure markings).

Christmas Beauty. The blossoming period of this large-flowering cultivar falls between October and mid-January. The official name is **Christmas Beauty 'St. Francis'**. It is a somewhat older cultivar which is remarkable for its good production. The flowers are white, with purple stripes on the back. The lip has a wide red edge.

'Gymer Nederhorst' is a very large-flowering cultivar with yellow, somewhat greenish high-lighted flowers and remarkable lip markings: a sharply delineated red edge. It keeps extremely well; the bloom falls in March/April.

'California Cascade'. A large-flowering cultivar with white blossoms, which is sold between April and the end of May. It is a fairly new cross between the cultivar 'Blue Smoke' and one of the first hybrids, *C. alexanderi*. It has clearly been gaining in popularity in recent years.

'Eliot Rogers C 290' is a large-flowering pink cymbidium cultivar of very good quality. The bloom falls between February and April.

'Isla Magic' is a cymbidium hybrid developed in southern Germany, with very lovely greenish flowers. The bloom falls quite early: between December and February.

121

Dendrobium phalaenopsis
Dendrobium

NAME: *Dendrobium* means 'living on a tree'; *phalaenopsis* = resembling a butterfly.

DESCRIPTION: The plant has pseudo-bulbs of 30-50 cm. The flowers are grouped in racemes in the axils of the upper leaves; in autumn, from 8 to 18 of them appear on each stalk, each with a diameter of 9-12 cm. The flower is usually lilac, with a purple lip; there are also white cultivars with a white lip. The perianth petals often have net-like venation.

ORIGIN: North Australia and the eastern part of Indonesia.

CULTIVATION: Chiefly Thailand and Singapore; on a limited scale in Western Europe and the United States.

AVAILABILITY: Chiefly in autumn; limited during the rest of the year.

CARE: Because the flower is sensitive to the ageing hormone, ethylene, it is immediately put in treated water after cutting. After purchase, use cut-flower food.

KEEPING PROPERTIES: 8-12 days. The flower is sensitive to temperatures lower than 15° C and to air pollution.

USE: In flower arrangement; to a limited extent, in a vase.

SCENT: None.

Dendrobium hybrids
Dendrobium

NAME: See *D. phalaenopsis*.

DESCRIPTION: The long stem (up to 1.5 m) bears fairly narrow leaves. In autumn, when the days are short, a flower stem of about 50 cm long with lilac blooms 7-9 cm across grows from the upper leaf buds. The lip is darker in colour; the margins of the petals are lighter.

ORIGIN: See *D. phalaenopsis*. The hybrid is a cross of this sort with *D.* Superbiens, which is again a hybrid of *D. discolor* and *D. bigibbum*.

CULTIVATION: Thailand, Burman, Malacca, Singapore.

AVAILABILITY: Chiefly in autumn.

CARE: After cutting, the flower is treated to prevent damage by ethylene. After purchase, use cut-flower food. Sensitive to temperatures lower than 15° C.

KEEPING PROPERTIES: 6-14 days.

USE: In a vase and in flower arrangement.

SCENT: None.

Epidendrum Rainbow hybrids
Epidendrum

NAME: *Epidendrum* means 'living on trees'.

DESCRIPTION: Orchid with climbing stems and a dense, umbel-shaped inflorescence. The numerous flowers, about 3 cm across, look like small cattleyas and come in a variety of shades of red, orange, yellow, lilac and pink to nearly white.

ORIGIN: The ancestors are native chiefly to Mexico and South Africa. The Rainbow hybrid is a back-cross of *E. obrienianum* on the ancestors *E. ibaguense* and *E. erectum*.

CULTIVATION: Ivory Coast, Thailand, Singapore, on a limited scale in Western Europe.

AVAILABILITY: All the year round.

CARE: After cutting, the flowers are put in treated water. After purchase use cut-flower food.

KEEPING PROPERTIES: 8-14 days.

USE: In flower arrangement; to a limited extent, in a vase.

SCENT: Weak.

Dendrobium phalaenopsis

Epidendrum Rainbow hybrid

'Golden Shower'

X Odontonia 'Lulli Menuet'

Odontoglossum crispum hybrids
Odontoglossum

NAME: The genus name is derived from the Greek words *odontos* (= tooth) and *glossa* (= tongue): a flower with teeth on the tongue (lip).

DESCRIPTION: The plant has ovoid pseudobulbs each of which bear 2-3 leaves. Each stalk bears 10-20 flowers. They are about 10 cm wide and vary in colour from white to pink, and brown-spotted. The lip sometimes has red spots and is yellow in the middle; its sinuate margin is finely dentate. The lumps in the flower are yellow and sometimes striped.

ORIGIN: This hybrid is a cross of *O. crispum*, *O. nobile* and others. The ancestors are native to Colombia and Peru. Humboldt brought the plant back from an expedition through Central and South America (1799-1804). At first, many new cultivars were obtained in Belgium and England; presently the latter country has gained prominence. *Odontoglossum* is an important ancestor of many sexual hybrids.

CULTIVATION: and other data: See x Odontiodia. Because the plant is very sensitive to air pollution and temperature, the world supply is decreasing.

X Odontioda hybrids
Odontoglossum

NAME: See *Odontoglossum*.
DESCRIPTION: See *Odontoglossum*.
ORIGIN: *Odontioda* is a sexual hybrid of *Odontoglossum crispum* and *O. nobile*, both of which bear lovely white flowers with strong markings, but which are difficult to cultivate, and *Cochlioda noetzliana* from Peru, a vigorous grower with orange-red flowers. The first crosses were obtained as early as 1898; after 1946, many new ones were added, in which the vitality and the colour assortment were chiefly increased. They were chiefly obtained by British orchid breeders. The ancestors came from Peru and Colombia.

CULTIVATION: Chiefly the United Kingdom; on a limited scale in Belgium, France and the Netherlands. The plants demand a cool summer climate and much fresh air.

AVAILABILITY: Nearly the year round.

CARE: When purchased, the last flower but one on the branch should be open. The flowers are treated. After purchase use cut-flower food.

KEEPING PROPERTIES: 8-12 days.
USE: In flower arrangement; sometimes in a vase.
SCENT: None.

X Odontonia 'Lulli Menuet'
Odontoglossum

NAME: See *Odontoglossum*.
DESCRIPTION: See *Odontoglossum*.
ORIGIN: This orchid is a sexual hybrid of *Miltonia* (mainly from Brazil), the 'violet orchid', with large flowers with lovely markings but moderate keeping qualities, with *Odontoglossum crispum* and *O. nobile*, both from Colombia. The first cross was registered in 1905 by the Liège breeder Lairesse. Later his compatriot, Vuylsteke from Loochristie (near Ghent), performed many crosses. The United Kingdom takes the lead in renewing the assortment of these hybrids.

CULTIVATION: See *Odontioda*.
AVAILABILITY: See *Odontioda*.
CARE: See *Odontioda*.
KEEPING PROPERTIES: See *Odontioda*.
USE: See *Odontioda*.
SCENT: See *Odontioda*.

Oncidium 'Golden Shower'
Oncidium

NAME: *Oncidium* is the Latin translation of the Greek *onkidoin*, which means 'swelling' or 'lump'. The name refers to the lumps on the lip.

DESCRIPTION: The plant has a dense mass of pseudo-bulbs of approx. 10 cm long and linear leaves. The predominantly yellow flowers have brown markings; they are 2-3 cm wide and are grouped in large, many-flowered plumes.

ORIGIN: The cultivar is a cross of *O. varicosum* 'Regersii' and *O. flexuosum*. The ancestors are native to Brazil, Uruguay and Paraguay.

CULTIVATION: Thailand, Malacca, Burma, Singapore, Hawaii.

AVAILABILITY: Chiefly in winter and spring.

CARE: After cutting, the flowers are placed in specially treated water. After purchase, use cut-flower food.

KEEPING PROPERTIES: 12-16 days.
USE: In a vase and in flower arrangement.
SCENT: None.

X *Vuylstekeara 'Cambria Plush'*
Cambria orchid

NAME: The hybrid is named after the Belgian flower breeder Vuylsteke from Loochristie, near Ghent.

DESCRIPTION: The flower shape of this hybrid resembles that of *Odontonia*. The colour and the lip markings, however, were improved by the contribution of two other sorts, *Cochlioda noetzliana* and *Miltonia vexillaria*. The flower colour is predominantly red; the lip is generally somewhat lighter and has lovely markings. Each stalk bears 10-20 flowers with a diameter of 10-12 cm.

ORIGIN: The first hybrid was obtained by Vuylsteke, who crossed *Odontioda* with *Miltonia*. Numerous new cultivars were registered until 1970, but none since then. The 'Cambria' was obtained in the United Kingdom in 1931. Later the 'Cambria Plush' was selected from it.

CULTIVATION: Temperate areas, especially the Netherlands.

AVAILABILITY: The year round, with a peak supply in spring and autumn.

CARE: When purchased, the last flower should be on the verge of opening. Use cut-flower food.

KEEPING PROPERTIES: 3-4 weeks.

USE: In a vase and in flower arrangement.

SCENT: None.

Phalaenopsis Amabilis hybrids
Moth orchid

NAME: *Phalaenopsis* means 'resembling a moth'. C.L. Blume (1796-1862), director of the National Botanical Gardens in Buitenzorg (now Bogor, Indonesia) and later director of the National Herbarium in Leiden, took the flower of one of the ancestors for a butterfly when he first saw it in the undergrowth. *Amabilis* = amiable.

DESCRIPTION: There is a pink and a white form of this hybrid. The plant, which grows from one point, has elongated, thick, fleshy leaves. The oblique flower stem is usually unbranched; the flowers are loosely grouped in racemes.

ORIGIN: The most important ancestors of this hybrid are *P. amabilis* (white flower, green leaves) and *P. schilleriana* (pink flower, dark grey, marbled leaves). In addition, it was crossed with *P. violacea, P. lueddemanniana* and *P. fasciata*. For *P. amabilis*, called *angreh boelan* on Java, where the native population eats its leaves as a vegetable, the sum of Dfl. 1200 per plant was paid in the United Kingdom in 1848. Many modern cultivars are of German or American origin, some obtained in Hawaii.

CULTIVATION: Temperate areas with cut-flower cultivation.

AVAILABILITY: All the year round.

CARE: When purchased, the last flower on the branch should be nearly open. Use cut-flower food.

KEEPING PROPERTIES: 2-3 weeks.

USE: In a vase, in flower arrangement and - the individual flowers - in corsages and in bridal work, for example.

SCENT: None.

X Vuylstekeara 'Cambria Plush'

Phalaenopsis Amabilis hybrid

Paphiopedilum hybrid

Paphiopedilum hybrids
Lady's slipper orchid

NAME: The genus name is derived from the town of Paphia on Cyprus.

DESCRIPTION: The plant has no pseudobulbs; its leaves are 15-25 cm long and green, but sometimes spotted. The stem is densely covered with short, stiff hairs. The two outer perianth petals are fused to form the 'flag'; of the inner three, one has grown into the 'slipper'. The flowers have lovely markings on a glittering background of white or various shades of green, red or brown.

ORIGIN: The ancestors are native to Asia (Thailand, Burma, South China, Vietnam and Malacca). The first hybrid blossomed in 1869 in the United Kingdom; it was a cross betweeen *P. villosum* and *P. barbatum* and was given the name *P. harrisianum*. After that the assortment grew very rapidly; by 1901, over 1000 crosses had been registered; at present there are many more than 20,000. Most new cultivars come from the United States. the United Kingdom, Australia and, to a much more limited extent, Germany and the Netherlands, also play a role.

CULTIVATION: United States. Also in the Netherlands, the United Kingdom, Germany and France.

AVAILABILITY: The year round.

CARE: When purchased, the flower should stand almost parallel to the stem. Do not put the stem too deep in the water (because of the hairs). Use cut-flower food; cut off a bit of the stem each week.

KEEPING PROPERTIES: 4-6 weeks.

USE: Primarily in flower arrangement.

SCENT: None.

Vanda caerulea
Vanda

NAME: *Vanda* is the Hindustani popular name of the plant. *Caerulea* means dark blue.

DESCRIPTION: The plant has a single long stem with numerous leaves. The 12-18 flowers, around 12 cm across, grow in racemes; they are bright blue, with darker, box-shaped markings. The petals are ovoid; the lip has spreading side lobes and a darker coloured central lobe. There are several cultivars.

ORIGIN: Thailand, the Himalayas. Introduced in the United Kingdom in 1847.

CULTIVATION: Thailand and Burma; because of the cultivation it is expensive. Only on a limited scale in Western Europe and the United States.

AVAILABILITY: From autumn until spring.

CARE: When purchased, the last flower should be open. Use cut-flower food.

KEEPING PROPERTIES: 3-5 weeks.

USE: In flower arrangement.

SCENT: None.

Vanda hybrids
Vanda

NAME: See *V. caerulea*.

DESCRIPTION: The plant has a single stem and 8-10 leaves which are $\pm$ 5 cm wide. The perianth petals are sinuate; the present cultivars are primarily red, carmine red and lilac with darker outline markings.

ORIGIN: The most important ancestors of this hybrid are *V. tricolor* of Java (yellowish-white flowers with brown spots and a violet-rose lip with purple stripes) and *V. teres* from north Indonesia, Vietnam and Burma (white with markings of pink to red and yellow).

CULTIVATION: On a limited scale in Thailand, Singapore and in Hawaii. The cultivation is expensive and requires much warmth; a plant only flowers after 8-11 years.

AVAILABILITY: Chiefly in autumn and winter.

CARE: When purchased, the top flower should be almost completely open. Use cut-flower food.

KEEPING PROPERTIES: 4-5 weeks.

USE: In flower arrangement.

SCENT: Very fragrant.

Vanda caerulea

Paeoniaceae

The crowfoot family (*Paeoniaceae*) has only one genus, *Paeonia*, which comprises 33 species. The plants, which were formerly included in the *Ranunculaceae*, are native to the temperate regions of the northern hemisphere. They are perennial herbs or sub-shrubs with a subterranean rootstock or tubers. The leaves are composed of numerous leaflets which are sometimes lobed. The hermaphrodite flowers are regular. The five green sepals do not fall off, as in the *Ranunculaceae*; they become thicker and smaller in surface area during the flowering. There are 5-10 petals (in the double-flowering cultivars naturally many more) and a large number of stamens. The fruit of the peony family is a follicle, and the seeds colour from red to black when they ripen. In some varieties they have a coloured appendage.

Paeonia lactiflora hybrids,
syn. *P. sinensis*
Chinese garden peony
NAME: The genus name is the Latin form of the Greek plant name *Paioni*, named after Panon, the doctor among the Greek gods. The name alludes to the medicinal characteristics of some species. *Lactiflora* means 'having milky white flowers'.

DESCRIPTION: The reddish stem bears double ternate leaves, the leaflets of which are oval lanceolate and terminate in a point. The base of the leaf is wedge-shaped. The simple or multiple flowers have a diameter of 10-12 cm and come in shades of white, pink or red. The multiple-flowering cultivars are primarily used for cut-flower cultivation. Two frequently grown cultivars are 'Sarah Bernardt' (pink) and the very fragrant white cultivar 'Duchesse de Nemours'.

ORIGIN: Central and East Asia; not in Japan, however. In China, the peony has been under cultivation for over 1000 years. It came to Europe in 1808. Most of the more than 260 cultivars were obtained in France, a few in the United Kingdom. Nowadays Germany plays an important role in the expansion of the assortment.

CULTIVATION: Temperate areas with outdoor cut-flower cultivation, mostly in the Netherlands.

AVAILABILITY: The peak is in the first half of July. The availability period can be lengthened by cooling the flowers.

CARE: When purchased, the buds should show good colour, but still be entirely closed. Use cut-flower food.

KEEPING PROPERTIES: 10-15 days. Florists can keep the flowers for 2-3 weeks with water by holding them at a temperature of 2° C with a relative humidity of 70 per cent.

USE: In a vase, in bouquets and in decorations.

SCENT: Fragrant to very fragrant, depending on the cultivar.

△ Phoenix dactylifera   ▽ Paeonia Lactiflora hybrid 'Sarah Bernhard'

Palmae

Papaveraceae

Most palms (*Palmae*) grow in the tropics and subtropics, although they are not entirely absent in temperate climates. Some of the nearly 3000 species prefer a warm, humid climate; others feel most comfortable in the desert. Many of these monocotyledonous plants have been under cultivation a very long time and several, such as the tropical date and coconut palms, play an important role in food supply, or are of economic importance for their fibres or their great abundance of oils and fats.

All palms - there are over 200 genera - have an unbranched stem with whorls of leaves at the top. The outside of the stem clearly exhibits leaf scars. The leaves are fan-shaped. In some species, the youthful form of the leaf is entire, but, as they grow, they develop swellings that push the folded leaves apart. The leaflets can be linear or shaped like fish tails, but also blunt or irregular.

Depending on the species, palms have varying flower shapes, from large plumes to spikes which are usually oblique. The flowers, unisexual or hermaphrodite and monoecious or dioecious, are short-lived; they are pollinated by the wind or by insects. The sepals are free-standing or fused. In female flowers, the petals may be imbricate (like roof tiles); in the male flowers, they are opposite. The stamens stand in two whorls of three. The superior ovary consists of three carpels which are sometimes fused. The fruits are single-seeded berries or stone fruits.

The *Papaveraceae* or poppy family (26 genera, around 250 species) are annual and biennial or perennial plants which primarily come from the temperate areas of the northern hemisphere. Their leaves are alternate, have no stipules, and have a single lobe or are deeply cut. All parts of the plant contain tubes filled with a white or yellow juice.

The flowers usually stand alone, sometimes in plumes. The two sepals drop off when the flower opens. The flowers are hermaphrodite and regular; most have two whorls of two petals which are finely folded in the bud, as in the poppy. The numerous stamens stand in several whorls; the filaments are sometimes petal-like in shape. A capsule develops from the superior ovary. The seed tissue is sometimes rich in oils, as in the poppy seed (*P. somniferum*) which may have an oil content of 50 per cent. Poppy seed oil, a raw material for expensive sorts of paint, is pressed from it. If the unripe seed capsules are slit, an allied sort yields a raw material for the production of several narcotics.

Phoenix dactylifera
Date palm

NAME: The genus name is the Latin version of the Greek *phoinix* = date, but also 'Phoenician' and 'purplish-red'. It is not impossible that the Greeks made the acquaintance of this palm through the Phoenicians. Perhaps the name also has to do with the colour of the ripe fruits. *Dactylifera* means 'bearing dates'.

DESCRIPTION: Palm with a fairly thick stem which can reach a height of 10 m. The leaves, initially erect, are later arched, and can grow up to 3 m long. They consists of numerous smaller leaflets. The leaf spathes are covered with long brown hairs. The plant bears an oblique inflorescence from a leaf axil. The inflorescence, which can reach a length of 1 m, is encircled by a large floral spathe in the bud. The flower is unisexual.

ORIGIN: The date palm is a very old plant which was cultivated long before our times, and is unknown in the wild.

CULTIVATION: For the unripe fruit, which is used in flower arrangement, primarily on the French and Italian Riviera. It is not warm enough there for the fruit to reach maturity.

AVAILABILITY: November (for Christmas).

CARE: None; branches and fruits are practically dry.

KEEPING PROPERTIES: 6-8 weeks.

USE: In Christmas floral work.

SCENT: None.

Macleaya cordata
Plume poppy

NAME: The genus is named after Scottish entomologist A. Macley (1767-1848), who worked in Australia and served as secretary of the Linnaeus Society there. *Cordata* means 'heart-shaped'.

DESCRIPTION: Perennial plant, around 2.5 m high, with unbranching, bluish-frosted stems which contain an orange milky juice. The nearly round leaves are seven-lobed, with a heart-shaped leaf base; the underside is silvery blue. The small flowers stand in large plumes; they have two creamy white sepals and numerous stamens; petals are lacking. The most frequently cultivated cultivar is 'Coral Plume', with ochre-coloured racemes.

ORIGIN: Eastern China, Japan; introduced into the United Kingdom in 1795.

CULTIVATION: Temperate areas with outdoor cut-flower cultivation.

AVAILABILITY: June-July.

CARE: When purchased, the first flowers of the plume should be open. Cut off a bit of the stem; use cut-flower food.

KEEPING PROPERTIES: The sepals drop off after 4-5 days. After that it can be used as a dried flower.

USE: In a vase with other summer flowers and in decorations. The flower plumes can be dried.

SCENT: None.

Papaver orientale
Oriental poppy
NAME: *Papaver* is derived from the Latin word *papa* = father. In ancient times, the seeds or the milky juice of this plant were mixed with the food of small children to allow them to sleep more soundly. *Orientale* means 'from the east'.
DESCRIPTION: A coarse perennial plant, 60-90 cm high and with a stiff, hairy stem. The finely divided leaves have lanceolate slips, and nearly all of them form a root rosette. The flower is orangish-red with a black centre. It has bluish-black stamens and 4-6 petals; bracts are absent.
ORIGIN: From the Caucasus to Iran. First cultivated in France in 1700.
CULTIVATION: Chiefly Western Europe.
AVAILABILITY: May-June.
CARE: When purchased, the bud should already show some colour. Cut off a bit of the stem; use cut-flower food for herbaceous plants.
KEEPING PROPERTIES: 4-7 days.
USE: In a vase and in mixed summer bouquets. The capsules are used, fresh or dried, in flower arrangement.
SCENT: None.

Papaver nudicaule
Island poppy
NAME: See *P. orientale*. *Nudicaule* means 'bare-stemmed'; this variety has leafless flower stems.
DESCRIPTION: Clump-forming perennial, up to 50 cm high, with bluish-green, finely divided leaves with lanceolate segments. The stems are covered with rough hairs. The flowers stand alone on a leafless stem. The petals have a yellow or a green base. The original colour was yellow; now there are cultivars in all shades of yellow, salmon, white and orange. This poppy is cultivated as a biennial, generally as a mixture of, for instance, 'Goodwin's Victory' and 'San Remo'. The plant has white milky juice.
ORIGIN: From Europe to eastern Asia; under cultivation since 1730.
CULTIVATION: In temperate and subtropical areas with outdoor cut-flower cultivation; much on the French and Italian Riviera.
AVAILABILITY: April-August.
CARE: When purchased, the bud should still be closed, but show its colour. Cut off a bit of the stem; use cut-flower food for herbaceous plants.
KEEPING PROPERTIES: 6-9 days.
USE: In a vase and in bouquets.
SCENT: Slightly fragrant.

Phytolaccaeae

Most members of the pokeweed family (*Phytolaccaceae*) are native to tropical America and the Caribbean. They are dicotyledonous trees, shrubs or climbing shrubs and herbaceous plants. Their leaves are alternate; some species have stipules. The family has 22 genera, with around 125 species.

The small hermaphrodite and regular flowers grow in a raceme at the end of the stem or from the leaf axils. The perianth consists of a whorl of four or five parts and is sometimes disc-shaped. The number of stamens is equal to or larger than the number of lobes of the petals. The ovary is superior; sometimes it is borne on a stem of the stigmas. It consists of one or even many more fused carpels. The number of styles is equal to the number of carpels. They are short and thread-like; in some species they are absent. The fruit is a fleshy berry, a dry nut or a capsule.

Phytolacca americana
Pokeweed, Pigeon berry
NAME: The genus name is a contraction of the Greek words *phuton* = plant and *lacca* = red lacquer. *Americana* refers to the area of origin.
DESCRIPTION: Perennial plant, 1.50-2 m high, with somewhat reddish stems. The fairly large leaves stand on short stems, are oval and have smooth margins. The long racemes of white flowers stand opposite the leaves. The flowers have ten stamens. The plant's ornamental value is determined by the fruit cluster of juicy berries, which turn from purplish-red to dark purple.
ORIGIN: United States; now all over the world in the wild.
CULTIVATION: On a limited scale, all over the world.
AVAILABILITY: End of July-September.
CARE: Remove the leaves. Cut off a bit of the stem and use cut-flower food.
KEEPING PROPERTIES: 10-15 days.
USE: In bouquets and in floral work.
SCENT: None.

Papaver nudicaule

Phytolacca americana

Plumbaginaceae

The plumbago family (*Plumbaginaceae*) consists of ten genera classified into around 560 species which grow all over the world, but generally show a preference for dry or salty growing places. They are usually annual or perennial herbaceous plants, with a few shrubs or climbing plants as the exceptions that prove the rule.

In many varieties, the simple leaves have nectaries. The flowers are arranged in plumes or racemes, or in a sort of head. They are hermaphrodite, regular and pentamerous. The sepals are fused to form a five-toothed or lobed tube which is membraneous, ribbed and coloured in some sorts. The sepals are fused at the base to form a long tube. The stamens stand on the base of the corolla, or are free-standing. The ovary is superior and unilocular, as a result of the fusion of the five carpels. The calyx usually remains on the fruit.

Armeria pseudarmeria

Armeria pseudarmeria
Thrift
NAME: The genus name is of Celtic origin and means 'growing by the sea'. This was true of the first sort described, *A. maritima*, at any rate. *Pseudarmeria* = pseudo armeria.
DESCRIPTION: A clump-forming perennial, 40-60 cm high, with bluish-green elongated leaves. They are a few centimetres wide and have 5-7 veins. The flower stem, approx. 50 cm long, bears heads of 5-7 cm wide, with pointed involucre leaves of nearly equal length. In the original sort the corolla was lilac-rose. The cultivated cultivars are pink, lilac-rose, carmine rose and white. A well-known cultivar is the rose-red 'Bees Ruby'.
ORIGIN: Coastal areas of Spain and Portugal. First cultivated in the United Kingdom in 1740.
CULTIVATION: Temperate and subtropical areas with outdoor cut-flower cultivation.
AVAILABILITY: End of May-July.
CARE: When purchased, the flower should be open but not yet fully-grown. Cut off a bit of the stem; use cut-flower food for herbaceous plants.
KEEPING PROPERTIES: 10-14 days.
USE: In a vase and in flower arrangement.
SCENT: None.

Goniolimon tataricum,
syn. *Limonium tataricum*
Sea lavender
NAME: The genus name is composed of the Greek words *gonia* (= corner) and *leios* (= bare, smooth). *Tataricum* means 'from Tartary'. Tartar, or Tatar, was the name formerly given to a rather vague area between south-eastern Europe and Asiatic Russia.
DESCRIPTION: Hardy perennial, with leaves in rosette form and long, bare stems of up to 50 cm. The ovoid leaves have entire margins with short points, and they change without transition into a long leaf stem. The flowers stand alone or in pairs in spikes, and form wide clusters on winged, arching branches. The calyx margin is white with green veins and five pointed teeth; the whorl is lilac.
ORIGIN: Chiefly western Europe.
CULTIVATION: Fresh from July until September; dried the year round.
AVAILABILITY: Western Asia; first cultivated in the United Kingdom in 1731.
CARE: When purchasing fresh flowers, the first flowers should be open. Use cut-flower food.
KEEPING PROPERTIES: Fresh flowers, 18-21 days.
USE: Usually as a dried flower. Fresh, in bouquets and in flower arrangement.
SCENT: None.

Limonium sinuatum,
syn. *Statice sinuata*
Statice, Sea lavender
NAME: The genus name is derived from the Greek *leimonion*: the name for a plant of wet grasslands, a meadow plant. *Sinuatum* = curving.
DESCRIPTION: An annual plant, 50-60 cm high, slightly hairy and with a rough feel. The lower leaves stand in rosettes and are lyrate pinnatifid. The flowers are grouped in wide clusters of three or four; the flower stem is winged. The calyx is hairless and white or pale lilac; the original flower colour was yellow. Nowadays there are dark blue, pink, white, yellow, and apricot coloured cultivars. Frequently cultivated: the blue cultivars and a mixture of pale shades under the name 'Pacific mixture'.
ORIGIN: Mediterranean area; first cultivated in the Netherlands in 1610.

CULTIVATION: Temperate and subtropical areas with outdoor cut-flower cultivation; much in the Netherlands and Israel.
AVAILABILITY: From western Europe, from June until September; elsewhere, all the year round.
CARE: When purchased, most flowers should be open. Use cut-flower food for herbaceous plants.
KEEPING PROPERTIES: 12-16 days.
USE: In a vase, in flower arrangement and, dried, in mixed dried bouquets.
SCENT: None.

△ Limonium perezii   ▽ Limonium sinuatum, syn. Statice sinuata

Limonium suworowii,
syn. *Statice suworowii*
(no popular name)
NAME: See *L. sinuatum*. The sort is named after I.P. Suwerow, of whom we only know that he was an inspector in a military hospital in Turkestan.
DESCRIPTION: Annual plant, up to 40 cm high, with angular stems. The leaves, 15-20 cm long, are narrow, spatula-shaped and basal; they have smooth or shallowly lobed margins. The flowers, bright lilac-rose, are arranged in twos or threes in long spikes; at the bottom, they have a few short sessile secondary spikes. The green base of the calyx has glandular hairs; the corolla is funnel-shaped.
ORIGIN: Turkestan; first cultivated in Germany in 1881.
CULTIVATION: See *L. sinuatum*.
AVAILABILITY: See *L. sinuatum*.
CARE: See *L. sinuatum*.
KEEPING PROPERTIES: See *L. sinuatum*.
USE: See *L. sinuatum*.
SCENT: See *L. sinuatum*.

Limonium latifolium
Sea lavender
NAME: See *L. sinuatum*. *Latifolium* = wide-leaved.
DESCRIPTION: Perennial, 40-50 cm high. The elongated oval, blunt leaves stand in rosettes and narrow to a long stem. The flowers, with lavender corollas and white-edged calyxes, are grouped in one-sided spikes. The clusters are very wide and strongly branched; the branches are round or somewhat angular and obliquely erect or somewhat arching.
ORIGIN: Caucasus; first cultivated in the United Kingdom in 1791.
CULTIVATION: Temperate and sub-tropical areas with outdoor cut-flower cultivation.
AVAILABILITY: Fresh, June-July; dried the year round.
CARE: When fresh flowers are purchased, the first flowers should be open. Use water with cut-flower food. With dried material, all flowers should be open.
KEEPING PROPERTIES: Fresh flowers, 18-21 days.
USE: Fresh, in bouquets and in flower arrangement. However, usually used dried.
SCENT: None.

Limonium perezii
Blue sea lavender
NAME: See *L. sinuatum*. The variety is named after P.J.B. Baron de Perez (1803-1859), governor of the Dutch East Indies.
DESCRIPTION: A perennial plant which is usually cultivated as an annual, 70-80 cm high and in composition almost the same as *L. sinuatum*, only somewhat coarser and dark blue. It is a fairly new introduction which is gaining popularity for cut-flower cultivation. Nothing is known about its origin.
ORIGIN: Not known.
CULTIVATION: See *L. sinuatum*.
AVAILABILITY: See *L. sinuatum*.
CARE: See *L. sinuatum*.
KEEPING PROPERTIES: See *L. sinuatum*.
USE: See *L. sinuatum*.
SCENT: See *L. sinuatum*.

Limonium ferulaceum
'Karel de Groot'
(no popular name)
NAME: See *L. sinuatum*. The name *ferulaceum* is ambiguous. It may have been taken from the old name of a plant with long branches which was used as a splint and a punishing rod (this derivation would come from *ferire* = beat), but it may have come from the Greek *fere* = ascending plant. The latter sounds more logical; this *Limonium* sort grows higher than most other species.
DESCRIPTION: Perennial plant with stems of 60-70 cm long and narrow leaves in rosettes. The main branch is composed of numerous smaller, sturdy but thin branches. The pale pink flowers stand in lovely feathery racemes at right angles to the branch.
ORIGIN: Mediterranean area; central and southern Portugal. The cultivar 'Karel de Groot' is a Dutch selection (Rijnsburg) from 1982.
CULTIVATION: In temperate and subtropical areas with outdoor cut-flower cultivation.
AVAILABILITY: Fresh, from July until September; dried, all the year round.
CARE: When purchasing fresh flowers, most flowers should be open. Cut off a bit of the stem; use cut-flower food. With dried material, all the flowers must be open.
KEEPING PROPERTIES: Fresh flowers, 18-21 days.
USE: In mixed bouquets and in flower arrangement; in the latter case, dried flowers are also used.
SCENT: None.

Polemoniaceae

The *Polemoniaceae*, the phlox family, consists of 18 genera with around 300 species of annual and perennial plants and climbers and a number of trees. They grow all over the world, but most of them come from the United States. They are dicotyledonous plants with simple or compound, alternate or opposite, leaves.

The usually regular and hermaphrodite flowers grow at the end of the stem or from the leaf axils and stand alone, in racemes or in dense heads. The five sepals are fused into a tube, the five petals to a flat, round bell- or tube-shaped corolla. The five stamens are fused with the petals.

The ovary of the *Polemoniaceae* is superior. It is borne by a disc and is usually trilocular. The number of stigmas on the style is the same as the number of cavities. The fruit is a capsule.

The phlox family is subdivided into five groups of genera. The only genus which plays a role in cut-flower cultivation, *Phlox*, belongs to the group of the *Polemonieae*, in which the stamens are often irregularly placed on the regular corolla.

Phlox maculata hybrids
Summer phlox

NAME: The genus name means 'flame' or 'glow' and refers to the flaming red flower colour in some varieties. *Maculata* = spotted.
DESCRIPTION: Perennial, 70-80 cm high, with somewhat hairy, reddish spotted stems. The sessile leaves are lanceolate. The flowers are grouped in many-flowered plumes which are longer than they are wide. The flowers have a diameter of 2.5-3 cm. The original colour was dark pink. Today, frequently cultivated cultivars are 'Alpha' (bright pink) and 'Omega' (white with a red eye).
ORIGIN: The eastern United States. Some cultivars may be hybrids between *P. maculata* and *P. carolina*, both of which were first cultivated in the United Kingdom, in 1740 and 1728 respectively.
CULTIVATION: Temperate areas, both in the hothouse and outdoors.
AVAILABILITY: June-October.
CARE: When purchased, a few flowers should be entirely open. After 4-5 days the first flowers will fall off. Cut off a bit of the stem; use cut-flower food. The flowers are often treated after cutting to improve their keeping qualities.
KEEPING PROPERTIES: 5-10 days.
USE: In a vase and in mixed bouquets. Disadvantage: their scent attracts insects.
SCENT: Fairly strong.

Phlox paniculata hybrids
Summer phlox

NAME: See *P. maculata* hybrids. *Paniculata* = plume-shaped.
DESCRIPTION: Perennial plant, 1 m high, with nearly sessile, elongated oval leaves with clearly visible side veins on the underside. The flowers, 2-3 cm across, stand in large plumes. The anther lobes are white to cream-coloured. The original flower colour was pink; the cultivars come in all kinds of shades of red, salmon, pink, lilac, purple, violet and white, sometimes with a different colour ring in the centre.
ORIGIN: Eastern United States; first cultivated in the United Kingdom in 1732. Many cultivars are of British or German origin; a few were obtained in the Netherlands.
CULTIVATION: Western Europe, in the hothouse or outdoors.
AVAILABILITY: From July until September. Sometimes before July, as a hothouse flower.
CARE: When purchased, the first flowers should be open. Cut off a bit of the stem; use cut-flower food.
KEEPING PROPERTIES: 6-11 days; after 6 days the first petals will fall.
USE: In a vase, especially in mixed bouquets.
SCENT: Strong and sweetish; attracts insects.

Cultivars

'**Rembrandt**'. A much cultivated white-flowering cultivar with an excellent colour, a lovely cluster composition and very good keeping qualities.

'**Bright Eye**' is a pink-white cultivar with a red eye: a beautiful colour contrast. Flower size and shape meet high standards, as do their keeping qualities.

'**Windsor**' is a lovely pale lilac cultivar, an exclusive colour which is ideal for mixed bouquets. A very good cultivar with excellent keeping qualities.

'Windsor'

Primulaceae

Most members of the primrose family (*Primulaceae*), some 1000 species in all and classified into nearly 30 genera, are native to the temperate climate zones of the northern hemisphere. They are dicotyledonous herbaceous plants, annual, biennal or perennial. Sometimes they overwinter with a rootstock.

The simple leaves are alternate or opposite, also forming ground rosettes in some sorts. The flowers are solitary or in umbels on usually unleafy branches. They are usually regular, have bracts and are hermaphrodite. In a number of cases, for example, in *Primula obconica*, they have styles of unequal length: in one plant, the style is short and the stigma is at the base of the flower; in another plant, the style is long and protrudes above the stamens.

The five sepals are fused into a tube with pointed lobes. The corolla usually consists of five petals fused into a tubular shape. The five stamens are fused with this corolla tube. The ovary, composed of five fused carpels, is superior or semi-inferior and unilocular. The style ends in a globular stigma. The fruit is a capsule.

Cyclamen persicum

Cyclamen persicum
Cyclamen

NAME: The genus name is derived from the Greek *kuklos*, which means 'circle' and refers to the round tuber. *Persicum* = from Persia. This is erroneous, however; most Cyclamen species come from the Mediterranean area.
DESCRIPTION: A herbaceous plant with a large, flat tuber. The ovoid, heart-shaped leaves stand in rosettes; the upper side is green with silverish markings. The long-stemmed flowers (one bloom per stem) come in varying colours. The salmon red cultivar 'Vuurbaak' is chiefly cultivated as a cut flower. Very long-stemmed cultivars are cultivated in Germany.
ORIGIN: The eastern part of the Mediterranean area; first cultivated in the United Kingdom in 1731.
CULTIVATION: As a hothouse cut-flower in temperate areas; very popular in Germany.

AVAILABILITY: The year round, with a peak between October and the end of February.
CARE: Split the stem over a length of about 3 cm for good water absorption. The flowers cannot stand cut-flower food.
KEEPING PROPERTIES: 8-12 days.
USE: In flower arrangement and, to a limited extent, in a vase.
SCENT: Generally none.

Lysimachia clethroides
Loosestrife

NAME: The genus is named after Lysimachus, a friend of Alexander the Great who is said to have discovered *L. vulgaris*, the loosestrife, which is also native to the Netherlands. *Clethroides* = resembling the shrub, *Clethra*.
DESCRIPTION: Perennial plant, 60-80 cm high, somewhat bluish-green in colour with a light pubescence. The elongated ovoid leaves stand on short stems. The white flowers, with a diameter of about 1 cm, are grouped in long, somewhat arching racemes.
ORIGIN: Eastern Europe and Asia Minor.
CULTIVATION: Temperate areas with outdoor cut-flower cultivation; mostly in the Netherlands.
AVAILABILITY: July-September.
CARE: When purchased, the first flowers should be well open. Remove the lower leaves, cut off a bit of the stem and use cut-flower food.
KEEPING PROPERTIES: 8-12 days.
USE: In a vase and in mixed bouquets.
SCENT: None.

Lysimachia punctata
Loosestrife

NAME: See *L. clethroides*. *Punctatis* means 'speckled'.
DESCRIPTION: Perennial plant with stems of 40-60 cm which often bear some glandular hairs. The leaves stand in whorls of 2-4; they are nearly sessile and lanceolate. The yellow flowers have a brown base and stand in groups, erectly, in the axils.
ORIGIN: Eastern Europe and Asia Minor.
CULTIVATION: Temperate areas with outdoor cut-flower cultivation.
AVAILABILITY: June-end of July.
CARE: When purchased, the first flowers should be open. Cut off a bit of the stem; use cut-flower food for herbaceous plants.
KEEPING PROPERTIES: 6-10 days.
USE: In mixed bouquets. They are not very attractive in a vase, because the petals fall off.
SCENT: None.

Primula x polyantha
Garden polyanthus

NAME: *Primula* is the diminutive of the Latin *primus*, meaning 'first'; it refers to the early flowering. *Polyantha* = many-flowered.

DESCRIPTION: Clump-forming perennial with elongated, wrinkled leaves which are somewhat hairy on the underside. The flower stem is 10-25 cm long; the flowers are grouped in umbels which often turn to one side. The diameter of the individual flowers is about 3 cm. The original colour was yellow; most garden polyanthuses used as cut flowers are still yellow. In addition, there are mixtures with numerous red, pink, yellow and cream-coloured shades.

ORIGIN: Hybrid origin, derived from *P. elatior* and *P. vulgars*; first cultivated in Switzerland in 1561.

CULTIVATION: Temperate areas with flower cultivation.

AVAILABILITY: March (from the hothouse) and April.

CARE: When purchased, the first two flowers should be open. Cut off a bit of the stem; use cut-flower food for herbaceous plants.

KEEPING PROPERTIES: 7-12 days.

USE: In flower arrangement, as in mixed Biedermeier bouquets. Also in floral work, the yellow cultivars especially at Easter.

SCENT: Slightly fragrant.

Primula Vialii hybrid

Primula obconica
Pot primrose

NAME: See *P.* x *polyantha*. *Obconica* means 'inversely cone-shaped' and refers to the shape of the ovary.

DESCRIPTION: Perennial, but not hardy, herbaceous plant with large oval, roughly dentate leaves. The calyx is funnel-shaped and pointed at the base. The flower, 4-5 cm across, is cultivated in the colours carmine red, rose-salmon, salmon-orange, blue and white.

ORIGIN: West China; first cultivated in the United Kingdom in 1880.

CULTIVATION: Temperate areas with hothouse flower cultivation.

AVAILABILITY: On a limited scale, with the main supply in summer and late summer.

CARE: When purchased, the first two or three flowers should be open. Cut off a bit of the stem; use cut-flower food for herbaceous plants.

KEEPING PROPERTIES: 10-14 days.

USE: In floral work; to a limited extent in a vase. Some people are allergic to this plant, skin contact causing dermatitis.

SCENT: Slightly fragrant.

Primula Bullesiana hybrids
Garden primrose

NAME: See *P.* x *polyantha*. *Bullesiana* refers to the cross ancestors.

DESCRIPTION: Perennial plant, the leaves of which have dentate or serrate margins and grow in rosettes. The flower stem is sometimes slightly powdery. The flowers in 'stacks' of whorls of 10-20 flowers on the roughly 60 cm long stem. They are red, orange, carmine red, pink, yellow or blue.

ORIGIN: A cross between *P. bulleyana* and *P. beesiana* and obtained by the famed perennial plant breeder, Moerheim, in the Dutch town of Dedemsvaart. By the way, the same cross was obtained in the United Kingdom and became known as 'Ipswich hybrids'.

CULTIVATION: Temperate areas; especially popular in the United Kingdom and Germany.

AVAILABILITY: June-July; from the end of May from the hothouse.

CARE: When purchased, a few flowers should already be open. Cut off a bit of the stem; use cut-flower food for herbaceous plants.

KEEPING PROPERTIES: 8-12 days.

USE: Chiefly in flower arrangement, but also as a special flower in a vase.

SCENT: Slightly fragrant.

Lysimachia punctata

Proteaceae

The proteas are a family of dicotyledonous trees and shrubs which grow exclusively in the southern hemisphere and show clear links between Australia, southern Africa and South America. The family has 62 genera and over 1000 species. The simple leaves are alternate and have no stipules. The flowers are usually hermaphrodite. The flower shape is irregular, with four perianth segments which are sometimes considered sepals. They have lobes which are turned back. Alternated by the perianth petals are two to four scale-shaped corolla petals. The four stamens are located on the perianth lobes; usually only the anther is free-standing and is visible. The ovary is unilocular and superior; it may be stemmed. The style is long and bent, sometimes fleshy, sometimes thread-like. The fruit is a nut, a follicle or a stone fruit.

Banksia serrata
Banksia
NAME: The genus is named after Sir Joseph Banks (1743-1820), an Englishman who travelled the world with James Cook and collected a great many plants. He possessed a large library and a very extensive herbarium, both of which he left to the British Museum. *Serrata* = serrate; it refers to the leaf margins.
DESCRIPTION: Tree with a height of 10 m and long, narrow serrate leaves. The plant has large flower heads which are pale orange when they open. A related sort, *B. grandis*, is yellow.
ORIGIN: Tasmania, Australia (Victoria, New South Wales).
CULTIVATION: Chiefly South Africa.
AVAILABILITY: All the year round, less so in summer.
CARE: Cut off a bit of the stem; use cut-flower food for woody plants and water at a temperature of 15-20° C.
KEEPING PROPERTIES: 1 month or more, depending on how fresh they are when purchased.
USE: In exclusive floral decorations.
SCENT: None.

Leucadendrum argenteum
Silvertree
NAME: The genus name is composed of the Greek words *leucos* (= white) and *dendron* (= tree) and refers to the colour of the bark. *Argenteum* means 'silvery-white', the colour of the leaf.
DESCRIPTION: Silverish-coloured shrub with downy silvery hairs and narrow, leathery leaves of 10-15 cm. The flowers are grouped in conical flower heads of approx. 4 cm wide at the ends of the branches; the heads are encircled by yellow bracts.
ORIGIN: South Africa; introduced in England in 1693.
CULTIVATION: Africa, including the Ivory Coast and South Africa.
AVAILABILITY: All the year round; less so in summer.
CARE: See *Banksia serrata*.
KEEPING PROPERTIES: See *Banksia serrata*.
USE: See *Banksia serrata*.
SCENT: See *Banksia serrata*.

Banksia serrata

Protea cynaroides

Leucospermum cordifolium,
syn. *L nutans*
Nodding pincushion
NAME: *Leucospermum* means 'having white seeds'; *nutans*, from *nutare*, stands for 'nodding'.

DESCRIPTION: A shrub, about 1 m high, with fairly small greyish-green leaves. The flower petals are curved inward somewhat; the centre of the flower is filled with the curving, orange-yellow stigma.

ORIGIN: The south-western part of the Cape of Good Hope (South Africa).

CULTIVATION: Chiefly in South Africa.

AVAILABILITY: All the year round, less so in summer.

CARE: Cut off a bit of the stem; use cut-flower food for woody plants and water with a temperature of 15-20° C.

KEEPING PROPERTIES: Around a month or longer, depending on how fresh they are when purchased.

USE: In flower arrangement, for exclusive work.

SCENT: None.

Protea cynaroides
King protea, Giant honeypot
NAME: The genus is named after the Greek sea god, Proteus, who herded the seals for Poseidon. The name (Proteus could assume various shapes) alludes to the various forms of this plant.

DESCRIPTION: Large shrub with ovoid leaves of 10-12 cm long on long stems. The stems are red; the flowers are grouped in heads sometimes as wide as 20 cm and are surrounded by pale pink (sometimes white) scales with silky hairs.

ORIGIN: South Africa; first cultivated in the United Kingdom in 1774.

CULTIVATION: Chiefly in Australia, South Africa.

AVAILABILITY: The year round, with a peak between September and May.

CARE: See *Banksia serrata*.

KEEPING PROPERTIES: See *Banksia serrata*.

USE: See *Banksia serrata*.

SCENT: See *Banksia serrata*.

Protea neriifolia
Oleander-leaved protea
NAME: See *P. cynaroides*. *Neriifolia* means 'having the foliage of the nerium oleander'.

DESCRIPTION: Richly blossoming shrub, up to 3 m high, with silvery-blueish, leathery, and elliptical leaves. The flower stands at the end of the stem and its colour varies from rose-red to pale pink. The tops of the petals are brownish-black and covered with hairs.

ORIGIN: South Africa (around the Cape of Good Hope) and Australia.

CULTIVATION: See *Banksia serrata*.

AVAILABILITY: See *Banksia serrata*.

CARE: See *Banksia serrata*.

KEEPING PROPERTIES: See *Banksia serrata*.

USE: See *Banksia serrata*.

SCENT: See *Banksia serrata*.

Protea barbigera
Giant woolly-beard
NAME: See *P. cynaroides*. *Barbigera* means 'having a beard' and refers to the woolly flowers.

DESCRIPTION: An evergreen shrub which can reach a height of 1.50 m. The leathery leaves, 15 cm long, are pale greyish-green with whitish hairs. The flower can reach a diameter of 20 cm. The outer petals are soft or pale pink; the tops are covered with fine, silvery-white hairs. They encircle a large number of soft, white and woolly flowers with at the bottom a dark violet centre.

ORIGIN: South Africa (the south-western part of the Cape Province) and Australia.

CULTIVATION: See *Banksia serrata*.

AVAILABILITY: See *Banksia serrata*.

CARE: See *Banksia serrata*.

KEEPING PROPERTIES: See *Banksia serrata*.

USE: See *Banksia serrata*.

SCENT: See *Banksia serrata*.

Leucadendrum argenteum

Leucospermum cordifolium, syn. L. nutans 'Hawaii'

Ranunculaceae

The buttercup family (*Ranunculaceae*) is not so very large in itself - 50 genera, 1800 species - but does exhibit a great variety of forms. With the exception of a few woody climbers, such as the clematis, they are generally herbaceous plants. The perennials winter with the aid of a root-stock or radical tubers. Most buttercups belong in the temperate and cooler regions of the northern hemisphere.

The leaves are quite diverse in shape: linear or heart-shaped, feather-shaped, palmate, composite, etc. Some genera have stipules.

The inflorescence is terminal, which means that the flowers stand at the end of the stem. Sometimes they are simple, as in the anemone, but usually they are grouped in plumes or racemes. The floral parts stand in a spiral on the receptacle; often they stand in whorls. The number of sepals is 3-5. With the exception of a few varieties, such as the Persian buttercup, a clear corona and corolla are lacking. The number of stamens is large; they spring open outwards. The number of carpels varies from one to many; sometimes, as in Nigella, they are fused into a capsule. The annual sorts are generally self-pollinating; meadow rue (*Thalictrum*) is pollinated by the wind; most others are pollinated by insects.

Aconitum napellus
Monk's hood

NAME: The genus is named after the Greek *akoniton*, the name of a plant which was used to poison wolves and other beasts of prey. *Napellus* is the diminutive of *napus* = tuber.

DESCRIPTION: Perennial, up to 1.20 m high, with deeply incised five to seven-part leaves. The outer leaf slips are narrow. The flower stem is not branched. The flower stems stand erect, the anther is slightly bent, the bracts are lanceolate-linear. The cultivated forms of this variety have dense, strong flower racemes in a number of shades of blue.

ORIGIN: Western and Central Europe, as far north as Sweden.

CULTIVATION: In temperate areas with hothouse and outdoor cut-flower cultivation.

AVAILABILITY: May-October.

CARE: When purchased, the first flower buds should be fully-grown, but not yet open. Remove lower leaves; cut off a bit of the stem; use cut-flower food.

KEEPING PROPERTIES: 12-14 days.

USE: In a vase, in mixed bouquets and in flower arrangement. The flowers may also be dried.

SCENT: None.

Aconitum carmichaelii var. arendsii
Monk's hood

NAME: See *A. napellus*. *Carmichaellii* means 'resembling the Carmichaelia' (papilionaceous plants).

DESCRIPTION: A tuberous perennial, up to 1 m high, with stems covered with kinky hairs. The leathery, dark green and shiny leaves are deeply cut into three parts, but clearly joined at the base. The flower racemes are somewhat branched at the base. The stamen is 1½ times to twice as high as it is wide. In the variety *arendsii*, the dark bluish-violet and very large flowers stand on a stem which can reach a length of 1.50 m.

ORIGIN: China; first cultivated in Germany in 1886.

CULTIVATION: Temperate areas with outdoor cut-flower cultivation.

AVAILABILITY: September-October.

CARE: When purchased, around one-third of the flowers should be open. Remove lower leaves; cut off a bit of the stem and use cut-flower food.

KEEPING PROPERTIES: 10-12 days.

USE: In a vase and in mixed bouquets.

SCENT: None.

Aconitum napellus

Anemone coronaria 'Mona lisa'

Anemone coronoria 'De Caen'
Garden anemone

NAME: The genus name is derived from the Greek word *anemos* = wind. Some anemone sorts are also called 'windflowers'. *Coronoria* means 'crowned' and refers to the crown of leaves on the stem below the flower.

DESCRIPTION: A plant with flat tubers. The ternate leaves stand in rosettes and have lightly cut linear tips. The double involucres (the corona on the flower stem) are feather-shaped. The simple flowers are 9-10 cm across and may be red, blue, pink, violet or white. The stamens are very dark. The flower stem is 25-30 cm long. The anemone mixture 'De Caen' is being replaced to an increasing extent by the large-flowering type 'Mona Lisa', with long, strong stems (up to 45 cm) and a flower diameter of 10-13 cm. They are F_1 hybrids of American origin, in the colours red, pink, blue, lilac, white, and two-coloured.

ORIGIN: The eastern part of the Mediterranean area and Asia Minor. The plant has been cultivated since ancient times.

CULTIVATION: As a hothouse cut flower, in temperate areas.

AVAILABILITY: From November, with a peak between February and the end of June.

CARE: When purchased, the flower should be fully-grown. Often they are sold wrapped in paper, to keep them straight. Use cut-flower food for bulb plants; first cut off a bit of the stem.

KEEPING PROPERTIES: 8-12 days.

USE: Primarily in a vase.

SCENT: None.

Anemone hupehensis var. japonica
Windflower

NAME: See *A. coronaria*. *Hupehensis* means 'from the Chinese province of Hu-pei'; the variety name refers to its origin in Japan.

DESCRIPTION: Perennial, 70-90 cm high, with slightly hairy stems. The leaves are ternate; their parts are ovate leaves which are three to five-lobed and have roughly serrate margins. The 10-15 flowers, with a diameter of around 8 cm, are grouped in loose plumes and have 5-6 silky-haired flower petals. The original colour was pink; in cultivation, dark pink, lilac-rose, dark red and white cultivars have also been developed.

ORIGIN: Central and western China; taken under cultivation in Italy in 1902.

CULTIVATION: Temperate areas with outdoor cut-flower cultivation.

AVAILABILITY: August-end of October.

CARE: When purchased, three-fourths of the flowers should be open. Use cut-flower food for herbaceous plants. If the flowers start to droop, put them in water with a temperature of 50-55° C.

KEEPING PROPERTIES: 6-9 days.

USE: In mixed bouquets and in flower arrangement.

SCENT: None.

Anemone hupehensis var. japonica

Cimicifuga racemosa
Bugbane

NAME: The genus name is a contraction of the words *cimicis* (= bedbug) and *fugare* (= to repel). The unpleasant odour of this plant repels bedbugs and other pests. *Racemosa* refers to the unbranched (racemose) inflorescence.

DESCRIPTION: Perennial plant, up to 1.50 m high, with an erect manner of growth. The leaves are twice to three times ternate and have elongated, lanceolate leaflets with serrate margins. The silvery-white flowers are arranged in somewhat pendulous racemes.

ORIGIN: The eastern United States; under cultivation since 1732.

CULTIVATION: Temperate areas with outdoor cut-flower cultivation.

AVAILABILITY: July-September.

CARE: When purchased, one-fourth of the flowers should be open. Cut off a bit of the stem; use cut-flower food for herbaceous plants.

KEEPING PROPERTIES: 6-7 days.

USE: Chiefly in mixed bouquets. In a vase only to a limited extent because of the unpleasant odour.

SCENT: Unpleasant.

'Prins Hendrik'

Clematis 'Prins Hendrik'
Clematis

NAME: *Clematis* means 'plant with vines'.

DESCRIPTION: Climbing plant with a maximum length of 2.5 m. The flowers have 6-8 fairly broad petals which partly overlap. The plant flowers both on the young, herbaceous stems and on the older, woody stems. The cultivar 'Prins Hendrik' is lavender-coloured; the flowers have clear veins.

ORIGIN: A cross of *C. lanuginosa*, from China, with the south-east European sorts *C. patens* and *C. viticella*. It was obtained in the United Kingdom, France and the Netherlands.

CULTIVATION: In temperate areas, on a very limited scale as a hot-house cut flower.

AVAILABILITY: May/June; limited in autumn.

CARE: When purchased, the flowers should be fully grown. Always keep them in water to prevent them from drooping. Use half the amount of cut-flower food.

KEEPING PROPERTIES: 7-11 days.

USE: In flower arrangement, for exclusive funeral work, and in floating dishes, etc.

SCENT: None.

Delphinium consolida
Larkspur

NAME: The Greeks called this flower after the Delphian Apollo, the god of the city of Delphi. *Consolida* means 'to strengthen'.

DESCRIPTION: Annual plant, 60-80 cm high, the lower leaves of which are tripinnate with linear slips. The long flower stem is covered with dozens of flowers which are slightly spreading. At the top, the axis is covered with short, crooked hairs. The original colour was blue; now there are also pink, salmon pink, lilac and various blue shades. The plant is also sometimes erroneously called *D. ajacis*. However, that species has shorter, somewhat branching flower stems.

ORIGIN: Mediterranean area and western Asia; nowadays native to all of southern Europe. The plant has been cultivated since ancient times.

CULTIVATION: Temperate areas with flower cultivation.

AVAILABILITY: Fresh flowers, from the end of May until mid-September. As a dried flower, all the year round.

CARE: When purchasing fresh flowers, the lower 6-8 flowers should be open; the others will develop later. Remove the lower leaves from the stem; cut off a bit of the stem, use cut-flower food for herbaceous plants.

KEEPING PROPERTIES: 8-12 days.

USE: In a vase and for decorations.

SCENT: None.

Delphinium hybrids
Larkspur

NAME: See *D. consolida*.

DESCRIPTION: Perennial plant, up to 1.80 m high in the Elatum cultivars and 1.40 in the Belladonna cultivars. The latter group of cultivars has loosely branching flower racemes and a decorative composition; the main colour is blue. The Elatum cultivars have very dense flower clusters with large flowers, and are cultivated in numerous shades of blue, lilac, lilac-rose, and greenish-white. Thanks to crosses with *D. nudicaule*, there is now also a limited supply of salmon-coloured and orange cultivars. These latest crosses were obtained by the Dutch professor, Legro.

ORIGIN: The original varieties came from China and eastern Europe; *C. nudicaule* is native to California.

CULTIVATION: Temperate areas with hothouse and outdoor cut-flower cultivation. At present much improvement work is being performed in the United Kingdom.

AVAILABILITY: June-November.

CARE: When purchased, a few flowers should be open. Usually the flower is treated with a special substance to prevent shedding. Cut off a bit of the stem; use cut-flower food.

KEEPING PROPERTIES: 10-12 days.

USE: In a vase and for decorations.

SCENT: None.

Delphinium hybrid

Helleborus niger subsp. niger

Nigella damascena

Helleborus niger subsp. niger
Christmas rose

NAME: The genus name is the Latin translation of the Greek plant name *helleboros*, the meaning of which is unknown. *Niger* = black; the colour of the roots.
DESCRIPTION: An evergreen perennial which grows to a height of 30 cm. The plant has radical leaves which are composed of wide, cuneiform leaflets with serrate tops. The flower stem protrudes above the foliage; the flowers, 8-9 cm wide, stand alone or in groups of 2-3 and point sideways. The style is longer than the stamens. The flowers are initially bright white, later fading to pink and green.
ORIGIN: Central Europe; first cultivated in Switzerland in 830.
CULTIVATION: Temperate areas.
AVAILABILITY: From mid-November until Christmas.
CARE: When purchased, the flowers and the first two whorls of stamens should be entirely open. Use half the amount of cut-flower food.
KEEPING PROPERTIES: 8-12 days.
USE: In Christmas decorations, mainly in Scandinavia.
SCENT: None.

Nigella damascena
Love in a mist, Devil in the bush

NAME: *Nigella* is the diminutive of *niger* (= black) and refers to the colour of the seeds. *Damascena* means from Damascus.
DESCRIPTION: Annual plant, up to 40 cm high, with finely cut and divided leaves. The simple flowers, 3-4 cm wide, are pale blue and surrounded by a five-leaved and finely cut involucre which is longer than the calyx. The perianth is pentamerous and has eight 'honey leaves'. The fruit, from which the plant chiefly derives its ornamental value, is a follicle; the carpels are fused.
ORIGIN: The Mediterranean area; under cultivation since 1542.
CULTIVATION: In temperate and subtropical areas; widely cultivated in the Netherlands for the dried fruits.
AVAILABILITY: As fresh flowers, very limited, from June to September. The dried fruits, all the year round.
CARE: Fresh flowers should be entirely open when purchased. Cut off a bit of the stem; use cut-flower food for herbaceous plants.
KEEPING PROPERTIES: Fresh flowers, 6-10 days.
USE: Fresh flowers, in a vase and in mixed bouquets. The dried fruits are used in flower arrangement and in dried flower bouquets.
SCENT: None.

Ranunculus asiaticus 'peony-flowered'
Persian buttercup

NAME: The genus name is declined form of the Latin *rana* (= frog) and refers to the place of growth, which is often swampy. *Asiaticus* = from Asia.
DESCRIPTION: Perennial plant with lobed tubers and hairy stems. The lower leaves are ovate and trilobate; the upper ones are singly or doubly ternate, with ovate, toothed segments. The usually simple flowers are about 5 cm wide, have a hair-covered calyx and are very filled out: they look like peonies. They come in all shades of red, pink, orange, yellow and white.
ORIGIN: From the eastern Mediterranean area to Iran.
CULTIVATION: In temperate areas as hothouse cut flowers; in the subtropics outdoors.
AVAILABILITY: Nearly all the year round, with peaks in March/April and December.
CARE: When purchased, the flowers should be open. Transport them erect to prevent them growing crooked. Use cut-flower food for bulb flowers.
KEEPING PROPERTIES: 8-14 days.
USE: In a vase and in small bouquets.
SCENT: None.

Ranunculus asiaticus 'peony-flowered'

Rosaceae

The rose family (*Rosaceae*) has an almost equally important role in flower cultivation as it does in fruit cultivation, where it is represented by plants such as the apple, pear, peach, prune, cherry, apricot, etc.; it forms one of true economic cornerstones of this branch. To a large extent, this is because of the genus *Rosa*, a very old cultivated plant of which many thousands of cultivars have been developed over the centuries, and in practically all the colours of the rainbow - with the exception of blue. The rose occupies a prominent position in cut-flower cultivation.

The family has around 120 genera and nearly 3400 species. They are deciduous or evergreen trees, shrubs, perennials and a few annual plants, and they mostly come from the northern hemisphere. A few sorts, such as the rose, have prickles.

The leaves are generally alternate and simple (in the cherry tree, for instance) or composite, as in the rose. They all have stipules. The leaf stem bears several pairs of nectaries.

The flowers are usually regular and hermaphrodite. In the rose, the carpels stand on an extended receptacle shaped like a vase, thus forming the rose hip. Many members of the rose family have a secondary calyx: a ring of five leaves which alternate with the sepals. The natural species mostly have five petals; in the cultivated double-flowering cultivars - of the rose, for instance - there are many more. The stamens, and sometimes the styles as well, have been replaced by petals. In this case, the centre of the flower may still be green, because the carpels have altered into flower petals. Such flowers are naturally infertile. In fertile sorts, the stamens are grouped in whorls. There are a great many of them; their number is twice to three times the number of flower petals. All *Rosaceae* are easy to pollinate; they form an abundance of pollen which has a strong attraction for all kinds of insects.

Trollius hybrid

Trollius chinensis
Globe flower

NAME: The genus name is a Latinized form of the German 'Trollblume'; trolls are evil spirits in Norse mythology. Another explanation says that the name is derived from *trullius* (= basin or wash-basin); in this case, it would allude to the shape of the flowers. *Chinensis* means 'from China'.
DESCRIPTION: Strongly branching plant, 60-80 cm high. The lower stem leaves are kidney-shaped and 5-lobed, with serrate lobes. The flowers, 3-4 cm wide, stand in clusters and have 7-12 blunt sepals which are spreading when the plant is in full bloom. The flower consists of 10-13 broadly oval, deep orange-yellow sepals, and has twenty orange-yellow 'honey leaves' which are twice as long as the stamens. The best cultivar is 'Golden Queen'.
ORIGIN: North-eastern China; brought to the United Kingdom in 1827.
CULTIVATION: Temperate areas with outdoor cut-flower cultivation.
AVAILABILITY: May-July.
CARE: When purchased, the flower buds should show colour, but still be closed. As soon as they are cut, the flowers should be set in deep water to prevent them drooping. Cut of a bit of the stem; use cut-flower food for herbaceous plants.
KEEPING PROPERTIES: 8-10 days.
USE: In a vase, in mixed bouquets and in flower arrangement.
SCENT: None.

Trollius hybrids
Globe-flower

NAME: See *T. chinensis*.
DESCRIPTION: Perennial plant, up to 60 cm in height, with leaves cut and divided into five parts, and toothed or deeply cut lobes. The lower leaves have long stalks; the upper ones are sessile. The flowers, 3-4 cm wide, have 10-15 sepals and 5-10 'honey leaves' which are as long as the stamens. There are several cultivars. The best for keeping quality is 'Orange Princess' (orangish-yellow); the cultivar 'Orange Globe' is large-flowering.
ORIGIN: The ancestors were native to south-eastern Europe and Asia. The hybrids are derived from *T. europaeus*, *T. asiaticus* and *T. chinensis*. Many crosses were obtained in the United Kingdom, Germany and the Netherlands.
CULTIVATION: Temperate areas with outdoor cut-flower cultivation.
AVAILABILITY: May-June.
CARE: When purchased, the buds should show their colour completely and be fully grown; the flowers must still be closed. Put them in deep water straight away (the flowers readily droop) and use cut-flower food for herbaceous plants.
KEEPING PROPERTIES: 8-10 days.
USE: In a vase, in mixed bouquets and in flower arrangement.
SCENT: None.

Alchemilla mollis
Lady's mantle

NAME: The genus name is derived from the Arabic word *alkimia*: our 'alchemy'. Before alchemists lost themselves trying to turn base metals into gold, they used to occupy themselves with obtaining healing herbal infusions. They even ascribed miraculous powers to the drops of water on the leaves of *Alchemilla*. *Mollis* means 'soft'.
DESCRIPTION: A perennial plant, 40-50 cm high, with a soft pubescence and fan-shaped leaves. They are seven to eleven-lobed, with sinuate and notched margins, and are bright green on the upper side. The underside is somewhat lighter coloured. The leaves are covered with a waxy layer on which water drops remain. The plant derives its ornamental value from these leaves. The tiny yellowish-green flowers are grouped in large panicles.
ORIGIN: The Balkans; introduced in Austria in 1874.
CULTIVATION: Temperate areas with outdoor cut-flower cultivation.
AVAILABILITY: May-September.
CARE: When purchased, most flowers should be open. Cut off a bit of the stem; use cut-flower food for herbaceous plants.
KEEPING PROPERTIES: 10-12 days.
USE: In mixed bouquets and floral work (foliage as well).
SCENT: None.

Aruncus dioicus
Goat's beard

NAME: *Aruncus* means 'goat's beard' and refers to the shape of the inflorescence. *Dioicus* = dioecious (male and female flowers on separate plants).

DESCRIPTION: Perennial plant with a height of 1-1.50 m. The somewhat wrinkled leaves are triangular and bipinnate to tripinnate, with pointed, doubly-serrate leaflets. The small flowers are creamy white and stand in large plumes at the ends of the flower stems. The plumes fade during the bloom to greenish-white.

ORIGIN: Northern hemisphere; first cultivated in Germany in 1561.

CULTIVATION: Temperate areas with outdoor cut-flower cultivation.

AVAILABILITY: June-August.

CARE: When purchased, most flowers in the raceme should be open. Cut off a bit of the stem; use cut-flower food.

KEEPING PROPERTIES: 10-14 days.

USE: Chiefly in mixed bouquets and in flower arrangement.

SCENT: None.

Malus Floribunda hybrids
Crab apple

NAME: *Malus* = apple tree. The hybrid name refers to one of the ancestors of the cross, *M. floribunda*.

DESCRIPTION: A shrub or small tree with serrate leaves. The flowers vary in colour from pale pink to red. The plant forms large numbers of tiny fruits which are yellow, red, or yellow with red.

ORIGIN: The species are native to Europe, Asia and America. The hybrid is a cross of numerous varieties, including *M. domestica* (the wild apple), *M. floribunda*, *M. baccata*, *M. prunifolia* and others.

CULTIVATION: As forced shrubs in temperate areas.

AVAILABILITY: As flowering branches, from February to April; as branches with fruits, from September until November.

CARE: The buds on flowering branches should be fully grown but not yet open. For branches with fruits, the apples should show colour, but they should not be ripe because then they readily drop off when they are used. Put the branches in water with cut-flower food for shrubs. Take care: never use the branches with fruits together with flowers. The fruits produce the ageing hormone, ethylene, which causes the flowers to wilt rapidly.

KEEPING PROPERTIES: Blossoms 7-10 days; fruits 12-16 days.

USE: In a vase, in mixed floral work (only flowering branches) and as a decoration.

SCENT: None.

Cultivars

'**Prof. Sprenger**', a profusely flowering cultivar with pale pink flowers and, in autumn, a large number of small, pale green apples with a lovely red blush.

'**Wintergold**'. As a flowering plant this cultivar has no value (the flower colour is too pale), but it is used as a fruit branch; in autumn it bears a large number of bright yellow apples.

Ornamental apples because of their fruits are *M. floribunda* and *M. sieboldii*, 'Gorgeous' and 'Red Sentinel'.

◁ Alchemilla mollis   ▷ Aruncus dioicus   ▷ Malus Floribunda hybrid

Mespilus germanica

Prunus 'Kanzan'

Mespilus germanica
Medlar

NAME: *Mespilus* is an old Latin name, a translation of the Greek *mespi* or *mespilon*; the meaning is unknown. *Germanica* means 'from Germany'.

DESCRIPTION: A tree or large shrub with thorny twigs which are covered with a dense, felty layer. The elongated leaves, with entire or finely dentate margins, are softly pubescent on both sides. The white flowers stand alone; they bear forty stamens and are around 3 cm across. The yellow-brown apple-like fruits have green calyx slips. A few cultivars are grown.

ORIGIN: Western Asia and, in the wild, in Europe. Has been under cultivation for a long time.

CULTIVATION: Often cut in the wild. Cultivated on a limited scale in temperate areas.

AVAILABILITY: From July until October (branches with fruits).

CARE: Remove the leaves, put the branches in water with half the usual concentration of cut-flower food for shrubs.

KEEPING PROPERTIES: 2-3 weeks.

USE: In mixed floral work, as for decorations. Sometimes in exclusive floral work.

SCENT: None.

Prunus avium
Wild cherry, Gean

NAME: *Prunus* is the Latin name for the plum tree. *Avium* is a reference to the fact that birds eat the fruits.

DESCRIPTION: Tree with pyramid-shaped branchings and short shoots which accumulate at the ends of the twigs. The leaves are elongated ovate, with hairs on the undersides; the leaf stem is purplish. The white flowers are grouped in leafless umbels; the bud scales are folded back during the flowering. The calyx has smooth margins.

ORIGIN: Western Asia and Europe; has been under cultivation for a long time.

CULTIVATION: Fruit growers in temperate areas.

AVAILABILITY: From the end of March until the beginning of May.

CARE: The buds should show colour when purchased, but preferably not yet be open. Cut off a bit of the stem; use cut-flower food for shrubs.

KEEPING PROPERTIES: 8-10 days.

USE: In a vase and in mixed bouquets.

SCENT: None.

Prunus glandulosa 'Alboplena'
White almond

NAME: See *P.-avium. Glandulosa* means 'gland-bearing', 'covered with glands'.

DESCRIPTION: A shrub with dark brown twigs. The buds come in groups of three. The leaves are ovate lanceolate and sharply double dentate. The base of the leaf is cuneate. The double white blooms are solitary or in pairs on stems along the entire branch.

ORIGIN: The wild form of this Prunus is native to China and Japan and was introduced in France in 1785. The cultivar 'Alboplena' was obtained in the United Kingdom in 1852.

CULTIVATION: Chiefly by shrub forcing houses in Aalsmeer, in the Netherlands.

AVAILABILITY: From December until the end of May, with a peak from January until the end of March.

CARE: After having been cut, the branches are put in specially treated water. Cut off a bit of the stem; use cut-flower food for shrubs.

KEEPING PROPERTIES: Around 2 weeks.

USE: In a vase, in mixed bouquets and in flower arrangement.

SCENT: None.

Prunus 'Kanzan',
syn. *'Hizakura'*
Japanese cherry

NAME: See *P. avium.*

DESCRIPTION: A shrub with ovate leaves which turn brownish-red when they open. The leaf margins are serrate, with long-needled teeth. The underside of the leaf is somewhat bluish-green. The flowers are grouped in bunches of two to five on short shoots: short side branches with blossom wood. The double flowers are dark pink and have two green styles.

ORIGIN: Japan; introduced in Germany in 1909.

CULTIVATION: Still on a limited scale, at the shrub forcing houses in Aalsmeer. The cultivation takes a long time and is labour-intensive, which makes it very costly.

AVAILABILITY: To a very modest extent, before Christmas; the main supply is from January until March. In May there is a modest supply of branches which have been cut outdoors.

CARE: When purchased, the buds should be fully grown but not yet open. After cutting, the branches are put in specially treated water for three hours. Cut off a bit of the stem; use cut-flower food for shrubs.

KEEPING PROPERTIES: 10-14 days.

USE: In flower arrangement and as an exclusive vase flower.

SCENT: Slightly fragrant.

Prunus triloba 'Multiplex'
Double-flowering almond

NAME: See *P. avium. Triloba* means
'3-lobed' (the leaves).
DESCRIPTION: Small shrub with a
stem of about 60 cm and a crown
resembling a pollard willow. The
invertly ovate leaves are somewhat
3-lobed past the middle. The leaf
margins are doubly serrate. The
deep pink, semi-double flowers
stand in pairs on either side of the
leaf buds.
ORIGIN: Eastern Asia; under cultivation in China for a very long
time. This sort is unknown in the
wild. First cultivated in the United
Kingdom in 1855.
CULTIVATION: Chiefly in the Netherlands.
AVAILABILITY: Branches from cooled shrubs in November/December.
The main supply period is in
January/February, and ends early
in April.
CARE: When purchased, the lower
buds should be fully-grown and a
lovely rose-red in colour, but still
closed. Immediately after cutting,
the branches are placed in specially
treated water for three hours. Cut
off a bit of the stem; use half the
concentration of cut-flower food
for shrubs.
KEEPING PROPERTIES: 7-8 days.
USE: In a vase and in mixed bouquets.
SCENT: None.

△ 'Veronica'   △ 'Sterling Silver'   △ 'Madelon'

△ 'Jaccaranda'   △ 'Disco'   △ 'Jack Frost'

Rosa hybrids
Rose

NAME: *Rosa* is the old Latin name
for the rose.
DESCRIPTION: Because of the crosses
of the numerous species, no uniform description of the rose is possible. The plant has a pinnate leaf.
The fully grown leaves, in the
middle of the stem, are composed
of usually 5-9 leaflets with two
stipules. At the bottom of the
stem, and just under the flower,
the leaves often have fewer leaflets.
The leaf colour varies with the cultivar, as do shape and colour of the
flowers and the colour of the
prickles. Despite the widely-held
belief, some roses have no thorns!
ORIGIN: The present roses have a
generous number of ancestors. The
most important one is a form of *R.
chinensis*, kown as the Bengal rose.
It was introduced in Europe from
Bengal in 1768. It is almost certainly a hybrid that had been cultivated in China for thousands of
years before that. By crossing the
Bengal rose with *R. gallica*, native
to Central Europe, the Bourbon
hybrids were obtained. The Noi-
sette hybrids were obtained from

crosses of the Bengal rose with *R.
moschata*, the musk rose from the
Himalayas, Iran and Ethiopia.
Other ancestors: *R. centifolia* from
the Caucasus and itself probably
also a hybrid; *R. foetida*, the Persian rose, from Asia Minor (this
brought the yellow colour into the
assortment) and *R. damascena*.
CULTIVATION: In all temperate and
subtropical areas of the world,
with the Netherlands as the largest
producer.
AVAILABILITY: The year round.
CARE: Immediately after cutting,
the roses are cooled and put in
treated water. They are also transported in it. After purchase, remove the lower leaves and the
prickles. Cut off a bit of the stem;
use cut-flower food.
KEEPING PROPERTIES: 8-18 days, depending on the temperature and
the cultivar.
USE: In a vase, in mixed bouquets
and in flower arrangement.
SCENT: Slightly to very fragrant,
depending on the cultivar and the
room temperature.

Cultivars

In rose cultivation, the assortment
is subdivided into four groups:
large-flowering roses, medium-
flowering roses, small-flowering
roses and bunch roses. Each group
has many dozens of cultivars in
numerous colours. We will here
list a few of the most important
and most frequently cultivated or
newer cultivars for each of these
types. The assortment is still
growing.

Large-flowering cultivars

'**Sonia**' is the most frequently cultivated large-flowering rose. The
colour of the flower is deep pink;
the cultivar keeps very well and
lends itself nicely to use in bouquets, etc.
'**Madelon**' is one of the newer
large-flowering roses; a cultivar
which is becoming more and more
important. The colour is a lovely
red; it keeps very well.
'**Jaccaranda**', another new large-
flowering cultivar, has a very different lilac-rose flower colour and
shiny dark green leaves. It does not
keep so well, but the flower has a
very pleasant scent. Other large-

flowering cultivars with a good
scent are 'Sterling Silver' (lilac) and
'Mainzer Fastnacht' (lilac).
'**Tineke**' is a new large-flowering
cultivar with a bright white colour: also - and this is special - during the months when there is little
light. The flowers are large, the
bud shape very lovely and it keeps
very well.
'**Veronica**' (red) has a very double, weak scented flower and many
prickles, some underneath the leaf
stem. It keeps well (about 9 days);
on water the flowers open very
well and do not discolour.
Other frequently cultivated large-
flowering rose cultivars are 'Ilona'
(syn. 'Varlon') (red), 'Red Success'
(red), 'Baccara' (red) and 'Cocktail
'80' (yellow with red edges).

Medium-flowering cultivars

'**Gabriella**' is a mutant of the
bright orange cultivar 'Mercedes',
which also brought forth the mutants 'Jaguar' (deep orange) and
'Gerdo' (pale pink). These cultivars
are sold with slightly opened buds,
so that they will keep longer.
'Mercedes' and its mutants are the
most frequently cultivated me-

medium-flowering roses. Their scent is weak.

'**Jack Frost**' is a medium-flowering greenish-white rose with beautifully formed buds and a good scent. It also keeps very well. Thanks to the colour, the cultivar is very popular.

'**Frisco**' is a fairly new cultivar in this group; the flowers are bright yellow. 'Frisco' has joined battle in the market with older yellow medium-size flowered cultivars such as 'Golden Times' and 'Evergold'; it is a cultivar which will surely increase in importance.

'**Laminuette**' takes up around 6 per cent of the acreage of medium-flowering roses. It is the most frequently cultivated two-coloured rose: white with red margins. It keeps well and its scent is good.

Small-flowering cultivars
'**Motrea**' is the most frequently cultivated rose cultivar and also the most important small-flowering rose. The cultivar, the flowers of which are a warm pink, is very productive, in winter as well, and is easy to work with because it has almost no prickles. The bud shape is not pretty and the flower has hardly any scent, but it keeps exceptionally well.

'**Carol**' is a pale pink small-flowering rose, a mutant of 'Garnette' (see below) and closely related to

△ 'Carol'   △ 'Motrea'   △ 'Garnette'

'Motrea'. The cultivar has small flowers on a light-coloured branch. The flowers have almost no scent, but they keep well.

'**Garnette**' is the oldest cultivar from the group of small-flowering roses. The flower colour is a somewhat matt red; the bud is short and stands somewhat open. The rose has almost no scent, but its production is high and it keeps very well.

'**Disco**' is a small-flowering red cultivar with double flowers which have no scent and do not discolour on water. Sometimes the flower shape differs. The stem has many prickles.

Bunch roses
This type of rose keeps a very long time; its cultivation is expanding and many new cultivars are coming on the market. In winter the supply is small, and the quality is also poor. Well-known bunch roses are the small-flowering 'Dorus Rijkers' (salmon pink) and the bright orange 'Gloria Mundi'. The newer cultivars have larger flowers and longer stems. Examples: 'Evelien' (bright pink), 'Porcelina' (cream-coloured), 'Mimi Rose' (pale pink), 'White Dream' (white) and 'Pink Delight' (pink).

Spiraea x bumalda
'*Anthony Waterer*'
Spiraea
NAME: *Spiraea* is the Latin form of an old Greek plant name, *speiraia*; nothing is known about the meaning of the word or about the plant in question. This is known as 'graeca obscura': cryptic Greek names. *Bumalda* is derived from Jo Antonius Bumalda, the fantasy name of Ovidio Montalbani (1601-1671), professor at Bologna and author of botanical publications.
DESCRIPTION: A shrub with striped twigs which often peel off somewhat. The glabrous leaves are ovate lanceolate; the dark red flowers have long stamens and stand in dense, wide clusters. The plant flowers on the young shoots.
ORIGIN: The ancestors *S. albiflora* and *S. japonica* are both native to Japan. The sort cross *S. x bumalda* was obtained in Belgium around 1890.
CULTIVATION: Limited, by shrub breeders in temperate areas.
AVAILABILITY: June-July.
CARE: When purchased, the first flowers should be well open. Remove the lower leaves; cut off a bit of the stem and use cut-flower food.
KEEPING PROPERTIES: 10-15 days.
USE: In mixed bouquets.
SCENT: None.

'Evelien'

Spirea x bumalda 'Anthony Waterer'

Rubiaceae

The madder family (*Rubiaceae*) is a very large family of dicotyledonous plants: chiefly trees, shrubs and semi-shrubs which
are native to the tropics and subtropics. Some members of the
madder family have great economic value, such as the coffee
plant and the cinchona or quinine tree.
The simple leaves of the Rubiaceae are in whorls or opposite
and generally have smooth margins. The stipules, usually
large, are fused on either side of the stem.
The flowers are grouped in panicles or clusters, sometimes in
heads. They are hermaphrodite and usually regular, with four
or five sepals, petals and stamens. The stamens are borne at the
base of the corolla. There are often thread-like hairs on the
throat of this tube. The ovary is usually composed of two
fused carpels. The fruit is a berry or a stone fruit.

Bouvardia longiflora
Bouvardia

NAME: The genus is named after
the Parisian physician Charles
Bouvard (1571-1658): in addition
to being a professor and director of
the Jardin des Plantes, he was also
personal physician to King Louis
XIII. In a single year, Bouvard
gave the monarch 200 different
medicines, 200 blood-lettings and
47 enemas. His Majesty seems to
have survived it. *Longiflora* =
long-flowering.
DESCRIPTION: A semi-woody shrub
with erect stems and pointed
leaves. The flowers are grouped in
clusters. They have a long corolla
tube with four spreading lobes.
The cultivar 'Albatros' is cultivated.
ORIGIN: Mexico; introduced in the
United Kingdom in 1854.
CULTIVATION: In temperate and
subtropical areas, in the hothouse
or outdoors in summer.
AVAILABILITY: Usually in autumn.
However, it is possible to spread
the flowering time by using artificial daylight. *Bouvardia* is a short-
day plant.
CARE: When purchased, the first
flower should be well open. After
cutting, the branches are put in
specially treated water. Use special
cut-flower food for bouvardias.
Make sure the flower branches do
not droop because of lack of water.
KEEPING PROPERTIES: 14-18 days.
USE: In a vase, in bouquets and in
flower arrangement.
SCENT: Very fragrant.

Bouvardia hybrids
Bouvardia

NAME: See *B. longiflora*.
DESCRIPTION: Sub-shrub with long,
erect branches and pointed leaves.
The white, pink, salmon pink or
bright red flowers, approx. 3 cm
across, are grouped in clusters. The
corolla is 1-2 cm long; the four
lobes spread widely. Frequently
cultivated cultivars are 'Arthemy'
(white), 'Arethusa' (pale pink),
'Daphne' (salmon pink), 'Sappho'
(dark red), 'Red King' (red) and
'President Cleveland' (bright red).
Double-flowered cultivars are being cultivated more and more.
ORIGIN: The species chiefly from
Mexico. The hybrid is a cross of *B.
longifolia*, *B. leiantha* and *B. ternifo-
lia*.
CULTIVATION: As a hothouse cut
flower, in temperate and subtropical areas; however, chiefly in the
Netherlands.
AVAILABILITY: On a limited scale in
February/March; in good supply
from May to end of December.
CARE: When purchased, two flowers should be open. After cutting,
the flowers are put in specially
treated water for three hours; they
are sold in covers to prevent too
much dehydration. Use special
cut-flower food for bouvardias.
KEEPING PROPERTIES: 19-22 days.
USE: In a vase, in flower arrangement and in bouquets. Their use is
increasing.
SCENT: Slight.

Gardenia jasminioides
Gardenia

NAME: The genus is named after
the Canadian doctor, botanist and
zoologist A. Garden (1730-1791),
one of Linnaeus' correspondents.
Jasminioides means 'similar to the
jasmine'; here it primarily refers to
the scent.
DESCRIPTION: Small evergreen
shrub with shiny green, somewhat
leathery, leaves with smooth margins. The double flowers, 6-8 cm
wide, are white and have thick,
sturdy petals. As they mature, the
flowers change to a creamy white.
The edges are spreading, with 8-9
lobes. The most frequently grown
cultivar is 'Fortunei'.
ORIGIN: China; introduced in the
United Kingdom in 1754.
CULTIVATION: As a cut flower,
widely in the United States; in
Europe, practically only as a pot
plant. In the United Kingdom,
where the gardenia was formerly
also popular as a cut flower, it has
been supplanted by longer-stem-
med sorts such as roses, pinks and
chrysanthemums.
AVAILABILITY: On a limited scale,
all the year round.
CARE: When purchased, the flowers
should be entirely open and still a
bright white. They can be arranged on damp cotton wool, for
example.
KEEPING PROPERTIES: Because of
their use (as a corsage), this is not
important.
USE: In flower arrangement, almost
exclusively in corsages.
SCENT: Very fragrant; a heavy,
sweet scent.

Bouvardia hybrid

Rutaceae

The rue family (*Rutaceae*) is a family of dicotyledonous plants, mainly trees, shrubs and a few herbaceous plants. It has 150 genera and around 900 species, of which the genus *Citrus* is economically the most important as the supplier of citrus fruits such as the orange, the lemon, the grapefruit, the manadarin, etc. Rues grow all over the world, although chiefly in the tropics and subtropics, especially in Australia and southern Africa. The leaves contain oil glands which can be observed as tiny, light points. When bruised, their presence becomes quite clear because they give off an aromatic odour. The leaves are alternate and have no stipules. They are trilobate to deeply cut; some, however, are simple (*Citrus*).

The flowers are grouped in cluster-like inflorescences and have four or five sepals and petals. They are free-standing and are often dentate or fimbriated (finely fringed). The disc of the receptacle bears 8-10 nectaries and the same number of stamens. The ovary is superior.

Dictamnus albus
Burning bush

NAME: The genus name is derived from the old Greek plant name, *diktamnos*, a contraction of the name of the mountain, Diktè, on Crete, and the word *tamnos* (= shrub). With this name, the Greeks referred to an entirely different plant sort. *Albus* is 'white' and refers to the sheer white roots of the burning bush.

DESCRIPTION: Perennial, 70-90 cm high, with hairy stems. The entire plant is covered with oil glands which give off a strong, aromatic scent. On warm days, the oil fumes can be set alight around the flower, which gave the plant its English name. The 7-8 leaves which make up the composite leaf are ovate and have finely serrate margins. In the wild, the 3-4 large flowers are dark lilac, with an even darker venation. In cultivation there are white and pink cultivars. The petals narrow at the base to a 'claw'. The fruits, which are highly decorative and keep very well, are also used in flower arrangement.

ORIGIN: Central and southern Europe; first cultivated in Switzerland in 1830.

CULTIVATION: Temperate areas with outdoor cut-flower cultivation.

AVAILABILITY: The flowers, in May/June; the branches with fruits in July and August.

KEEPING PROPERTIES: The flowers 8-12 days, the fruits 18-21 days.

CARE: When purchased, the first flowers should be open. Use cut-flower food.

USE: In bouquets and in flower arrangement. The fruits are also sometimes used in flower arrangement.

SCENT: Strongly aromatic.

Skimmia japonica 'Rubella'
(no popular name)

NAME: *Skimmia* is the Latinized form of the Japanese popular name, *shikimi*. *Japonica* = from Japan; *rubella* is 'reddish'.

DESCRIPTION: Fairly squat evergreen shrub with somewhat pointed lanceolate spatula-shaped leaves. They have short stalks and are shiny green on top. The tops of the twigs are purplish, as are the leaf stems and the flower buds. The exclusively male flowers are ashen white and stand in extended racemes.

ORIGIN: Japan; introduced in the United Kingdom in 1838. The cultivar 'Rubella' was obtained in 1865, also in the United Kingdom; the colour of the buds is a deeper red than that of the original sort.

CULTIVATION: Shrub growers in temperate areas.

AVAILABILITY: From October to April.

KEEPING PROPERTIES: When purchased, the buds should show colour but should not yet be open. Use cut-flower food for shrubs.

CARE: 4 weeks or longer.

USE: The branches with the reddish flower buds are used in floral work. The open flowers are not used.

SCENT: Highly scented when the flowers are open.

Skimmia japonica 'Rubella'

Salicaceae

The willow family (*Salicaceae*) includes around 350 species of dicotyledonous trees or shrubs, classified into four genera. The most important genera are the willow (*Salix spp.*) and the poplar (*Populus spp.*); willows are small trees or shrubs, the poplars are large trees. Their wood does not wear very well, and is used in making matches and wooden shoes. The family is chiefly native to the temperate areas of the northern hemisphere.

All willow family members are deciduous plants with simple leaves that have stipules. The plants are monoecious; male and female flowers are never found on the same plant. The flowers stand in catkins which blossom before the leaf appears; they stand in the axil of a bract and have no sepals or petals.

In the willow, each flower has two glands which give off a sweet-smelling nectar. This attracts the insects that pollinate them. The willow has stiff, erect catkins; the poplar (pollinated by the wind) long and pendulous ones.

The fruits are usually small capsules; the seeds generally have a whorl of hairs which makes spreading by the wind possible.

Salix caprea
Willow

NAME: *Salix* is the Latin name for the willow. *Caprea* means 'goat'; these animals love to eat the plant.
DESCRIPTION: Shrub with leaves of 6-11 cm which can have quite a variety of shapes, from broadly oval to lanceolate. The leaf margin is entire or irregularly serrate; the top is often crooked. The very striking male catkins appear before the foliage and generally blossom in March/April.
ORIGIN: North-eastern Asia; has been under cultivation for a very long time.
CULTIVATION: The branches with catkins are generally cut in the wild.
AVAILABILITY: From December (not wild but forced) until March/April.
CARE: The catkins should show their colour when purchased. Cut off the dried ends of the branches and place them in clean water. The water will stay clean if you add cut-flower food.
KEEPING PROPERTIES: 3-4 weeks.
USE: In flower arrangement, for special occasions such as Christmas and in spring floral work.
SCENT: None.

Salix matsudana 'Tortuosa'
Dragon-claw willow

NAME: See *S. caprea. Matsudana* honours the Japanese botanist Sadahisa Matsuda (1857-1921), a student of the Chinese flora. The cultivar name tortuosa means 'curving' and refers to the shape of the branches.
DESCRIPTION: Tree with glabrous, yellowy-green twigs which are spirally twisted. The narrow, lanceolate leaves are yellowy-green on the undersides. The catkins are small and have no ornamental value.
ORIGIN: The species is native to north China and was introduced in the United States in 1906. The cultivar 'Tortuosa' was first cultivated in France in 1924. It originated in China.
CULTIVATION: In temperate areas, for the twisted branches.
AVAILABILITY: From June until April.
CARE: Remove the leaves; set the branches in clean water.
KEEPING PROPERTIES: 4-6 weeks.
USE: In flower arrangement and in decorations.
SCENT: None.

Salix sachalinensis 'Sekka',
syn. *S. 'Setsuka'*
Willow

NAME: See *S. caprea. Sachalinensis* means 'from the island of Sakhalin' (Asian Russia); *sekka* and *setsuka* are Japanese cultivar names.
DESCRIPTION: Shrub with thick, erect and nearly bare twigs which later turn colour from green to yellow. Some branches are bent and conspicuously widened; this manner of growth is termed 'fasciated'. The catkins are long and numerous, but they do not give the plant its ornamental value.
ORIGIN: Japan. Only the cultivar 'Sekka' is under cultivation.
CULTIVATION: In temperate areas, for the wildly contorted branches.
AVAILABILITY: From July until April.
CARE: The branches are only cut when they have become woody enough. In the summer months, remove the leaves to show off the shape better. See further *S. caprea*.
KEEPING PROPERTIES: 4-6 weeks.
USE: In flower arrangement and in exclusive floral work.
SCENT: None.

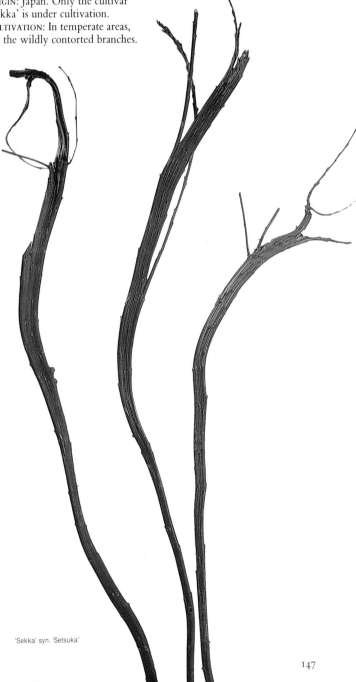

'Sekka' syn. 'Setsuka'

Sarraceniaceae

Saxifragaceae

A small family of insectivorous pitcher plants with only three genera, it is native to the marshy Atlantic and Pacific coasts of the United States and South America. The leaves in which the insects are trapped have acquired a special form. The family is related to the *Nepenthaceae* (p. 113) and, according to some classifications of insectivorous plants, to the sundew (*Drosera*).

The saxifrage family (*Saxifragaceae*) is related to the *Rosaceae*. It includes 50 genera and around 1500 species of small trees, shrubs, semi-shrubs, perennial and annual plants which grow all over the world, but particularly in the northern hemisphere; they are dicotyledonous.

The simple leaves, which have no stipules, are often alternate but sometimes opposite. In some varieties the leaves are composite.

The number of petals, if any, is four or five. The number of stamens is twice this number, but may be more. The 2-4 carpels are fused, at least at the base. The fruit is a small capsule, except in the subfamily *Ribesoideae* (some members of this subfamily are the red and the white currant and the blackberry), which bear berries.

Sarracenia flava
Yellow pitcher plant
NAME: The genus name commemorates Dr. M.S. Sarrazin (1659-1734), a Canadian doctor. *Flava* means 'pale yellow', the colour of the leaves.
DESCRIPTION: Plant with an underground root-stock on which rosettes of pitcher-shaped leaves grow. These yellowish-green leaves are narrowly tubular, with a green edging on the outside. The quite crooked pitcher is covered by a hood-shaped appendage. The mouth of the tube contains honey glands which attract insects inside. At the bottom of the pitcher is an acerbic liquid in which the prey is digested. The plant blossoms with 4-6 overlapping sepals, five white petals and many short stamens. The fruit is a capsule.
ORIGIN: The marshy areas of the southern United States and countries to the south.
CULTIVATION: On a limited scale, in the hothouse, in the Netherlands and elsewhere.
AVAILABILITY: All the year round.
CARE: When purchased, the pitcher should be fully grown. Use cut-flower food in half the usual concentration.
KEEPING PROPERTIES: Approx. 2 weeks.
USE: In flower arrangement, for exclusive work.
SCENT: None.

Sarracenia leucophylla
White pitcher plant
NAME: See *S. flava*. *Leucophylla* = having white leaves.
DESCRIPTION: See *S. flava*; the only difference is formed by the silvery-white ends of the leaves.
ORIGIN: See *S. flava*.
CULTIVATION: See *S. flava*.
AVAILABILITY: See *S. flava*.
CARE: See *S. flava*.
KEEPING PROPERTIES: See *S. flava*.
USE: See *S. flava*.
SCENT: See *S. flava*.

Astilbe x arendsii hybrids
False spiraea
NAME: *Astilbe* means 'plant without sheen' and recalls the first sort described, *A. rivularis*, which has inconspicuous yellowish-green flowers. The hybrid is named after its originator, the German perennial breeder Arends.
DESCRIPTION: Perennial, up to 1 m high, with two to three times ternate leaves; the lower leaves are large. The flowers are grouped in dense panicles. A large assortment is cultivated in white, dark red, lilac and many shades of pink.
ORIGIN: The ancestors are native to China, Korea and Japan. The *Arendsii* hybrid dates back to 1910 and was derived from *A. astilboides*, *A. japonica*, *A. davidii* and *A. thunbergii*. The Frenchman Lemoine started with the crossing as early as 1895.
CULTIVATION: Temperate areas with outdoor cut-flower cultivation.
AVAILABILITY: July-September.
CARE: The flowers should nearly all be open when purchased; flowers which are not yet open will droop. After cutting, they are immediately placed in specially treated water of 50-60° C. During handling they should be kept in water as much as possible. Always use cut-flower food.
KEEPING PROPERTIES: 5-8 days.
USE: In a vase and in mixed bouquets.
SCENT: None.

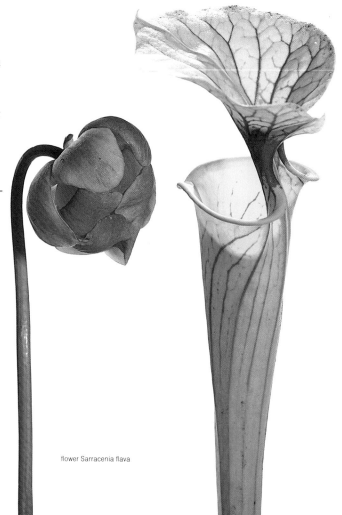

flower Sarracenia flava

Astilbe japonica hybrids
Florist's spiraea

NAME: See *A. arendsii* hybrids. The *Japonica* hybrids are so named because *A. japonica* greatly predominates in them.

DESCRIPTION: The two to three times ternate leaves have red hairy stems; the leaflets which make up the compound leaves are ovate with serrate margins. The leaf colour ranges from purplish-red to green. The flowers are grouped in dense, hairy, erect plumes on somewhat arched branches. The petals are at most twice as long as the sepals. The stamens are shorter than the petals. The Japonica hybrids blossom earlier than the Arendsii hybrids; the flower colour is dark red, purplish-red, white, pink or salmon pink. The plant grows to be about 60 cm high.

ORIGIN: The original species is native to Japan and was introduced into Belgium in 1830.

CULTIVATION: Temperate areas with outdoor cut-flower cultivation.

AVAILABILITY: May-June.

CARE: See *A. x arendsii* hybrids.

KEEPING PROPERTIES: See *A. x arendsii* hybrids.

USE: See *A. x arendsii* hybrids.

SCENT: See *A. x arendsii* hybrids.

Hydrangea macrophylla

Heuchera hybrids
Coral bell, Alum root

NAME: The genus is named after the Austrian botanist, J.H. von Heucher (1677-1747), director of the botanical gardens in Wittemberg and author of several botanical publications.

DESCRIPTION: Perennial plant with flower stems of 35-40 cm and heart-shaped, round leaves grouped in rosettes; they are usually somewhat brown spotted. The leaf is borne on a long stem, has 7-9 lobes and serrate margins. The flowers are grouped in somewhat pilose racemes; the stamens are shorter or longer than the calyx lobes. The most frequent flower colour is red; in addition, there are cultivars in shades of white and pink. A frequently grown cultivar is the red 'Pluie de Feu'.

ORIGIN: Southern and eastern United States and northern Mexico. The hybrid is a British cross from the beginning of this century, of *H. sanguine* with *H. micrantha* and *H. americana*.

CULTIVATION: Temperate and subtropical areas with outdoor cut-flower cultivation.

AVAILABILITY: June/July.

CARE: When purchased, half the flowers should be open and the stem should be firm. Use cut-flower food for herbaceous plants; cut off a bit of the stem.

KEEPING PROPERTIES: 12-15 days.

USE: In a vase, in fine summer bouquets and in floral work.

SCENT: None.

Hydrangea macrophylla
French hortensia

NAME: *Hydrangea* means 'water barrel' and refers to the shape of the fruit after it has sprung open. *Macrophylla* = large-leaved.

DESCRIPTION: Shrub with thick twigs and large, fairly thick leaves with deeply serrate margins. The inflorescence is globular, with large sterile flowers. The sepals are white, red or carmine red. The pink flowers may turn blue if they absorb aluminium. The flowers turn greenish after they have finished blooming and, after drying, can be kept a long time.

ORIGIN: Japan, where the plant has been under cultivation for a very long time. The original form is unknown. Introduced into the United Kingdom in 1788.

CULTIVATION: Temperate areas, outdoors or forced in the hothouse.

AVAILABILITY: March-July. Overblown flowers from August until December.

CARE: When purchased, the flower should be fully grown. Remove most leaves; cut off a bit of the stem; use cut-flower food for shrubs. Watch them for drooping.

KEEPING PROPERTIES: Fresh flowers, 10-12 days; overblown flowers, about 4 weeks.

USE: In flower arrangement and sometimes in modern bouquets.

SCENT: None.

Astilbe x arendsii hybrid

Scrophulariaceae

The figwort family (*Scrophulariaceae*) is a large family of dicotyledonous, mainly herbaceous plants, a few shrubs and climbing plants and only one tree: the beautiful blue-flowering *Paulonia* from China. The 220 genera, with approximately 3000 species, are distributed all over the world; however, most of them grow in the northern hemisphere. In an economic sense, the family chiefly derives its importance from the ornamental value of several varieties. A species of foxglove, *Digitalis lanata*, is cultivated for medicinal use.

The leaves of the figworts are alternate or more usually opposite and simple or with feathery lobes. Usually stipules are absent. If there are any, then their shape and size are rather varied, as are those of the bracts.

The flowers are hermaphrodite; the shape is nearly always asymmetrical. In some sorts the flowers are spurred or almost regular. The shape of the asymmetrical corolla is adapted to the types of insects that pollinate the plant. Flowers with a short style are visited by wasps, flowers with a short corolla base by bees and flies. Stamens and stigmas are so positioned that they touch the abdomens of the insects. The superior ovary, with a honey-producing disc at the base, consists of two fused carpels and a bilobate stigma.

Antirrhinum majus
Snapdragon

NAME: The genus name is a contraction of *anti* (= taking the place of) and *rhinos* (= nose) and refers to the shape of the flower, which resembles a calf's snout. *Majus* = larger than.

DESCRIPTION: Glabrous perennial which is always cultivated as an annual; it can reach a height of 1 m. The lanceolate leaves vary in colour from green to reddish, according to the flower colour. The large flowers, about 5 cm across, are grouped in racemes. The flower has a five-lobed calyx, as well as a five-lobed corolla with two lips. Both the two long and two short stamens are attached to the corolla. The original flower colour was pink; nowadays they are cultivated in white and all shades of red, pink, orange and yellow. In the hothouse, the cultivars are cultivated by name.

ORIGIN: Mediterranean area; the plant was first cultivated in Switzerland in 1561.

CULTIVATION: As a hothouse cut flower all over the world; popular in the United States.

AVAILABILITY: Limited supply in February/March. Two peaks: May/June and from August until the end of October.

CARE: When purchased, the lowest flower should be open. Immediately put them in water with cut-flower food.

KEEPING PROPERTIES: 8-10 days.

USE: In a vase and in mixed bouquets.

SCENT: None.

Cultivars

In addition to the many hothouse snapdragons grown by cultivar, there is the colour mixture '**Rocket**', which blooms outdoors. These plants are somewhat squatter than their hothouse counterparts (stem length 50-50 cm) and are usually deeper and warmer in colour. They keep somewhat less well, because when the lowest flowers are cut, they have often been pollinated. The flower quickly wilts after it is pollinated.

Chelone obliqua
Turtle-head, **Snake-head**

NAME: *Chelone* means 'turtle'; the upper lip of the flower corolla has the shape of this animal's shell. *Obliqua* = crooked.

DESCRIPTION: Perennial plant, up to 60 cm high, with square stems. The leaves are elongated lanceolate and fairly deeply serrate or cut. The flowers, 2-3 cm long, are grouped in short, spike-shaped racemes. The carmine red bracts are finely fringed.

ORIGIN: The south-eastern United States; first cultivated in the United Kingdom in 1752.

CULTIVATION: Temperate areas with outdoor cut-flower cultivation.

AVAILABILITY: June/July.

CARE: When purchased, the lowest flowers in the raceme should be open. Cut off a bit of the stem; use cut-flower food for herbaceous plants.

KEEPING PROPERTIES: 8-12 days.

USE: Especially in mixed bouquets.

SCENT: None.

Digitalis purpurea
Foxglove

NAME: The genus name is derived from the Latin *digitus*, meaning 'finger'. The name refers to the shape of the flower. *Purpurea* = purple.

DESCRIPTION: Biennial plant, up to 1.50 m high, with hairy stems. The large, elongated ovate leaves are grouped in rosettes; the underside of the leaf is hairy. The flowers, 3-5 cm long, are grouped in racemes turned to one side; they have a tubular, somewhat pendulous corolla. The original colour was pink, with a somewhat lighter and spotted inside. Nowadays red, carmine red, yellow, brownish and white forms are also cultivated.

ORIGIN: Central and Western Europe; first cultivated in Switzerland in 1830.

CULTIVATION: Temperate areas with outdoor cut-flower cultivation.

AVAILABILITY: June and July.

CARE: When purchased, the lower four or five flowers should be open. Cut off a bit of the stem; use cut-flower food for herbaceous plants.

KEEPING PROPERTIES: 7-12 days.

USE: For decorations and, to a limited extent, in mixed bouquets.

SCENT: None.

Antirrhinum majus

Penstemon hybrids
Beard tongue
NAME: *Penstemon* is Greek, meaning 'five stamens'.
DESCRIPTION: Semi-shrub with densely leafy stems. The leaves are oval, with a wedge-shaped base. The upper side is dark green, the underside pale green. The flowers, 4-6 cm long, are grouped in large racemes. The most frequent colour: all kinds of shades of red.
ORIGIN: The ancestors were native to the south-western United States, Mexico and Central and South America. The hybrid is a cross of *P. barbatus, P. scouleri* and mainly *P. hartwegii*.
CULTIVATION: Subtropical areas or regions with a mild temperate climate: the plants are insufficiently hardy.
AVAILABILITY: July-September.
CARE: When purchased, one-third of the flowers should be open. Use cut-flower food for herbaceous plants.
KEEPING PROPERTIES: 5-8 days.
USE: In a vase, in mixed bouquets and in flower arrangement.
SCENT: None.

Chelone obliqua

Veronica longifolia
Speedwell
NAME: *Veronica* is an old plant name, the meaning of which is not known. Some assume that it is a contraction of *vera unica* = the only truth: this would be related to its presumed medicinal qualities. Others say the genus is named for St Veronica. *Longifolia* = long-flowered.
DESCRIPTION: Perennial plant with short, hairy stems of 60-90 cm long. The lanceolate leaves often stand in whorls; their margins are singly or doubly serrate. The base of the leaf is heart-shaped or truncate. The flowers stand in profusely flowering narrow racemes. They are blue and have bracts which are longer than the flower stems.
ORIGIN: Europe and Asia; first cultivated in Switzerland in 1561.
CULTIVATION: Temperate areas with outdoor cut-flower cultivation.
AVAILABILITY: June-August.
CARE: When purchased, the flowers should be 50 per cent open. Use cut-flower food.
KEEPING PROPERTIES: 5-8 days.
USE: In a vase, in mixed bouquets and in flower arrangement.
SCENT: None.

Digitalis purpurea

Veronica virginica
Speedwell
NAME: See *V. longifolia. Virginica* means: 'from the American state of Virginia'.
DESCRIPTION: Perennial plant with lanceolate leaves in 4-6 whorls. The leaves have finely serrate margins. The pale blue flowers are grouped in many spike-shaped racemes or in the leaf axils. The stamens extend far out of the flowers.
ORIGIN: The eastern United States; first cultivated in the United Kingdom in 1714.
CULTIVATION: Temperate areas with outdoor cut-flower cultivation.
AVAILABILITY: From July until the end of August.
CARE: When purchased, nearly half the flowers on the raceme should be open. If they are not, the top of the stem will droop. Cut off a bit of the stem; use cut-flower food.
KEEPING PROPERTIES: 5-8 days.
USE: In a vase, in mixed bouquets and in flower arrangement.
SCENT: None.

Phygelius capensis
Cape figwort
NAME: *Phygelius* means 'shunning the sun' and refers to the position of the flowers, which is averted from the sun. *Capensis* = from the Cape of Good Hope.
DESCRIPTION: Perennial plant with square stems which are woody at the base. The elongated oval leaves are stemmed; the margins are serrate. The flowers are grouped in long plumes, mostly with the opening rotated slightly towards the axis of the plume. They are 4-5 cm long. The base of the corolla is long and curved, with short lobes. The stamens protrude from the throat. The colour of the flower is bright orange-red, with a yellow throat.
ORIGIN: South Africa; introduced into the United Kingdom in 1855.
CULTIVATION: In areas with a subtropical or mild temperate climate. Cultivated on a limited scale.
AVAILABILITY: July-September.
CARE: When purchased, the lower flowers should be open. Put them in water which is not too cold; cut off a bit of the stem and use cut-flower food.
KEEPING PROPERTIES: 9-12 days.
USE: In flower arrangement and as an exclusive flower in a vase.
SCENT: None.

Solanaceae

The sizeable nightshade family (*Solanaceae*) contains 90 genera with some two or three thousand species of dicotyledonous plants, many of which are poisonous, such as black nightshade (*Solanum nigrum*), henbane (*Hyoscyamus niger*), thorn apple (*Datura stramonium*) and – in two senses – tobacco. Incidentally, the poisonous substances are also used in medicine. The other side of the coin is that some members of this family are useful nutritional plants of often great economic importance, such as the potato, the tomato, the eggplant, the sweet pepper and several other pepper varieties. Many ornamental plants also contribute to the economic significance of the family.

The *Solanaceae* have many representatives in Central and South America and in Australia. The family is taken to have its origins in South America. Most varieties are annual or perennial herbaceous plants. There are also a few climbing plants and shrubs.

The leaves are usually alternate, varying in shape from simple to deeply cut. Generally they have no stipules. The flowers are regular and hermaphrodite, usually with five sepals and five to ten petals. The sepals are fairly often fused. Sometimes they encircle the flower, as is the case in the Chinese lantern. The petals are somewhat fused, forming a flattish bell-shaped or tubular flower. Five stamens are generally implanted on the base of the corolla, alternately with the corolla lobes. The ovary is superior and has a single style; the fruit is a berry or a capsule.

Salpiglossis sinuata

Nicandra physalioides
Nicandra

NAME: The genus is named after the Greek physician Nicandros ($\pm$ 275 B.C.), author of several medical works. *Physalioides* = resembling physalis; the fruit resembles that of the winter cherry.
DESCRIPTION: Annual plant, 70-80 cm high, with an unpleasant smell. The stems are angular; the ovate leaves are widely cut and stand in pairs. The single, hanging flowers stand on short stems; are cup-shaped and about 4 cm wide. The colour is white with a purplish-blue margin. The deeply parted calyx has five wide slips which enlarge after flowering. The globular fruits have a diameter of about 5 cm and determine the ornamental value of the plant.
ORIGIN: Peru; grows in Europe often in the wild. Introduced into the United Kingdom in 1759.
CULTIVATION: Subtropical and temperate areas with dried cut-flower cultivation.

AVAILABILITY: Dried, all the year round.
CARE: For dried flower, none.
KEEPING PROPERTIES: Once dried, about one year.
USE: Dried in floral work and dried bouquets.
SCENT: None (when dried).

Physalis alkekengi var. franchetii
Winter cherry, Chinese lantern

NAME: *Physalis* means 'water blister' and refers to the swollen orange fruit calyx. *Alkekengi* is an Arabic plant name. The variety name is taken from Adrien Franchet (1834-1900), who began collecting plants at the young age of 16 for the Marquis de Viltraye, and who did much botanic research in China.
DESCRIPTION: Perennial plant with creeping root-stock, up to 50 cm high, with a slightly pilose stem. The large oval leaves have entire margins and narrow into a winged leaf stem. The flowers stand alone, sometimes with one or two others; they are about 2 cm wide and white, with yellow spots inside. The plant derives its ornamental value from the deep orange berries which are encircled by the swollen orange, lantern-shaped calyx. It has a diameter of 5-6 cm.
ORIGIN: Japan. The variety franchetii has larger lanterns than the original species and was first cultivated in the United Kingdom in 1895.

CULTIVATION: Temperate areas with outdoor cut-flower cultivation.
AVAILABILITY: All the year round.
CARE: The plants are sold when the lantern shows good colour. Hang them up upside down to dry.
KEEPING PROPERTIES: Once dried, 1-2 years.
USE: In dried bouquets.
SCENT: None.

Nicandra physalodes

Salpiglossis sinuata
Trumpet flower
NAME: The genus name is a contraction of *salpinx* (= trumpet) and *glossa* (= tongue). The words refer to shapes of the corolla and style respectively. *Sinuata* means curving.
DESCRIPTION: Annual plant with a height of 70-80 cm. The stems and leaves are slightly sticky, the ovate leaves serrately cut. The funnel-shaped flowers are grouped in racemes. At the top, the flower is slightly lobed. The flowers appear in different colours and are often striped.

ORIGIN: Western South America; introduced into the United Kingdom in 1820.
CULTIVATION: On a limited scale, in subtropical and temperate areas.
AVAILABILITY: June-end of August.
CARE: When purchased, the first flower should be open. Cut off a bit of the stem; use cut-flower food for herbaceous plants.
KEEPING PROPERTIES: 7-9 days.
USE: In a vase and in mixed bouquets.
SCENT: None.

Typhaceae

The 15 species of monocotyledonous plants which together form the cat-tail family (*Typhaceae*) all belong to one genus: *Typha*, the reed mace or cat's tail. They grow in temperate, subtropical and tropical areas, from the polar circle to 30° south of the equator. Their favourite growing places are reed marshes and the banks of lakes and rivers. The water, in most cases, is fresh. The plants can reach a height of 2 m; their stem is sometimes partly under water. The long leaves are thick and spongy.

The flowers of *Typhaceae* are unisexual; the inflorescence is a spike. The male flowers are at the top of the spike, the female ones near the bottom. It is the latter which give the plant its ornamental value.

The sepals and petals consist of thread-like appendages or spoon-shaped scales; this gives the perianth a rather conspicuous appearance. The perianth petals stand in between the carpels or the stamens. The female flowers have a unilocular ovary with a ribbon-like stigma. The male flowers have two to five stamens; sometimes they are free-standing, in other sorts they are fused. The fruit, an achene, has a long stem which is covered with brown hairs; these hairs serve to make propagation by the wind possible. The economic importance of the family is slight. Only the leaves of *Typha latifolia* are still used here and there to weave mats and chair seats.

Typha latifolia
Cat-tail, Reed-mace
NAME: *Typha* is the Latin version of the old Greek name *tuphe*, which indicated the genus. *Latifolia* = having wide leaves.
DESCRIPTION: Perennial plant, up to 1,50 m high, with long, band-like leaves of 2 cm wide. The floral spikes are initially greenish. The female part is longer; it grows to about 3 cm thick and 15 cm long and turns brown (the 'cigar').
ORIGIN: Northern hemisphere.
CULTIVATION: Cut in the wild.
AVAILABILITY: Dried, the year round.
CARE: For dried flowers, none.
KEEPING PROPERTIES: Around one year; after this the spike will start to shed.
USE: In dried form, in floral work.
SCENT: None.

Typha minima
Cat-tail, Small reed-mace
NAME: See *T. latifolia. Minima* = the smallest.
DESCRIPTION: Same as *T. latifolia*, but smaller (60-80 cm high) with very narrow leaves; the female part of the spike is smaller than the male part.
ORIGIN: From Europe into Central Asia.
CULTIVATION: See *T. latifolia*.
AVAILABILITY: See *T. latifolia*.
CARE: See *T. latifolia*.
KEEPING PROPERTIES: See *T. latifolia*.
USE: See *T. latifolia*.
SCENT: See *T. latifolia*.

Physalis alkekengi var. franchetii   Typha latifolia

Umbelliferae

Broadly speaking, the carrot family (*Umbelliferae*) grows all over the world, although its representatives are rare in the tropics, being primarily concentrated in areas with a temperate climate. The family has some 200 genera; the species number somewhere between two and three thousand. They are all herbaceous: annual, biennial, or perennial plants. Several sorts are remarkable for their scent, taste or toxicity, or for their significance as cooking herb or nutritional plant.

The leaves of the carrot family are alternate and usually cut and divided. The flowers are generally grouped in simple or composite umbels, often with involucres at the point where the flower or umbel stems join. The flowers in the umbels open from the edge inwards. The stamens are generally ripe before the stigmas. The edge flowers in the umbel are sometimes irregular and have larger petals, to attract the insects which are to pollinate them. Sometimes the involucres serve to attract; then they are larger and coloured, as in the blue thistle (*Eryngium*).

The flowers almost always have five petals and five sepals. The calyx is greatly reduced; the ovary is inferior and consists of two carpels. The base on which the style stands is variable in shape, and is characteristic of this family. The fruits take a wide variety of shapes. It is remarkable that hybridization almost never takes place in the *Umbelliferae*.

Astrantia major

Astrantia major
Masterwort
NAME: *Astrantia* is an old plant name with an unclear meaning. The word *astron*, meaning 'star', most certainly plays a role: the flowers are star-shaped. *Major* = larger.

DESCRIPTION: Perennial plant, 60-70 cm high, with pentamerous or deeply five-part cut leaves. The leaflets of which they are composed are inversely oval and have doubly serrate margins. The small pink flowers stand on stems in wide umbels. The flowers are shorter than the involucre. The involucre leaves are petal-like and white or red, with a feathery venation.

ORIGIN: Central Europe to the Caucasus; first cultivated in Belgium in 1574.

CULTIVATION: Temperate areas with outdoor cut-flower cultivation.
AVAILABILITY: June-August.
CARE: When purchased, the main umbel should be open. Cut off a bit of the stem; use cut-flower food for herbaceous plants.
KEEPING PROPERTIES: 7-10 days.
USE: Much in flower arrangement; also in mixed bouquets.
SCENT: None.

Heracleum mantegazzianum
Giant cow parsnip

NAME: The genus is named after Heracles or Hercules, the powerful Greek demigod who is said to have discovered the medicinal qualities of the plant. The species is named after the Italian professor and scientific author, Paolo Mantegazzi (1830–1910).

DESCRIPTION: Very large perennial plant which can reach a height of 2.5 to 3 m. The stem is thick, with reddish-brown spots at the bottom. The leaves are more than 1 m long; the lower ones are bipinnate to tripinnate. The leaflets of which they are composed are elongated, with narrow, triangular and pointed, notched leaf segments. The underside of the leaf is hairy. The white flowers stand in umbels which have over 50 rays and may reach a diameter of 1 m.

ORIGIN: The Caucasus; first cultivated in Russia in 1890.

CULTIVATION: On a limited scale, in temperate areas. Also grows much in the wild.

AVAILABILITY: June-July.

CARE: When purchased, the umbel should be fully-grown; an unripe umbel will quickly droop. Cut off a bit of the stem; use cut-flower food for herbaceous plants.

KEEPING PROPERTIES: 7-9 days.

USE: In decorations. Many people are allergic to this plant when they touch it - the sap may cause severe blistering, especially in sunny weather.

SCENT: The entire plant smells somewhat of aniseed.

Eryngium alpinum
Alpine thistle

NAME: The genus name is the Latin translation of the old Greek name *erungion* or *erungein*, which is associated with the healing effect of the plant for colic. *Alpinum* = from the Alps.

DESCRIPTION: Perennial plant, up to 60 cm high, with a stem which is steel-blue at the top. The lower leaves are deeply heart-shaped, with doubly serrate margins; the upper ones are roundish, heart-shaped and cleft into three to five parts. Their colour is bluish-green. The blue flowers are grouped in cylindrical flower heads. The involucral bracts are twice lightly cut, with very narrow segments.

ORIGIN: The Alps and the Balkans; the plant was first cultivated in England in 1597.

CULTIVATION: Temperate areas with outdoor cut-flower cultivation.

AVAILABILITY: July-August.

CARE: When purchased, the first flowers should be open. Use cut-flower food.

KEEPING PROPERTIES: 12-16 days.

USE: In mixed summer bouquets and in flower arrangement; sometimes as dried flowers.

SCENT: None.

Eryngium alpinum

Eryngium planum
Sea holly
NAME: See *E. alpinum*. *Planum* = flat.

DESCRIPTION: Perennial plant, 80–100 cm high, with stems that are blue toward the top. The fairly thin leaves are heart-shaped and sharply dentate near to the bottom of the stem; the upper ones are cut and divided into three to five parts, with prickly teeth. The flower heads are small and stand in fairly dense clusters. Their colour is a bright pale blue. The 6 to 7 involucral bracts are lanceolate and somewhat prickly dentate.

ORIGIN: From Central and South-ern Europe to Siberia. This variety was first cultivated in Belgium in 1567.

CULTIVATION: Temperate areas with outdoor cut-flower cultivation.

AVAILABILITY: July-August.

CARE: When purchased, the first flowers should be slightly open. Cut off a bit of the stem; use cut-flower food.

KEEPING PROPERTIES: 12-16 days.

USE: In mixed bouquets and in flower arrangement.

SCENT: None.

Heracleum mantegazzianum

Anethum graveolens var. graveolens

Eryngium planum

Ammi majus
Lace flower

NAME: *Ammi* is the old Greek and Latin name for the flower. *Majus* is 'larger than usual'. The plant bears an outward resemblance to the - related - dill plant.

DESCRIPTION: Annual plant with a height of about 80 cm. At the tops of the stems are umbels with a large number of tiny white flowers. Their lacy structure is reminiscent of Brussels lace.

ORIGIN: Mediterranean area, from the Canary Islands to Iran; it is now wild in Western and Central Europe and in large parts of North America.

CULTIVATION: The Netherlands; in the winter months, also in Israel and Kenya.

AVAILABILITY: From early May from the hothouse; July until autumn, outdoors. Some imported in the rest of the year.

CARE: The flowers in the umbel should be at least one-third open when purchased. Remove the lower leaves, cut off a bit of the stem; use cut-flower food for herbaceous plants.

KEEPING PROPERTIES: 8-10 days, depending on the temperature.

USE: Usually in mixed summer bouquets.

SCENT: Slightly aromatic.

Anethum graveolens var. graveolens
Dill, Anethum

NAME: *Anethum* is the Latin form of the Greek name of the plant: *anethon*. *Graveolens* = heavy-scented, strong-smelling.

DESCRIPTION: Annual plant, up to 60 cm high, with bipinnate to tripinnate leaves. The leaflets of which they are composed have linear segments. The yellowish-green leaves are grouped in 30-50 rayed umbels. There are no involucres.

ORIGIN: Unclear; probably from Asia. The plant is unknown in the wild, but was cultivated as long ago as in ancient Egypt.

CULTIVATION: Areas with a subtropical or temperate climate.

AVAILABILITY: Nearly all the year round.

CARE: When purchased, the main umbel should be fully grown; if they are harvested unripe, the stem will droop. Cut off a bit of the stem; use cut-flower food for herbaceous plants.

KEEPING PROPERTIES: 7-10 days.

USE: Especially in mixed bouquets.

SCENT: Strongly aromatic.

Ammi majus

Valerianaceae

The majority of the 400 sorts of the valerian family (*Valerianaceae*) come from the northern hemisphere. However, a number of southern varieties are also known, chiefly from the South American Andes mountains.

The dicotyledonous valerians, which are classified into over 13 genera, generally have opposite and deeply cut and divided leaves with a stem-encircling leaf base. Some genera, such as valerian, give off a strong and characteristic odour. The essential oils which cause this scent are mainly found in the roots; among other things, a sedative is made from them.

The inflorescence is usually a two-branched compound umbel, often with many flowers close together, sometimes with large bracts. In most cases, the flowers are hermaphrodite and irregular. The calyx is scarcely visible in the inflorescence; it stands on an edge of the ovary. Theoretically, the ovary has five lobes, but in some sorts it has an entirely different shape. The petals have five lobes and form a long tube which may be spurred. The 1-4 stamens are implanted on the upper side of the corolla. The ovary is unilocular and inferior; it is composed of three fused carpels.

Centranthus ruber
Centranthus

NAME: *Centranthus* means 'having spurred flowers' and is derived from the Greek words *kentron* (= spur, spore) and *anthos* (= flower). *Ruber* = red, the flower colour.

DESCRIPTION: Perennial plant, about 70 cm high, with ovate lanceolate, fleshy leaves. The leaf margins are entire or weakly dentate. The lower leaves have short stems; the upper ones are sessile. The carmine red, spurred flowers are grouped in dense panicles at the end of the stem. There is also a white-flowering cultivar, 'Albiflorum'.

ORIGIN: Mediterranean area; first cultivated in Belgium in 1557.

CULTIVATION: Temperate and subtropical areas with outdoor cut-flower cultivation.

AVAILABILITY: June-August.

CARE: When purchased, the first flowers should be open and the other buds should show their colour. Cut off a bit of the stem; use cut-flower food for herbaceous plants, or else the flowers will shed.

KEEPING PROPERTIES: 8-12 days.

USE: In mixed bouquets and, to a limited extent, in a vase.

SCENT: Slightly fragrant.

Centranthus ruber 'Albiflorus'

Violaceae

In the violet family (*Violaceae*), one genus (*Viola*) consists of herbaceous plants; the rest - there are a total of 22 genera - are small shrubs and trees. Altogether the family comprises around 1000 species. They are dicotyledons. The family is re-presented all over the world, but primarily in areas with tem-perate climates and, in the tropics, in mountainous areas. The leaves are usually alternate; they are simple and have small stipules. The hermaphrodite flowers stand alone and grow from the leaf axils. They have five sepals and five petals; the five stamens are usually fused at the base of the filaments to form a ring around the superior ovary. The stigma and the style are normal in composition. The fruit has a single cavity; the seeds are round. The *Viola* species have flowers which can only be divided into two equal halves in one way (bilaterally symmetrical). The lower petals are larger and form a spur. At the base of the lower two stamens, honey is formed, which runs into the flower. Incidentally, in many violets self-pollina-tion occurs before the flower opens. The oil of one sort, *Viola odorata*, is used in perfumes and in liqueurs.

Viola Cornuta hybrids
Horned violet
NAME: *Viola* is an old Latin plant name with unknown meaning. The Romans also called other pleasant scented plants 'viola', such as the wallflower and the stock. *Cornuta* = horned.
DESCRIPTION: Perennial plant, around 20 cm high, with round or oval leaves with notched edges. The upper ones are narrower than the lower ones. The oval stipules are roughly serrate and just as long as the leaf stems. The original flower colour was lilac to purplish-blue, with a small, yellow eye. Crosses with *V. gracilis*, *V. tricolor* and other sorts has made the col-our assortment larger. Cultivars are now cultivated by name in yel-low, blue, lilac and white shades. The flowers have a spur (the 'horn') of 10-12 mm.
ORIGIN: The Pyrenees and the east-ern part of the Alps. *V. cornuta* was first cultivated in the United Kingdom in 1776, where much improvement work has also been done.

CULTIVATION: Chiefly in temperate areas.
AVAILABILITY: May-June.
CARE: When purchased, the flowers should be nearly open. Use cut-flower food for herbaceous plants.
KEEPING PROPERTIES: 6-9 days.
USE: In corsages and in a vase. The flowers are sometimes arranged with a sleeve of leaves.
SCENT: Sometimes very fragrant, depending on the cultivar.

Viola odorata
Sweet violet
NAME: See *V. cornuta*. *Odorata* = fragrant.
DESCRIPTION: Perennial plant with stemless leaves; they are round heart-shaped with notched mar-gins. The stipules are narrower and have smooth margins. The dark violet flowers have short spurs and stand on stems of 5-8 cm.
ORIGIN: From Western Europe to the Caucasus; Mediterranean area; in cultivation since ancient times.
CULTIVATION: Especially on the French Riviera (originally for the perfume industry).

AVAILABILITY: February-May.
CARE: When purchased, the flowers should be open. Use cut-flower food for herbaceous plants. The flowers are often sold in bunches with a sleeve of leaves.
KEEPING PROPERTIES: 4-7 days.
USE: In a vase and in flower ar-rangement, including corsages and Biedermeier bouquets.
SCENT: Very fragrant; in fact, the scent gives this species its value.

Viola Cornuta hybrid

Zingiberaceae

Of the around 1300 sorts of herbaceous plants which belong to the ginger family (*Zingiberaceae*), many are not only remarkable for their flowers, but also for their aromatic scent. This is due to volatile oils, in the plant itself or in the root-stock. A good example of this is *Zingiber officinale*, the fleshy root-stocks of which yield the familiar ginger. The ginger family grows in the tropics, chiefly in Indonesia and Malaysia. The monocotyledonous plants have branching fleshy root-stocks or tuber-like roots. An above-ground stem is short or absent. The leaves stand in two rows on the root-stock; the leaf sheaths may be open or closed. The side veins of the leaves are close together and emerge at oblique angles to the central vein.

The flowers are sometimes alone or in bunches, but usually in dense flower heads or clusters. Their composition is rather unique. The lowest segment of the inner whorl of perianth petals is two or three-lobed; it is formed by the fusion of two infertile altered stamens. The flower, which has only one fertile stamen, is encircled by a tubular calyx and a bract. The style is somewhat reduced; as a result, it is thin and weak and fused with the anther. Only the stigma protrudes above this growth. The ovary is inferior; the fruit (sometimes a fleshy capsule) is brightly coloured. The large seeds are usually surrounded by a red appendage.

The essential oils of some members of the ginger family are used as spices or dyes or for their medicinal qualities.

Alpinia zerumbet,
syn. *A. speciosa*

NAME: The genus is named after doctor and botanist Prospero Alpino (1553-1616), director of the botanical gardens in Padua and author of a treatise on Egyptian plants. *Zerumbet* is the original name, probably Arabic, for the plant.

DESCRIPTION: The plant has erect, lanceolate and somewhat pointed leaves. The flowers are grouped in a pendulous inflorescence which is around 30 cm long. They have ivory-white sepals and red with yellow petals. *A. purpurata*, with a red inflorescence, is rising.

ORIGIN: Eastern Asia, China and Japan; under cultivation since 1792.

CULTIVATION: On a limited scale, in the tropics, e.g. Ivory Coast and Thailand.

AVAILABILITY: Late summer and autumn.

CARE: When purchased, one-third of the flowers should be open. Use cut-flower food.

KEEPING PROPERTIES: 2-3 weeks.

USE: In exclusive floral work and decorations.

SCENT: Slightly fragrant.

Alpinia purpurata

Curcuma roscoeana
Hidden lily

NAME: *Curcuma* is the Latinized form of the Arabic plant name *kurkum*. The variety is named after W. Roscoe (1753-1831), founder of the botanical gardens in Liverpool and a specialist in the field of the plant families *Cannaceae* and *Zingiberaceae*.

DESCRIPTION: The tubers of this plant, which are white inside, have an aromatic scent. The large leaves, 30 cm long, 12 cm wide, are elongated lanceolate. The flowers are yellow, the bracts a striking orangish-red.

ORIGIN: Burma; introduced into the United Kingdom in 1837.

CULTIVATION: Very limited, as a cut flower in the hothouse, all over the world.

AVAILABILITY: Late summer and autumn.

CARE: When purchased, most bracts should show good colour. Use cut-flower food for herbaceous plants.

KEEPING PROPERTIES: Around 2 weeks.

USE: In flower arrangement and in decorations, for exclusive and costly work.

SCENT: Slightly aromatic.

Globba winittii
Globba

NAME: The genus name is derived from the original Moluccan name of the plant, *galoba*. The variety is named after a certain Winitt, about whom nothing is known.

DESCRIPTION: Perennial, erect plant with large, wide and lanceolate leaves which are pointed at the tips. Their underside is slightly pilose; the colour is a soft pale green. The inflorescence is remarkable for the large, pendulous branch with spreading lilac bracts and soft yellow flowers, a unique colour combination.

ORIGIN: Thailand.

CULTIVATION: Very limited, as a hothouse cut flower, all over the world.

AVAILABILITY: Late summer and autumn.

CARE: When purchased, about a quarter of the flower should be open. Use cut-flower food.

KEEPING PROPERTIES: 10-14 days.

USE: In exclusive floral work.

SCENT: None.

Hedychium gardnerianum
Kahili ginger

NAME: The genus name is derived from the Greek words *hedus* (= sweet) and *chion* (= snow); a plant with snow-white and sweet-smelling flowers. The sort is named after British colonel Edward Gardner, who was stationed in Nepal. He sent many then unknown plants to the botanist Wallich, whose real name was Nathan Wolff.

DESCRIPTION: The plant has elongated, bluish-green leaves with smooth margins; they are around 60 cm long and 10 cm wide. The yellow flowers have red anthers and sometimes stand on six-sided spikes up to 50 cm long.

ORIGIN: India; introduced into the United Kingdom in 1819.

CULTIVATION: On a limited scale, as a cut flower in the hothouse, all over the world.

AVAILABILITY: Late summer and autumn.

CARE: When purchased, one-fifth of the flowers should be open. Put them in tepid water; use cut-flower food.

KEEPING PROPERTIES: 10-16 days.

USE: In exclusive and costly floral work and decorations.

SCENT: Very fragrant.

Nicolai elatior,
syn. *Phaeomeria magnifica*
Torch ginger

NAME: The genus is named after Czar Nicholas I of Russia (1796-1855). *Elatior* means 'high', 'elevated'. *Phaeomeria* is a contraction of the Greek words *phaios* (= dark in colour) and *neris* or *neros* (= part) and refers to the flower colours. *Magnifica* = beautiful.

DESCRIPTION: Herbaceous plant, up to 6 m high. The elongated leaves are 60 cm long and stand in two rows. The inflorescence consists of wax-like bracts which are red with white edges. The flower lies in the bracts, as in a nest. Its upper petals are red; the lip is yellow.

ORIGIN: Java and Celebes; under cultivation for a very long time.

CULTIVATION: Tropical countries, such as Ivory Coast and Kenya. The plant is too large to be cultivated in the hothouse.

AVAILABILITY: From June until autumn.

CARE: When purchased, the flowers should be fully-grown. Use cut-flower food.

KEEPING PROPERTIES: 2-3 weeks.

USE: In large exclusive floral work.

SCENT: Slight.

Nicolaia elatior

Glossary

Adpressed (or **appressed**) - pressed flat to a surface (e.g. hairs).

Adventitious - occurring in places outside its normal range and habitats.

Alternate (of **leaves**) - occurring successively on a different level of a stem.

Annual - completing its life cycle from germination to death within one year.

Anther - terminal part of a *stamen*, containing the pollen grains.

Appendage (usually of *anthers*) - point, wing or knob attached to any part.

Axil - the angle between the leaf and stem; hence axillary flower or bud.

Axis - central part of a plant, around which the organs are developed.

Basal - at base of part of a plant.

Berry - fleshy fruit, not splitting to release seeds.

Biennial - requiring two years to complete its life cycle, growing in the first year, and flowering and fruiting in the second.

Bilaterally symmetrical - symmetrical about only one axis.

Bilobed - having two lobes.

Bipinnate - twice pinnate, i.e. the divisions of a *pinnate* leaf are themselves pinnate.

Bisexual - both sexes (*stamens and pistil*) in one flower.

Bract - a small modified leaf (intermediate between the sepals and normal leaves).

Bracteole - a minute bract.

Bristle - stiff hair.

Bulb - an underground organ, which is really a modified plant bud with fleshy scales, yielding stem and roots.

Bulbous - swollen part resembling a bulb.

Bulbils - small, bulblike organs or plantlets formed vegetatively on an older plant.

Calyx - the sepals as a whole; often joined together in a tube.

Capitulum - close cluster of sessile flowers.

Capsule - a simple, dry, *dehiscent* fruit.

Carpel - a modified leaf, one or several of which make up the *pistil*.

Caryopsis - naked grass-fruit or grain in which the seed coat is united with the ovary wall.

Cladode - branch or stem simulating a leaf.

Clavate - club-shaped.

Cleft - deeply cut, but not into the midrib.

Cluster (of flowers) - inflorescence.

Compound - made up of several similar parts.

Corm - a swollen underground stem or roof of one year's duration.

Corolla - the petals as a whole; often joined together in a tube.

Cotyledon(s) - first leaf or leaves of an embryo.

Crossbreeding - *pollination* of the *pistil(s)* of a flower by *pollen* of another plant of the same species.

Cultivar - cultivated variety.

Cuneate (or **cuneiform**) - wedge-shaped, with the narrow end at the attachment point.

Cyme - broad, more or less flat-topped inflorescence in which the central flowers open first.

Deciduous - losing the leaves annually.

Decurrent - extending down and fused to the stem or other organ.

Dehiscent - splitting to release the seeds.

Dentate - toothed, with tooth-like notches.

Dicotyledonous - with two seed-leaves.

Dioecious - with male and female flowers on separate plants.

Disc-floret - central, tubular flower in the head (*capitulum*) in *Compositae*.

Elliptical - oval, tapering at both ends.

Elongated - much lengthened.

Endosperm - substance enclosed with embryo in seeds; usually the eatable part.

Ensiform - sword-shaped.

Entire - with a continuous margin, without any lobes or indentations.

Epidermis - outer layer of plant skin.

FLORAL PARTS

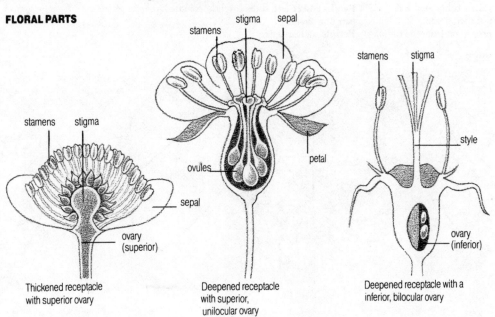

Thickened receptacle with superior ovary

Deepened receptacle with superior, unilocular ovary

Deepened receptacle with a inferior, bilocular ovary

Epiphyte - plant growing on (usually not fed by) another.

Erect - upright, vertical.

Evergreen - retaining its leaves throughout the year.

Family - a group of related *genera*.

Fasciate (of contiguous parts) - compressed or growing into one.

Feather-shaped - see *pinnate*.

Fibrous - threadlike.

Filament - stalk of a stamen, which bears the anthers.

Fimbriate - *fringed*.

Fleshy - thick and moist, succulent.

Floret - one of the small flowers forming a cluster or disc as in *Compositae*.

Flower stalk - see *pedicel* and *peduncle*.

Fringed - with hair-like appendages on the edges.

Fruit - the ripened seeds with their surrounding structure.

Genus (pl. genera) - smallest natural (plant) group containing one or more species.

Glabrous - smooth, without hairs.

Glandular - having glands, i.e. secreting structures on the surface of any part of a plant.

Globular - spherical.

Glume - small bract with a flower in the *axil* as in *Gramineae*.

Grooved - channeled.

Head (or **flower head**) - cluster of stalkless flowers.

Herb - non-woody flowering plant.

Herbaceous - not woody; green and of a soft texture.

Hermaphrodite - with stamens and pistil(s) in the same flower.

Hybrid - plant produced by the fertilization of one *species* by another.

Inferior ovary - ovary situated below petals, sepals and stamens in the flower.

Inflorescence - arrangement of the flowers on a stem or branch.

Involucre (or **involucral bracts**) - the whorl of bracts enclosing a flower cluster as in *Compositae* and *Umbelliferae*.

Keel - lower united petal(s) in a leguminous flower.

Kernel - softer part within hard shell of nut or stone-fruit; grain of wheat.

Lanceolate - lance-shaped, tapering at both ends with the widest part below the middle.

Leaflet - leaf-like part of a compound leaf.

Ligulate - with strap-shaped florets.

Ligule - small, thin projection from the top of the leaf-sheath in *Gramineae*.

Linear - flat and narrow with more or less parallel sides.

Lobed - referring to deeply toothed leaves, but not divided into separate leaflets.

Lyrate - lyre-shaped, pinnatifid with the terminal lobe enlarged.

Membrane - dry, thin, flexible, not green structure.

Monocarpic - flowering and seeding only once, then dying, after more than two years.

Monocotyledonous - with one seed-leaf.

Monoeciuous - having separate male and female flowers borne on the same plant.

Multilocular - having more than one cavity (of a capsule).

Nectary - a gland of a flower, which secretes nectar.

Nerve - vein or slender rib.

Notched - indented.

Nut - one-seeded fruit with a hard outer covering.

Oblong - longer than wide, parallel-sided with rounded ends.

Obovate - inversely ovate, broadest near the apex.

Opposite - growing at the same level on opposite sides of a stem.

Oval - broadly elliptic.

Ovary - base of a *pistil* containing *ovules*.

Ovate - flat, egg-shaped, narrowed to the apex.

Ovate-oblong - flat, egg-shaped, but much longer than broad.

Ovoid (of fruit) - egg-shaped.

Ovule - an immature seed before fertilization.

Palmate - lobed or divided into more than three leaflets arising from a central point.

Panicle - a raceme with branching *pedicels*.

Parietal placenta - part of *carpel* to which ovules are attached, being the wall of the ovary.

Pedicel - the stalk of a single flower (in a cluster).

Peduncle - the stalk of a flower cluster or a solitary flower.

Pendulous - drooping, hanging down.

Pentamerous - having five parts.

Perennial - living for more than two years (usually flowering annually).

Perianth - collective term for the whorls of petals and sepals.

Perianth lobes - loose parts of joined perianth segments.

Petal - flower leaf, often brightly coloured, part of a *corolla*.

Petiole - a leaf-stalk.

INFLORESCENCE TYPES

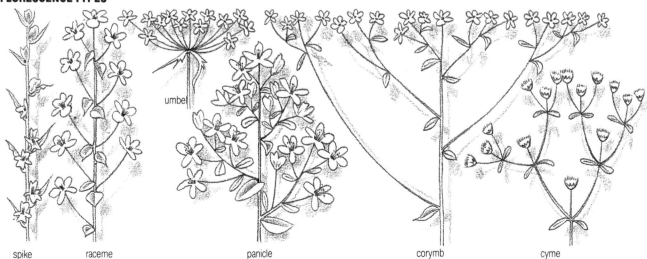

spike   raceme   panicle   corymb   cyme

Pilose - hairy, usually with long, soft hairs.
Pinnate - with leaflets arranged on opposite sides of a central *axis*.
Pinnatifid - divided in a pinnate way, but not cut to the midrib.
Pistil - female part of a flower, consisting of *ovary*, *style* and *stigma*.
Pollen - the male reproductive cells produced by and discharged from the *anthers* of a seed plant.
Pollination - fertilization or sprinkling with pollen.
Prickle - small spine.
Pubescent - covered with fine, soft hairs.

Quadipinnate - four times pinnate, cf. *bipinnate*.
Raceme - simple elongated *inflorescence* with flowers borne on equal *pedicels*. The oldest flower at the base.
Radiate - spreading from a common centre.
Radical - growing from the root.
Ray-floret - the outer ring of florets of a compound radiate flower.
Receptacle - the modified apex of a stem bearing the floral parts.
Reniform - kidney-shaped.
Rhizome - underground stem.
Rosette - a cluster of leaves in circular form.

LEAF TIPS

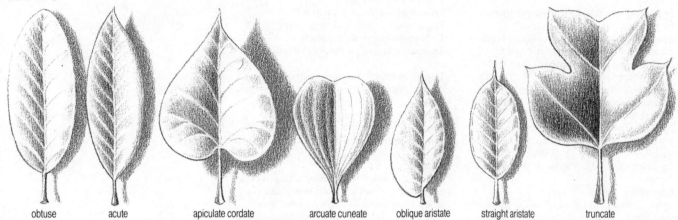

obtuse · acute · apiculate cordate · arcuate cuneate · oblique aristate · straight aristate · truncate

LEAF SHAPES

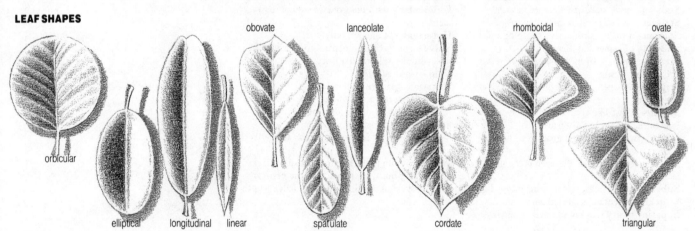

orbicular · elliptical · longitudinal · linear · obovate · lanceolate · spatulate · cordate · rhomboidal · ovate · triangular

LEAF MARGINS

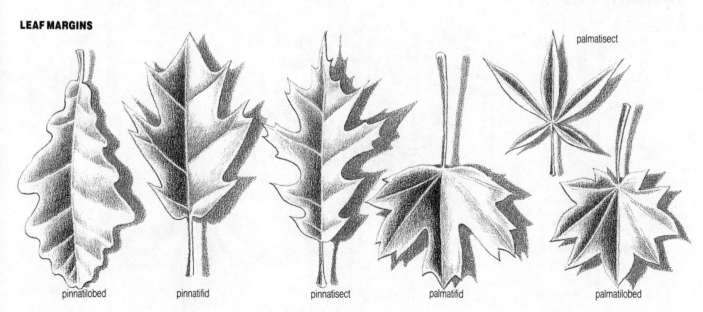

pinnatilobed · pinnatifid · pinnatisect · palmatifid · palmatisect · palmatilobed

Scutellate - formed like scales.

Scale - thin, scarious structure, often a degenerated leaf.

Schizocarp - a dry, indehiscent fruit, splitting into two valves.

Secretory - see *glandular*.

Sepal - a leaf of the *calyx*, the outer ring of the *perianth*.

Serrate - with saw-like teeth, which point forwards.

Sessile - without a stalk.

Shrub - woody plant, much branched and smaller than a tree.

Simple - not compound.

Sinuate - having a pronounced wavy margin.

Smooth (edged) - not lobed or toothed.

Solitary - flower singly on a stalk or at base of a leaf.

Spadix - thick, fleshy spike bearing *sessile* flowers.

Spathe - a large, sometimes coloured bract enclosing a flower cluster, usually a *spadix*.

Spatulate (or **spatula-shaped**) - spoon- or paddle-shaped.

Species - group of individual plants having common characteristic, which do not normally fertilize other species.

Spike - unbranched inflorescence of more or less sessile flowers with the oldest flowers at the base.

Spikelet - a secondary spike or the floral unit in a grass.

Spreading - directed outwards.

Spur - a slender, usually hollow extension from the base of a perianth segment as in *Violaceae*.

Stalk - primary stalk of a flower: *peduncle*.

Stalklet - secondary stalk of a flower: *pedicel*.

Stamen - a male reproductive organ of a plant, consisting of *anther* and *filament*.

Stem - main stalk from which stalks of leaves and flowers spring.

Stigma - the apex of the *pistil* which receives the pollen.

Stipule - a leaf-like appendage, usually at the base of the *petiole*; usually paired.

Striate - with fine ridges, grooves or lines of colour.

Style - part of the *pistil* between *ovary* and *stigma*.

Sub- - under or below (as in subfamily); slightly (as in sub-dentate, slightly toothed).

Superior ovary - ovary situated on the *receptacle* above the petals, sepals and stamens in the flower.

Sword-shaped - long and straight, evenly narrowed from base to apex.

Teeth - small marginal lobes.

Tendril - a slender, often coiled extension of stem or leaf used for climbing.

Terminal - borne at the top of a stem.

Ternate - divided into threes.

Terrestrial - growing in the soil.

Tetramerous - having four parts.

Thorny - bearing stiff, sharp-pointed processes.

Toothed - with *teeth*.

Tree - a large plant with a single woody trunk.

Trichome - hair, scale, prickle or other outgrowth from the *epidermis*.

Trichotomous - divided into three.

Trilobate - with three *lobes*.

Trilocular - with three cavities.

Tripartite - consisting of three parts.

Tripinnate - three times *pinnate*.

Truncate - as though abruptly cut off at the end.

Tuberous root - thick and fleshy like a *tuber*, but without buds.

Tuber - a thickened part of an underground stem or root of one year's duration, not creeping.

Tubular - with united parts (of calyx or corolla).

Tussock - clump.

Umbel - an inflorescence in which equal pedicels proceed from a common centre (like the spokes of an umbrella); hence *Umbelliferae*.

Umbellate - (of flowers) arranged in an *umbel*.

Unilocular - with only one (seed) compartment.

Unisexual - of one sex only.

Valve - one of the segments into which a *capsule* naturally splits at maturity.

Vein - nerve of a leaf.

Venation - pattern of the veins.

Verticillasters - a whorl-like structure composed of a pair of opposed cymes as in the inflorescence of *Labiatae*.

Whorl - a ring of leaves or flowers at one level around a stem.

Winged - with flat, membranous appendages.

Zygomorphic - symmetrical in the vertical plane only, thus divisible into two halve lengthwise.

COMPOUND LEAF TYPES

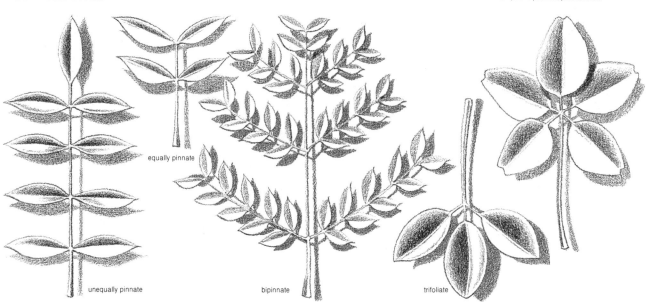

compound palmate, pentamerous

equally pinnate

unequally pinnate

bipinnate

trifoliate

Keeping properties

The value of a cut flower is largely determined by its keeping properties, or its 'vase life' as it is sometimes called. Once cut off the plant, flowers begin to age and after a while they will wilt. This is a natural and irreversible process; although numerous methods and substances have been found to delay it and to lengthen the life of a cut flower, it can never be made to live longer than if it had not been cut.

The ageing process is more rapid in one sort than in another; there are even differences between cultivars of one species. The length of time a cut flower will keep is influenced by numerous factors. The first study of it was performed by C. Buys from Aalst, Belgium; he went on to invent and then market a range of cut flower foods. Today, a number of companies manufacture in this field. The Floristry Research Station in Aalsmeer, Holland, has done much research to improve keeping. The Bulb Cultivation Research Station in Lisse, Holland, does similar research for bulb flowers. Both stations work closely with the Sprenger Institute in Wageningen, Holland. This research has given the Netherlands its present authoritative position in the study of factors influencing the keeping properties of cut flowers.

Ripe for harvesting

Nature intended a flower for propagation. In the course of its evolution, a flower has developed a number of traits which make it highly suited to the production of seed. These traits very often contrast with the unnatural demands that we make of a cut flower.

In cut flower cultivation, a flower is termed 'ripe' if it has developed in its full beauty. The professional grower needs to anticipate this stage by several days and so must identify the best moment for picking. This stage differs with the species and sometimes even the cultivar.

'Unripe' flowers, flowers in the bud, contain fewer sugars; as a result they absorb less water and will keep less well. Cutting flowers in the bud has a number of advantages. The flower is easier to work; it is less susceptible to damage and thus will stand up better to transport; and for the consumer, such a flower is more dynamic, because he sees part of the development from bud to flower. This extra pleasure is absent in varieties such as the gerbera which do not develop further after purchase.

Unlike the growth of a plant, the development from bud to flower is not the result of cell division, but of an increase in the cell surface area. During the development from bud to ripe flower, the cell surface area of the well-known rose 'Sonia' increases by 400 per cent.

Cutting flowers in the bud may have its advantages, but it may not be done too early. Flowers that are cut too early will droop sooner and keep less well than ripe flowers, and they often remain behind in their development, which means they have less effect in a vase.

In general, it may be stated that cut flowers should preferably be purchased when the buds are not yet open, but are already budding. The descriptions in this book usually indicate the ideal stage for purchase.

Water

The first rule in the care of cut flowers: always use clean water. Cut flowers will absorb both clean and dirty water, but the latter clogs their vessels and thus obstructs the water absorption. If the flowers themselves pollute the water (some sorts do), then it is a good idea to change the water from time to time. Nor should the water be too cold. Usually lukewarm water is best. The flowers absorb it better and it contains less oxygen, which inhibits the oxidation of certain organic substances in the plant (e.g. phenols). In this connection, it is also useful to know that alkaline tap water contains more oxygen than slightly acidic water (rainwater, for example).

Vases

Vases for cut flowers should be made of glass, pottery or plastic. The use of metal vases is discouraged, especially when the flowers have been treated or cut flower food is used. These substances corrode the metal and lose their effectiveness. For the same reasons, never buy cut flowers that are standing in zinc pails.

It is very important that cut flower vases be extremely clean. After use, they should always be cleaned with a normal household cleanser or, better still, with a bleach solution: 0.5 ml of bleach (with 10 per cent chlorine) to 1 litre of water.

Temperature

Room temperature has a great influence on the keeping properties of cut flowers. Some plants, such as the tulip, react favourably to low temperatures. But roses, too, last longer at 10° C than at 20° C.

Generally speaking, high temperatures make a cut flower finish flowering more rapidly and they shorten the vase life. Temperatures between 5° and 10° C increase the keeping qualities of many sorts. Others, such as the tail flower and euphorbia, flourish best if the temperature does not go below 16° C. Special temperature requirements are always mentioned in the descriptions in the book.

Evaporation

Cut flowers also need an equilibrium between water absorption and evaporation. The amount of water that a plant evaporates varies with the species and depends on the size and the number of stomata. Other factors which affect the amount of evaporation are the temperature and the relative humidity of the surroundings. In a warm, dry room - for example, a living room in a centrally heated house in winter - a cut flower evaporates considerably more moisture than in a warm and humid tropical hothouse.

Evaporation, no matter how great, is no problem as long as the flower can absorb enough water. This is why flower growers usually try to take their flowers to auction in water. The problems only arise during handling and transport, when it is practically impossible to keep the flowers in water; many sorts lose as much as 10 to 20 per cent of their weight at this point, and this loss is never entirely restored. If a flower has lost too much moisture and has withered completely, very little can be done to save it.

Flower traders limit evaporation by wrapping the cut flowers in plastic foil or by packing them in boxes, or by keeping the temperature low and the relative humidity high. The purchaser of cut flowers can make his contribution by putting the flowers in water as soon as possible and not leaving them too long in a vehicle, especially in hot weather. The evaporation can also be limited by removing the lower leaves, primarily in leafy plants such as roses and chrysanthemums.

Food for cut flowers

Plants absorb energy from light by means of their green colouring-matter (*chlorophyll*) and store it in the form of sugars. During the vegetal breathing process, this energy is broken down and used for life processes such as growth, flowering, seed formation, fruiting, etc. This respiration is very intensive, especially in the flower; an apple blossom, for example, respires ten times more rapidly than an apple, and more intensely than the leaves.

After cutting, the flowers have too little energy to breathe well. Further development, such as budding, is delayed or even prevented altogether.

This energy shortage can be eliminated by giving the flower sugars. Usually this is done in the form of carefully balanced cut flower foods. They contain approximately 95 per cent sugars, such as saccharose and glucose, and a disinfectant. This composition explains why some 'household remedies', such as the addition of plain crystal sugar to the water or even the use of sweet soft drinks, also work. But these are emergency measures; the right balance is lacking, as is the disinfectant. Cut flower food is added to the water straight after picking. And that is necessary; because it usually takes from three to five days before the flowers reach the consumer, they can use that extra stock of sugars very well. By the time they are purchased, this stock is usually used up, so the consumer should add more cut flower food to the water.

The use of cut flower food has several advantages.

* The flowers keep longer.
* They retain their natural colour better.
* Thanks to the extra energy, the flowers can develop well.
* The flowers will stand up better to a water shortage because the sugars close the stomata and thus combat evaporation.
* The flowers are less sensitive to damage by ethylene.
* The flowers can be cut less ripe; because of the extra sugar, they continue to develop.
* The buds develop into fully grown flowers. Without cut flower food this is often not the case especially with bunch chrysanthemums, bunch pinks or freesias.

Sorts of cut flower food

There are various sorts of cut flower food. Their use depends on the sort of plant and the degree of ripeness of the flowers. All manufacturers of cut flower food have several types on the market; the largest assortment includes the following types:

White, for roses and, in general, for all cut flowers not otherwise mentioned;
Pink, for pinks, orchids and herbaceous cut flowers;
Tulip, a special product which makes it possible to combine daffodils with tulips and other cut flowers in the same vase;
Food for bulb flowers such as tulips, hyacinths, ornamental onions and dahlias;
Bouvardia, for bouvardias, which allows them to be kept very long;
Shrub, for woody plants such as lilac, forsythia and guelder rose;
All these products are available both in small packages (in dry or liquid form) and in packages of 1 and 2 1/2 kg. The latter, however, are only sold by suppliers to professional florists.

Clogged vessels

All plants, including cut flowers, absorb water via tracheae or vessels in the stem. When these vessels are clogged, it means drooping leaves, bent or broken stems and wilting flowers. Clogged vessels can be caused either by an *air embolism* or by bacteria. In the case of an air embolism, there are air pockets in the stem of the flower which impede the water transport or may even entirely obstruct it. An air embolism can occur if the flowers lie about dry for a while. Because evaporation continues, water is sucked out of the vessels and air takes its place, particularly at the bottom of the stem. 'Old-fashioned' florists combat this by cutting off bits of the stems under water, so that water immediately penetrates into the vessels. The consumer can reach approximately the same effect by cutting off a piece of the stem before putting the flowers in water. *Clogged vessels caused by bacteria* often occur in cut flowers which first stood in water, then were left dry for a while at relatively high temperatures (in the back of the car!). In such a situation, the bacteria in the vessels or in the water left on the flowers will rapidly multiply: after 8 hours, one hundred of them in 1 ml of water may have grown to more than a million specimens, feeding on the plant's sugars. In some cut flowers, such as the gerbera, this can cause serious problems: the stems may bend and break.

The professional combats this shortcoming by keeping cut flowers in cold storage (low temperatures inhibit the development of bacteria), by cleaning the water and the container with chlorine bleach, or by treating the water with ultraviolet light or chemicals. All water treatment substances and flower foods contain a disinfectant to control the bacteria.

The consumer can combat clogged vessels caused by bacteria by using very clean vases, by cutting off bits of the stems of the flowers (and repeating this from time to time), by using clean water in the vase and changing it now and then, and by using cut flower food.

Treating cut flowers

Hormones made by the plant itself have a great influence on the life processes. One of them, the ageing hormone *ethylene*, influences the life of cut flowers unfavourably.

Ethylene is a gas which is produced by all plant parts. Some of it remains in the plant; some is released into the surrounding air. The richer the concentration of ethylene in the air, the more of this ageing hormone the plant produces. This is of importance for the keeping qualities of cut flowers because ethylene is not only produced by the flowers themselves (and by other plants in a room), but also by some bacteria and moulds, by ripening fruits and vegetables (tomatoes, aubergines, etc.). In addition, air pollution also yields extra ethylene.

The more ethylene the air in a room contains, the earlier cut flowers wilt. Florists combat ethylene formation by placing the flowers in water with a treatment substance for a few hours. The active ingredient in such substances usually is a silver compound. Its effect lasts so long that the consumer can suffice with the use of cut flower food. The flower auctions in the Netherlands have made it compulsory to treat flowers. All cut flowers which come from the Netherlands will thus last longer. In some cases, these substances also stop the leaves from turning yellow and the vessels from being clogged by bacteria.

10 golden rules for handling cut flowers

1. *Buy good quality flowers in the proper stage of ripeness, but make sure they are not too immature.*
2. *Buy only treated flowers.*
3. *Do not allow the flowers to lie dry too long after purchase.*
4. *Use lukewarm, clean water.*
5. *Prevent ethylene damage; do not put cut flowers in a room with ripening fruit.*
6. *Cut the flower stems with a sharp knife; repeat this after a few days.*
7. *It is advisable not to dethorn roses; the damage to the stem may affect their keeping qualities.*
8. *Make sure the room temperature is suitable for the variety.*
9. *Be careful about combining different varieties: they may influence each other's keeping qualities.*
10. *Always use cut-flower food.*

For cut flowers to keep well, it is important to trim stems or branches properly. The cut must be as straight and as clean as possible. The wound surface is essential: if the cut is not made cleanly, the stem will start to rot sooner, thus shortening the vase life of the flower. For this reason, it is sheer foolishness to flatten chrysanthemum stems or lilac or ornamental cherry branches with a hammer, a suggestion which is still heard today. It is said that this treatment will enable the stem to absorb more water. But it has the opposite effect: the hammer destroys too many cells; they start to rot, and the bacteria they produce clog up the vessels, which obstructs the water absorption.

The best tools for cutting or trimming the stems are a knife, a pair of scissors or pruning-shears.

A knife must be razor-sharp in order to make a clean cut. The best ones are special florist's knives; their only drawback is that they are quite expensive. A good-quality potato-parer will do very well, provided it is really sharp.

Kitchen scissors can be used to cut off thin-stemmed flowers. But the result will not be ideal, because it bruises the stem somewhat and does not give a clean cut. A pair of sharp pruning-shears is often needed to cut off woody stems such as lilac. As long as they are of good quality, pruning-shears also make a reasonably clean cut.

A special kind of pincers is sold to strip the thorns from the stems of roses. This instrument does the job quickly, but it is not the best tool, because it may damage the outer skin of the stem too much. The result: decay and bacteria which pollute the water. A much better result is obtained by using a face flannel or a bath towel to remove the prickles from the stem.

Cultivation methods

The manner in which a plant is cultivated depends on a number of factors; one of the most important of them is climate. Many cut flowers are still cultivated out of doors. Although this cultivation method is by far the cheapest, it has a few disadvantages. A cool climate, for example, is unsuitable for the cultivation of tropical or subtropical sorts. Other drawbacks of outdoor cultivation are that the blossoming period remains limited to the natural flowering season, and the plants quite readily become dirty and damaged.

For these reasons, modern flower growers are more and more frequently moving to greenhouse cultivation; generally heated in Western Europe and areas with a similar climate, generally unheated in somewhat warmer countries like France and Italy. And in tropical or subtropical countries, such as Israel, more and more flowers are being cultivated under plastic or wide-mesh cloth called saran gauze. The latter method protects the plant from dirt and damage; cultivation in the hothouse makes it possible to spread out the flowering time and to cultivate plants from warmer regions.

In countries with intensive cultivation methods, hydroponics, or substratum cultivation, is becoming quite popular. With this method, a plant is not cultivated in soil, but in boxes containing mineral wool or a peat substratum. The fertilizer is mixed with water. Cultivation in a substratum requires high investments, but it gives a high yield and a good quality.

Propagation

All plants, including those producing cut flowers, can nowadays be propagated in three ways: by seed, vegetatively, and by tissue culture or *in vitro* cultivation.

Cultivation by seed is the oldest and most natural method. The advantages are that it is quick and that the plants obtained from seed are generally free of diseases. The largest disadvantage is that the offspring very often deviate slightly from the parent plants: propagation by seed does not usually yield uniform quality. The propagation by seed of hybrid cultivars, also termed F1 hybrids or heterosis cultivars, is presently gaining popularity. Such cultivars are the result of costly controlled breeding.

First, pure or *homozygotic* parent lines are obtained by inbreeding (by means of self-pollination). By crossing parent lines that are as little related as possible, F1 hybrids are obtained. They are entirely uniform and of better quality than the parent plants thanks to *heterosis*: the characteristics of such a crossing product surpass those of the parents because of the accumulation of favourable dominant genes. Heterosis is an important modern technique that makes possible great advancement.

Vegetative or asexual propagation is used for plants that are infertile (and thus form no seeds) and with sorts obtained from crosses that do not recur in a pure form. There are many types of vegetative propagation. It takes place naturally by the formation of bulbs, tubers, rootstocks and shoots; artificial methods are division or separation and taking slips - a plant cutting which is allowed to take root. Slips are often assisted in taking root by growth regulators, mist and soil heating. A third artificial form of vegetative propagation is grafting. Using this technique, which was known in ancient times and was probably borrowed from a natural example, a part of a plant, usually a small branch, is joined to the stem of another sort in such a way that the two grow together and form a whole. Conditions for a successful graft are that the graft and the understem are closely related and that their cambium layers fit together well. There are numerous grafting methods, such as oculation, triangular grafting and crown grafting.

A special form of vegetative propagation which is rapidly advancing is tissue culture or *in vitro* cultivation. This is the cultivation of plants, parts of plants or even a single plant cell in a test tube (*vitrum* = glass) on an artificial culture medium and under sterile conditions. The cultivation of cymbidiums and other orchids has particularly flourished thanks to *in vitro* cultivation. The tail flower (*Anthurium*), for instance, used to be propagated by seed, but the plants thus obtained were far from uniform in colour, production and keeping properties. Thanks to tissue culture, there are now uniform tail flower cultivars which keep well and have a high yield.

Another advantage of tissue culture is that the plants obtained are free of disease: the method is much used to combat viruses. Another advantage: *in vitro* cultivation is a very rapid method of propagation. Theoretically, one growing point of a cymbidium can produce one million descendants in 10 months. But this is not actually done, because mutations can easily occur over such a long period.

Tissue culture requires much expertise. A great deal of research has been done in the United States as well as in England, France, Israel, the Netherlands and Belgium. These countries also produce numerous plants by *in vitro* cultivation on a large scale.

Manner of cultivation

The various plants that play a role in ornamental flower cultivation are grown in several different ways. *Annual plants*, such as sowing asters, snapdragons and marigolds, are propagated by means of seeds. The cultivation lasts one growing season; in this period they grow from a seed into an adult plant that flowers, again forms seeds and then dies. Many of these plants originally come from deserts and semi-deserts; because of their short growing season, they can take advantage of the rainy period. Perennial plants would not survive the dry period in such areas.

Biennial plants, such as Sweet William and the wallflower, form a leaf rosette during the first year after they are sown, with which they overwinter. They do not flower until the year afterwards. In general, biennial plants are propagated by seed. The flowering can often be influenced by keeping them at cold temperatures, which makes the plant blossom earlier. This is done with Sweet William, for example.

Perennial plants can be propagated both by seed and vegetatively (cuttings, division). Most of them have a limited blooming season. Using a combination of cultivation methods, including different planting times, cultivation in hothouses and artificial daylight treatment, it is possible to spread the flowering period of such plants.

Bulbous plants with annual bulbs, such as the tulip, reproduce themselves spontaneously by forming buds: small new bulbs that appear on the old one. Bulbous plants with perennial bulbs, such as the hyacinth, multiply too slowly for flower growers. They are therefore artificially propagated by hollowing, cutting or scaling, methods which are comparable to taking a leaf cutting. The principle of all these methods is that young bulbs form on the wound surfaces from undeveloped buds, which are termed adventitious. Forced early flowering of bulbs is on the increase.

Tuberous plants, such as the crocus, freesia and gladiolus, are named after the thickened part of their stem, the underground tuber. Most sorts multiply by the formation of numerous small tubers called beads. In some sorts, such as the dahlia, the tuber is not part of the stem, but of the root (radical tuber). These tubers do not have buds and so cannot form any beads. Dahlias are therefore propagated by cutting shoots from the bulbils (stem buds).

The tubers of cyclamens do not multiply either. They come about from the *hypocotyl*, the stem below the cotyledons, which forms no buds. Cyclamens are therefore propagated by seed.

Shrubs, such as the lilac and the ornamental cherry, are woody plants which are usually propagated by grafting and sometimes, as with forsythia, by cuttings. Shrubs are often hardy and are therefore cultivated out of doors.

Shrubs that blossom in the spring, such as the lilac, are cultivated for their flowers. The plants are often forced to bloom early in the hothouse. Other shrubs, such as callicarpa and holly, are cultivated for the decorative value of their fruits in autumn and winter; still others, such as the convoluted and banded willow, for the shape of the branches; or, in other willow sorts, for their catkins. The leaf of some sorts, such as mahonia, is used in flower arrangement.

Spreading the flowering period

Most plants naturally have a limited flowering period which is also linked to a fixed season. Tulips, for example, bloom in spring, roses in early summer.

Selection and refinement have made it possible to spread the flowering periods of many sorts. The rose is a good example of this: the cultivar assortment has become so differentiated that it is now possible to spread the flowering period of roses throughout the year.

However, cultivation methods have also been developed

which make it possible to spread the flowering period in another manner. Using these methods, the plants are 'hoodwinked' by manipulating the two most important factors that influence the flowering: the temperature and the amount of light.

By manipulating the *temperature*, it is possible, for example, to influence the blossoming time of the tulip and other bulb plants. To make tulips blossom earlier than usual, the bulbs are given a heat treatment immediately after being lifted in the summer months. This extra warmth imitates and speeds up the natural summer rest period. Then the bulbs are frozen, which imitates the winter for the plant; at the end of the treatment, the tulip 'thinks' that it is already spring and it comes to blossom. In a similar manner, tulips are brought to flower in September/October by keeping the bulbs frozen until shortly before the desired flowering period. These tulips are called 'ice tulips'; they are generally somewhat weaker than untreated ones. Something similar is done with lilies of the valley. They can be brought to blossom throughout the year by freezing the buds with roots and thawing them just before the desired flowering time. Another example is the lilac, which naturally flowers in spring. But by treating it with high temperatures, it can be made to flower as early as November.

Manipulation with light is another way of changing the flowering period of all kinds of plants. This method is called *artificial daylight treatment*. Plants can be distinguished into short-day plants and long-day plants. The former flower in autumn or winter; the poinsettia is one example. By artificially lighting these plants when the days are short and darkening them in periods with long days, such short-day plants can be brought to blossom throughout the year. Similarly, autumn flowers can be forced to bloom early by artificially shortening the length of the day. This is done, for example with the Michaelmas daisy, which can nowadays be brought to blossom at the beginning of July. Long-day plants naturally flower in summer. Spreading the flowering period of these plants by artificial daylight treatment still only takes place on a limited scale; an example is cattleya.

Assortment: expansion and refinement

Flower growers are constantly seeking new plants, other colours, surprising shapes. In part, this is a question of ambition and love for the trade; another, surely equally important, aspect is a matter of healthy company management. In this field as well, the consumer constantly asks for something new, and product renewal and innovation is necessary for a firm's survival.

'New' plants are sometimes found by accident. For instance, the eustoma became popular after it had been brought back from Japan, and the well-known carthamus became an important plant after a breeder accidentally encountered this annual, summer-flowering thistle at a seed cultivation company and went to work with it. In other cases a 'new' plant may come about by *in vitro* cultivation. The orchid X *Vuylstekeara* had been known for over fifty years: a cross between the genera *Odontoglossum*, *Cochlioda* and *Miltonia*. The plant, however, could only be propagated by division, a method which is so slow that X *Vuylstekeara* could not become a popular plant because of the cost price alone. This changed when, thanks to *in vitro* cultivation (whereby a full-grown specimen can be quickly cultivated from a miniscule part of the plant), unlimited numbers of the plant could be obtained - and at a low cost. The cultivation of X *Vuylstekeara* considerably increased after this.

Refinement also brings about new cultivars, mostly with better characteristics than the parents. This work primarily focuses on resistance to disease, a short cultivation period, a higher yield and better keeping qualities.

Plant refinement is a science in itself and is generally very expensive. It is frequently amateur plant breeders who make the crosses. If they succeed in obtaining a valuable new cultivar, it is often bought up by florists and brought on the market. But even if the exploitation of such a new cultivar is successful, it does not usually imply that its 'inventor' is in clover. Sufficient patenting of new cultivars has not yet been internationally regulated.

Several Western European countries recognise what is known as plant breeder's rights, which are intended to encourage breeders to obtain new cultivars by offering them remuneration. This right entitles the finder of a new cultivar to a sum per specimen sold from the florist who cultivates it.

The names of many cultivars are protected by the Patent and Trade Mark Act. This is valid internationally, but it is often evaded by bringing the cultivar on the market under another name.

Nomenclature of flowers

Most plants have popular names that vary with the country and very often even the region. To exchange information internationally without confusion, botanists described the plants in Latin, the international language of science. But these descriptions were so extensive as to be far from practical. The sweet pea, for example, was originally called Lathyrus distopathyphullus, hirsutus, mollis, magno et peramaero floro, odore, meaning something like sweet pea with binary composite broad leaves, downy hairs and bearing large, lovely, odoriferous flowers. Using this method, to give a scientific description of the plants in a very tiny garden would require several reams of paper.

Swedish botanist Carl Linnaeus (1707-1778) changed this by the introduction of binary nomenclature, a system by which each living thing, plant and animal, was given a scientific name consisting of only two parts: a genus name followed by a specific epithet. The sweet pea, for example, he called Lathyrus odoratus.

Many plant names are of Latin or Greek origin; numerous others are derived from persons whose names have been Latinised. A good example is Gerbera; this genus is named after the Jutland physician, Traugott Gerber, who collected many plants in Russia in the 18th century.

Cultivated plants, such as the chrysanthemum, have a third name, the cultivar name. This is a fancy name; since 1959 it may not be derived from Latin.

The assignment of generic names and specific epithets comes under the rules of the International Code for Botanical Nomenclature. The committee that administers this code determines the proper name of a plant. If there is confusion - for instance, if a sort is known by several scientific names - then the decision of the committee is binding. For example, the official generic name of the arum lily is now Zantedeschia. The earlier name, Calla, is no longer used, or used only as a synonym. In the descriptions of the plants further on in this book, the synonym, if commonest any, is given: Zantedeschia aethiopica, syn. Calla aethiopica.

The cultivar names fall under the International Code for the Nomenclature of Cultivated Plants. One stipulation of this code is that the cultivar name, in contrast to the specific epithet is spelled with a capital letter if coined after 1958 and must be derived from a modern language. Other conditions are that the cultivar name may not consist of more than three words and that it may not greatly exaggerate the characteristics of a cultivar: for instance, a cultivar may not be called 'Earliest of All'.

Although not forbidden, the use of names of politically important persons for cultivars is discouraged, as it can lead to problems later. This was the case with a new azalea cultivar obtained in the thirties; called 'Adolf Hitler' by an admirer, it had to be renamed after 1945!

Although the present scientific plant nomenclature is very adequate in a practical sense because the names are used the world over, it cannot prevent some differences of opinion about certain names. From time to time it happens that the scientific name of a species is officially changed. Such a change can involve the generic name, the specific epithet, or both. Even the cultivar name can be changed.

International flower cultivation

The cultivation of cut flowers has become a highly international business in the past twenty-five years. Nowadays, flowers are not only cultivated in rich countries with a high domestic demand, such as the Netherlands, West Germany, the United States and Japan, and in areas with a favourable climate (Israel, French Riviera, the Canary Islands), but also in countries that have available cheap labour, such as Kenya, Colombia, Thailand and Singapore. These developments have internationalized the flower trade - a process which has also been encouraged by the greater possibilities of air transport and the availability of modern methods and substances to help flowers keep longer.

In this internationalized market, the Netherlands - always an important flower cultivating area - has developed into the largest flower exporter in the world. At the cooperative auctions which were set up at the beginning of this century and which laid the foundation for modern Dutch flower cultivation, the country sells not only the products of its own breeders, but also those of their counterparts in practically all countries of the world. Sometimes these foreign products are flowers which cannot be cultivated in the hothouse in Western Europe because of their size (mimosa from southern France, proteas from southern Africa); in other cases, they are flowers that cannot be cultivated here in the winter months (roses, bunch pinks).

The most important auction is the VBA (Verenigde Bloemenveilingen Aalsmeer - Associated Aalsmeer Flower Auctions). Its annual turnover of more than one and a half billion guilders makes it the largest flower auction in the world. The VBA and other Dutch flower auctions, such as the Westland flower auction in Naaldwijk and the Flora auction in Rijnsburg, thus serve as commercial centres for international flower cultivation. The following survey gives a broad description of the cultivating areas.

Europe

Not only is Europe, and Western Europe in particular, the most important flower growing area in the world; it is also a very important consumer area.

The Netherlands has a high standard of flower cultivation. The growers possess much expertise and work with most modern, high-technology equipment.

The area around Aalsmeer is mainly known for its forced shrubs such as lilac and ornamental cherry, and is also a leading area in rose cultivation. The area around Rijnsburg, adjacent to old bulb-cultivating centres such as Hillegom, Lisse and Sassenheim, has developed into an important centre for the cultivation of summer flowers and of bulbs and tubers such as tulips, hyacinths, daffodils and gladioluses, which are often forced. But the largest production area of the country is the glasshouse district around Naaldwijk, in South Holland. Flower growing started here at the end of the last century, often in combination with vegetable cultivation, and it has greatly expanded in the past twenty years. The most important products of the area are hothouse chrysanthemums, tail flowers, freesias, arum lilies and bunch pinks. In addition to these three centres, the Netherlands has several smaller flower-growing areas. They are spread throughout the country and produce all kinds of flowers of very good quality.

West Germany has a high flower consumption; however, because its own production cannot meet it, the country is the largest cut-flower importer in the world. The supply comes chiefly from the Netherlands and also from Israel, Kenya, Italy and a few other countries. West Germany has a high standard of flower cultivation. Although it primarily grows potted plants, there are also a few important cut flower areas: Vierlanden, near Hamburg, and the area around Straelen, Neusz and Moers. Flower cultivation in the latter area has a Dutch look to it, partly because the flowers are auctioned. In other parts of Germany, the flowers are marketed at wholesale markets. Germany has made a name for itself chiefly by obtaining a large number of important rose cultivars such as 'Mercedes', 'Aalsmeer Gold' and 'Jaccaranda'.

France has a number of flower-cultivating areas. Roses, lilacs, and orchids are cultivated around Paris; the country has traditionally played an important role in the development of the

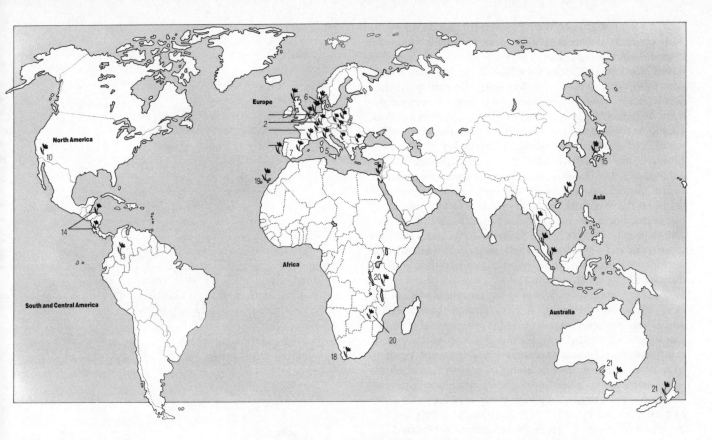

cultivar assortment of these sorts. By making crosses with the Persian rose, Pernet-Ducher developed the first yellow cut roses, and the firm Meilland in Cap d'Antibes obtained the important rose cultivars 'Baccara' and 'Sonia'.

The most important cultivating area for pinks is the French Riviera, from Toulon to the Italian border, where the climate is mild thanks to its proximity to the Mediterranean Sea. Because of increasing tourism and the rising cost of land, cultivation now takes place further inland as well. The climate here is less suitable, so that more and more growing is done in hothouses. In addition to pinks, the western part of the Riviera grows anemones, turban buttercups and other herbaceous cut flowers.

In the eastern part of the French Riviera (Nice, Cannes, Menton) mimosa cultivation is of great importance, mostly of *Acacia Dealbata* hybrid, the 'cut mimosa', which is chiefly intended for export. Thanks to modern conservation methods, the commercial value of this product has greatly increased. In the winter months this area also grows many pinks and a few roses (it is much too hot for them in summer), and, especially around Christmas, products such as dates, mistletoe, eucalyptus, ornamental peppers, etc. In spring the area yields *Viola odorata* and mixed bouquets with turban buttercup, anemone, marigold, oxeye daisy, and so on. French flower consumption is higher than their own production; the country therefore imports many quality flowers, chiefly from the Netherlands.

The *United Kingdom* has a low domestic flower consumption and has no large-scale cultivation under glass. The most important product is the chrysanthemum. Daffodils are also cultivated in large quantities and, on a limited scale, pinks, roses and bulb flowers. The most important cultivation areas are in the south and south-west and in a large circle around London. The island of Guernsey grows many roses and daffodils for export. The flowers are chiefly marketed in New Covent Garden, the main London wholesalers' market for flowers, fruit and vegetables. Considerable quantities of imported flowers are marketed there as well. The Royal Botanic Gardens at

CULTIVATION AREAS OF CUT FLOWERS FOR EXPORT

Europa
1. *The Netherlands*: Roses, chrysanthemums, lilacs, tulips, daffodils, gladioluses, freesias, lilies, pinks, tail flowers, sunflowers.
2. *West Germany*: Roses.
3. *France*: Roses, lilacs orchids, pinks, mimosa, anemones, buttercups, dates, eucalyptus.
4. *The United Kingdom*: Chrysanthemums, daffodils, roses. New cultivars: alstroemeria and freesias.
5. *Italy*: Pinks, gladioluses, roses, chrysanthemums.
6. *Denmark*: Pinks, fern (adiatum).
7. *Spain*: Pinks.
8. *Portugal*: Pinks, oleanders.
9. *Eastern Europe*: Pinks, gerberas, roses.

North America
10. *United States*: Leather fern, sword fern, bear's-grass; new cultivars.
11. *Hawaii*: Tail flowers.
12. *Haiti*: Roses.

South and Central America
13. *Colombia*: Pinks, roses.
14. *Costa Rica* and *Honduras*: Dracaena and yucca stems.

Asia
15. *Japan*: Chrysanthemums, lilies (bulbs and seeds).
16. *Israel*: Pinks, roses, gypsophila, blue sea lavender, ruscus.
17. *Thailand, Malaysia, Singapore* and *Hong Kong*: Orchids.

Africa
18. *South Africa*: No export.
19. *Canary Islands*: Roses.
20. *Kenya* and *Zimbabwe*: Pinks, protea, summer flowers.

Australasia
21. *Australia* and *New Zealand*: Protea, bankia, leucospermum.

Top-ten Flower-buying nations
(per head of the population 1987)
1. The Netherlands   £ 22
2. Italy   £ 20
3. Switzerland   £ 20
4. West Germany   £ 18
5. Sweden   £ 14
6. Norway   £ 14
7. Belgium   £ 13
8. Austria   £ 12
9. France   £ 11
10. The United Kingdom   £ 4

Derived from: Bloemenburo Holland. *Publication 1988*

Kew, on the outskirts of West London, are world famous. Now generally knows as Kew Gardens, they were founded in 1759 and house a very large scientific collection of plants. The Royal Horticultural Society, established in 1804, is an important organization with a large demonstration garden in which new plants are tested. It arranges a great many flower exhibitions, including the annual Chelsea Flower Show in London. Thanks to the RHS and its many, many thousands of members (specialized amateurs, one of whose activities is obtaining new cultivars), the United Kingdom is of great significance for international flower cultivation. Many of these new cultivars, such as alstroemeria and freesia cultivars, are ultimately introduced on the market in the Netherlands. The RHS plays a prominent role in the registration of orchid cultivars. In the formulation of cultivar lists of daffodils, tulips and a few other species, the RHS works closely with the Royal Dutch Society for Flower Bulb Cultivation. Many plants were first cultivated in England.

Italy has an important flower growing area on the Italian Riviera, adjacent to the French Riviera. Flower cultivation, which has developed since 1900 and is concentrated around San Remo and Ventimiglia, consists chiefly of pinks, with some gladioli, roses and chrysanthemums. The nurseries here have a fairly difficult time of it, due to frost damage (cultivation generally takes place out of doors), rising wages and the advance of mass tourism. Perhaps this is why the cultivation of pinks is presently on the increase in southern Italy and on the island of Sardinia. Part of the production is exported, much of it to West Germany. The flowers are sold at the markets to agents. Sales and transport are unfortunately poorly organised, which is an obstacle to the further development of the Italian flower growing industry.

Sicily cultivates cut foliage (asparagus) for seed production; in southern Italy, with its favourable climate and low wages, Western European companies engage in the cultivation of chrysanthemum slips. Italy cultivates too little for its own consumption (centred in the wealthy north) and therefore imports many high-quality flowers from the Netherlands.

Switzerland has numerous good potted plant nurseries, but cut flowers are only cultivated there in small quantities. Because Swiss flower consumption is high, much is imported from the Netherlands and Italy.

Denmark's flower growing industry, among the best in the world, specializes in the production of potted plants. The modern cultivating companies are highly mechanised and automated. Important cut flowers are the pink and the *Adiantum* fern. The entire Danish cut flower production is intended for domestic use and must be supplemented by import. All products are marketed and transported (and exported) via the auction by cooperatives.

Belgium can be regarded as the cradle of European flower growing. The most important cultivating area is Ghent and its environs; the most important products are potted plants, such as the azalea and many foliage plants. Cut flower cultivation in Belgium is small in volume; most cut flowers are imported from the Netherlands.

As a potential flower cultivating area, *Portugal* has two advantages: a good climate and cheap labour; however, its flower cultivation is still of little importance. A few Dutch firms grow pinks and oleanders in Portugal. However, it is expected that Portuguese flower growing will increase in importance now that the country has joined the EEC.

Spain has several advantages (good climate, good soil, relatively cheap labour) as a flower growing area. The export (to the Netherlands and West Germany) consists chiefly of pinks and

comes from the environs of Barcelona, where the climate is similar to that of the French and Italian Riviera. Since Spain joined the EEC, flower production has expanded, as have imports from the Netherlands and other countries.

Eastern Europe shows great interest in flower growing (examples: Czechoslovakia, Hungary, Yugoslavia, Bulgaria and Poland) but is inhibited in its development by currency problems and other trade obstacles which make it difficult to purchase good plant material, new cultivars and treatment substances. Cultivation is generally concentrated on pinks and, here and there, gerberas and roses.

America

Until recently, flower growing in the western hemisphere was limited to North America, primarily the United States. In recent years, however, capital and know-how have been exported from that country to some parts of Central and South America.

United States. Although the flower consumption in the United States is low in comparison with Western Europe, its own production cannot meet domestic demand. There is a rapidly growing import of cut flowers. Most of them come from the Netherlands, such as tulips, lilacs and roses; others from Thailand and Singapore (orchids), Hawaii (tail flower), Haiti (roses) and Colombia (pinks). For the exporting countries, the United States is a rather exacting client; Americans set high standards for imported plants.

American flower growing takes place at large, modern and highly mechanised companies. Cultivation, often in plastic hothouses or under saran gauze, is preferably concentrated on products that can be cultivated all the year round, such as chrysanthemums, roses, pinks and orchids. California is the most important growing area; the states of Florida, Iowa, Illinois and Colorado also play a role.

The American universities perform much research in the field of flower growing. For instance, they developed inhibitors and obtained numerous new cultivars of the pink, the year-round chrysanthemum, the euphorbia, several orchid species, and others. The most important lily group, that of the Mid-Century hybrids, was developed in the United States. The American export, in addition to lily bulbs and flower seeds (sweet pea, snapdragon and zinnia hybrids), consists mainly of the leather fern (*Arachniodes*), the Boston or sword fern (*Nephrolepis*) and bear's-grass (*Beaucarnea bigelovii*).

South and Central America. Starting from the United States, large flower-cultivating firms have developed in countries with more or less stable political climates such as Costa Rica, Honduras and Colombia. Colombia has a significant export of pinks and roses to the United States and Western Europe. Other Latin American countries chiefly produce plant material for potted plant cultivation, such as dracaena and yucca stems.

Asia and The Near East

Traditionally, Japan has been the largest and most important flower-growing area of the Asian countries. The export consists chiefly of lily bulbs and seeds and new chrysanthemum cultivars. Several other Asian countries chiefly grow flowers which cannot be cultivated cost-effectively in Europe and the United States. Israel, which primarily exports to the United States and Western Europe during the months when production there is lower, has a different position.

Israel. Since the founding of this state in 1948, Israel has developed a flower-growing industry based on Western patterns which is almost entirely focused on export. Part of the production is exported to the United States, Great Britain (the wholesalers' market in London) and West Germany; but the largest part is sold at the Dutch flower auctions.

Israeli flower production is designed to supplement the Western European range in the winter months when production is lower there due to lack of light. From May until autumn, no cultivation can take place in Israel: the temperature is simply too high. The Israeli growers chiefly use plastic hothouses. It would be theoretically possible to work with cooling systems in the summer months, but this would make it too expensive to be able to compete with Western European cultivation. Israeli flower cultivation is of a high standard, comparable to that of the Netherlands as to quality control and marketing, which is cooperative. The most important products of the Israeli flower growers are bunch pinks, gypsophila, roses, blue sea lavender, ruscus and several other sorts.

Japan has a very high flower consumption and, as a result, a growing import, mostly Western plants gaining in popularity: pinks, roses, gerberas, alstroemerias. Import from the Netherlands is greatly increasing. The imported plants must meet very high standards: at Dutch auctions, all flowers intended for Japan are checked by specialists of the Japanese Phytopathological Service who are stationed in the Netherlands.

In Japan, the flower often has symbolic significance: the chrysanthemum must be mentioned in this context. It is found in the imperial emblem and the imperial flag, is the basis of several military distinctions and even has a national holiday devoted to it. In addition to the chrysanthemum, many shrub flowers are cultivated such as ornamental cherry, cherry, azalea, viburnum, etc. All of them are important in Japanese flower arrangement, one style of which, *ikebana*, is known all over the world. *Bonsai*, or the cultivation of dwarf trees, is also universally renowned; incidentally, it is of Chinese origin.

Japan exports practically no flowers, but does export lily bulbs, newly developed chrysanthemum cultivars (e.g. 'Refour') and seeds of new cut flower cultivars (such as eustoma, gentian and cirsium).

Other Asian countries. Thanks to a favourable climate and low wages, countries such as Thailand, Malaysia/Singapore and Hong Kong can produce and export cut flowers which it would not be profitable to grow in Western Europe and the United States because their cultivation takes so long or because they need so much warmth. This is chiefly true of orchid sorts such as *Vanda, Dendrobium, Oncidium*; these countries possess the high degree of knowledge needed for the cultivation of these flowers. Although some flowers are exported to the United States, most of them go to the Netherlands; from the Dutch auction, they find their way to the farthest corners of the earth.

Africa

South Africa has traditionally been a flower cultivating area of great importance. In principle, the country has four significant advantages: an excellent climate, much expertise, cheap labour and a rich local flora. Cut flower and potted plant sorts originating from South Africa are freesia, gerbera, zantedeschia, tritonia, some gladiolus sorts, pelargonium, clivia, streptocarpus and euphorbia, and the protea, which, because of its sheer size, can never be grown in a European hothouse.

Until recently, South African flower growers not only produced their 'own' local flowers, but also sorts which were well nigh impossible to grow in the northern hemisphere in the winter months because of high costs: alstroemeria, agapanthus, liatris, several zantedeschia sorts, hippeastrum, roses and cymbidiums. Because of the political situation, however, the role of South Africa as a flower-exporting country is diminishing.

Another African growing area is the *Canary Islands*, the most important of which is Tenerife. The islands belong to Spain and lie off the west coast of Morocco in a subtropical climate. Flower cultivation takes place in plastic hothouses and outdoors. The quality of the flowers, including roses, is excellent; they are generally traded in Aalsmeer. A problem in this cultivating area is water: good water is scarce and has to be brought in over long distances.

Bit by bit, other African countries are starting to play a role. *Kenya* and *Zimbabwe* stand out in particular for their development of pink growing and for an increasing cultivation of summer flowers. They are beginning to take the place of South Africa for plants such as the protea. Growers in these countries come chiefly from England, Germany and Denmark. They profit by the excellent climate and the very cheap labour and they grow a good product. However, matters such as presentation, harvesting, product range, packaging and shipment are still capable of improvement.

Australia and New Zealand

Australia and *New Zealand* mostly export plants which, until recently, came primarily from South Africa, such as protea, banksia and leucospermum. They also do some cultivation of cymbidiums.

Literature

DR. C.A. BACKER: *Verklarend woordenboek van wetenschappelijke plantennamen*, 1936.

JOHN BERGMANS: *Vaste planten en rotsheesters*, 1939.

DR. B.K. BOOM: *Flora der gekweekte kruidachtige gewassen*, 1970.

DR. B.K. BOOM: *Flora van Kamer- en Kasplanten*, 1968.

DR. B.K. BOOM: *Nederlandse Dendrologie*, 1968.

R. BOSSARD: *Cultures Florales* (bibliothèque d'horticulture pratique), 1982.

DARTHUIZER BOOMKWEKERIJEN: *Darthuizer Vademecum*, 1987.

ENCKE BUCHHEIM: *Zander Handwörterbuch der Pflanzennamen*, 1984.

DR. FRIEDRICH ESCHER: *Die Schnittblumenkultuur in der Erwertsgärtnerei*, 1971.

GANSLEMEIER/HENSELER: *Schnittstanden*, 1985

ING. C. GELEIN: *Bloementeelt*, 3 delen, 1978-1982.

A.B. GRAF: *Exotica*, 2 delen, 1984.

A.B. GRAF: *Tropica*, 1978.

INT. PROTEA ASSOCIATION: *Proteaceae*, 1988.

H.J. VAN DE LAAR: *Naamlijst van houtige gewassen*, 1985.

DR. J. LARJAM: *Compendium van Pteridophyta en Spermatophyta*, 1960.

PROF.DR. R.L.N. PIERIK: *Planteteelt in kweekbuizen*, 1975.

WERNER RAUH: *Bromelien*, 2 delen, 1973.

RUDOLF SCHLECHTER: *Die Orchideen II*, 1986.

Winkler Prins Agrarische Encyclopedie, 1954.

Winkler Prins Encyclopedie van het plantenrijk, 1981.

SPRENGER INSTITUUT: *Snijbloemen en kwaliteitsbehoud in de afzetketen*, 1986.

VERENIGDE BLOEMENVEILINGEN AALSMEER: VBA-catalogi, 1976-1984.

VERENIGDE BLOEMENVEILINGEN AALSMEER: *Codeboekjes*, 1987-1988.

Further reading

BEAN, W.J., *Trees and Shrubs Hardy in the British Isles*, ed. 8, vol. 1-4, 1970-1980.

BECKETT, KENNETH J., *R.H.S. Encyclopedia of House Plants*, 1987.

GRAF, A.B., *Exotica*, 2 vols., 1984.

GRAF, A.B., *Tropica*, 1978.

Hillier's Manual of Trees and Shrubs, ed. 4, 1988.

RAUH, WERNER, *Bromeliads*, 1979.

RICE, GRAHAM, *A Handbook of Annuals and Bedding Plants*, 1986.

THOMAS, GRAHAM STUART, *Perennial Garden Plants*, ed. 2, 1982.

Index